A Handbook of

STOCK EXCHANGE LAWS

Affecting the Members and their Customers Brokers and Investors

By

SAMUEL P. GOLDMAN

A Handbook of STOCK EXCHANGE LAWS

GOLDMAN

STOCK EXCHANGE LAWS

A Handbook of Stock Exchange Laws

Affecting members, their customers, brokers and investors

BY

SAMUEL P. GOLDMAN

OF THE NEW YORK BAR

GARDEN CITY NEW YORK

DOUBLEDAY, PAGE & COMPANY

1914

PREFACE

THE present agitation for the compulsory incorporation of the Stock Exchange and the enactment of numerous laws having as their object the regulation of the business of stock brokerage as it is now conducted on the Stock Exchange in the City of New York has caused many inquiries to be made of the author of this book for some general statement of the law which could be used as a guide by stockbrokers in the pursuit of their occupation.

In response to such inquiries, and to requests both from members of the Stock Exchange and from lawyers, this compilation has been made.

It is not the purpose of the book to provide a complete and exhaustive treatise for lawyers. The book is intended to be serviceable to stockbrokers, as well as lawyers. For the brokers, it should provide a ready reference book which they may read understandingly, and from which they may obtain a fairly safe guide to their conduct in their ordinary affairs, without necessitating a long course of reading or study or a conference with a lawyer to determine their duty in simple matters. For the members of the legal profession, it should provide a ready hand-book from which they can easily get the leading cases and principles applicable to those matters which are most frequently the subject of conference with their clients.

In preparing to advise his clients, the author was impressed with the completeness of the machinery provided by the Exchange for the safeguarding of the public. It was found that the power of the Governing Committee of the Exchange for purposes of discipline was almost without limit, and that the constitution, by-laws, and rules of the Exchange and its governors prohibited every pernicious practice that has been so loudly inveighed against in the public prints, and has made the mad rush for legislation upon the subject a truly senseless clamor.

To enumerate the more important laws, to explain them and show their application, and to cite the main authorities in regard thereto, would hardly be a sufficient presentation of the subject. This can be accomplished only by setting forth the constitution and by-laws of the Exchange, and the rules of the Governing Committee, and showing their coördination with the Statutes, so that it may be apparent to whomever may be interested that even a slight departure from the standards set by the Stock Exchange itself will bring double punishment upon the offending member, first, by way of penalty for a violation of the law of the State, and second, the more drastic consequences that follow an infraction of the rules of the Stock Exchange.

Before undertaking the work an effort was made to ascertain whether there was any general need for such a compilation. Inquiries were made, not only of numerous stockbrokers and of their customers, but also of many lawyers; and in perhaps a half dozen instances bank officials were questioned. The unanimous verdict seemed to be that if the book could be contained within reasonable limits, and could be couched in phraseology that would serve bankers, brokers, and customers, as well as lawyers, it would become a handbook indeed, and would fill a real want.

It is hoped that the book will serve this purpose, and that its kindly critics will not fail to recognize that considerable discrimination and choice were necessary to get so large a subject within so small a space, and to find words that would prove equally suitable to both lawyer and layman.

For their valuable assistance in preparing this manuscript, I wish to express my sincere appreciation to my partners, Mr. M. L. Heidenheimer and Mr. Wm. F. Unger.

Dated, New York, 1914.

TABLE OF CONTENTS

PART ONE

	PAGE
The Exchange and Its Constitution	1

PART TWO

Summary of Laws and Decisions	43

PART THREE

The Broker and His Customer	73

PART FOUR

Constitution, By-laws, and Rules of the New York Stock Exchange	117

PART FIVE

Laws of the State of New York Relating to Stockbrokers	195
Table of Cases Cited	253
Index	267

PART I

THE EXCHANGE AND ITS CONSTITUTION

THE New York Stock Exchange is governed by a constitution of thirty-eight articles, which has been amended from time to time to meet exigencies as they arose, and which has, for its members, the force of laws. In this Constitution and the rules accompanying it the interests of the public dealing with members of the Exchange are carefully safeguarded, even to the minutest detail, and the effort is made so to regulate the conduct of the members among themselves as to hold them up to the very highest standards of honesty and fair dealing. Of necessity the rules are strictly enforced. Sales and purchases are made and contracts undertaken involving thousands of dollars, without any written memoranda, a nod of the head or a wave of the hand being all that is used to bind the bargain. The infractions of the rules are very few, so few in fact that it may fairly be said that no more honorable body of men exists anywhere in the world.

The purposes of the Exchange are denoted in the words of its first article:

"Its object shall be to furnish exchange rooms and other facilities for the convenient transaction of their business by its members, as brokers; to maintain high standards of commercial honor and integrity among its members; and to promote and inculcate just and equitable principles of trade and business."

The solicitude of the Exchange to maintain the high standard set by this article is manifest from, among others, the disciplinary provisions of the Constitution which follow, as well as from those creating safeguards against members deemed insolvent.[1]

---

[1]The rules of a Stock Exchange or Board of Trade, as between the members, have the force and effect of existing laws. Contracts are governed by the rules in force at the time the contracts are made.

Hess Malting Co., v. Warren, 15 Ill. App. 507.
Thorne v. Prentiss, 83 Ill. 99.
Paton v. Newman, 51 La. Ann. 1428.
Pacaud v. Waite, 218 Ill. 138.
Nat. League of Comn. Merchts. v. Hornung, 148 App. Div. 355.
Haight v. Dickerman, 18 N. Y. Supp. 559.

By becoming members, the members impliedly agree to be bound by the rules.

People v. Board of Trade, 45 Ill. 112.
Board of Trade v. Nelson, 162 Ill. 431.

The constitution and by-laws constitute a law which the members have established for themselves. "The very existence of this body depends upon the faithful observance of its organic law by all its members."

White v. Brownell, 2 Daly, 329, 338.
Weston v. Ives, 97 N. Y. 222.

To the same effect:

Thompson v. Adams, 93 Pa. St. 55 (Philadelphia Board of Brokers).

The contracts may be made with specific reference to the rules.

Albers Commission Co. v. Spencer, 205 Mo. 105.
Bassett v. Irons, 8 Mo. App. 127.

In a suit between members of the New York Stock Exchange it was held that the parties were bound by the constitution and by-laws of the association, and that by-laws prescribing the mode of performing contracts of the kind in question became part of the contract. Peabody v. Speyers, 56 N. Y. 230. And parties outside of the board of the Gold Exchange may agree to be governed, in regard to their contract, by rules which, by their terms, are expressly confined to contracts made at the board. Mills v. Gould, 42 N. Y. Super. Ct. 119.

But, while the association may adopt rules obligatory on its own

The Governing Committee.

The government of the Exchange is vested in a Governing Committee, composed of the President and Trea-

members, by which their rights may be summarily determined between themselves, such determination has no force to injure or impair the rights of outside persons not voluntarily subject to the jurisdiction of the tribunal.

Morris v. Grant, 34 Hun. 377.

See also Waugh v. Seaboard Bank, 54 N. Y. Super. Ct. 283 (Petroleum Exchange).

Stock exchanges have power to enact such rules and regulations as are necessary to carry out their purposes, if not contrary to the law of the land.

Cohen v. Budd, 52 Misc. 217.

By-laws should be strictly construed and should not be extended by implication so as to effect a forfeiture of membership.

Albers v. Merchants' Exchange, 140 Mo. App. 446.

The Open Board of Stockbrokers, organized in 1864 and consolidated with the N. Y. Stock Exchange in 1869, was described in White v. Brownell, 2 Daly, 329, 355, as "an association of persons engaged in the same kind of business, who have organized together for the purpose of establishing certain rules, by which each agrees to be governed in the conduct and management of his separate transactions or business."

A member admitted in subordination to existing rules is estopped from denying their reasonableness.

Bostedo v. Board of Trade, 130 Ill. App. 560.

The courts will construe such rules. In re Fisk & Robinson, 185 Fed. 974.

But they will not interfere to control the enforcement of reasonable by-laws, which infringe no rule of law or public policy.

Green v. Board of Trade, 174 Ill. 585.

Board of Trade v. Nelson, 162 Ill. 431

Board of Trade v. Weare, 105 Ill. App. 289.

A by-law is not invalid merely because it is different from the common law rule, if it is not against the policy of the law.

Goddard v. Merchants' Exchange, 9 Mo. App. 290.

A by-law providing for the suspension of a member for dishonorable conduct has been held valid.

Board of Trade v. Nelson, 162 Ill. 431.

A by-law of an Exchange that if a member fails to comply with a business contract made with another member he shall be expelled is valid.

People v. Board of Trade, 45 Ill. 112.

Board of Trade v. Nelson, 162 Ill. 431.

A by-law prohibiting the representation of parties by professional counsel in investigations before committees has been held reasonable and enforceable.

Green v. Board of Trade, 174 Ill. 585.

surer of the Exchange, and of forty members.[1] This committee is divided into four classes of ten members each, each class holding office for four years, but the expiration of the term of each class is so arranged that one class goes out of office each year.[2] It has power to determine the manner and form of its own proceedings; to appoint and dissolve all committees; define, alter and regulate their jurisdiction; direct and control their proceedings; try and punish members; control finances; compensate officers; and all other powers necessary or incidental to the proper regulation of business,[3] but no member may participate in the adjudication of any case in which he is personally interested.[4]

This committee may also choose an acting President in the absence of the President and Vice-President; and it may choose counsel each year.

Officers of the Exchange, Their Powers and Duties.

The President may call special meetings of the Exchange and the Governing Committee, and must call such special meetings on the written request of one hundred members and of the Governing Committee on the written request of ten committee members.[5] He may appoint committees *ad interim.*[6]

The Vice-President, who is chosen by the Govern-

[1] Art. II.
[2] Art. III, Sec. 1.
[3] Art. III, Sec. 2.
[4] Art. III, Sec. 4.
[5] Art IV, Sec. 2.
[6] Art. IV, Sec. 3.

ing Committee each year, assumes the powers and duties of the President in his absence.[1]

The Treasurer acts under the Finance Committee, which may appoint one of its members to act, with either the President or Vice-President, as Treasurer *pro tem.*[2]

The Secretary is appointed by majority vote of the Governing Committee.[3]

The Chairman is appointed by the Governing Committee. His duty is to preside over the Exchange during business hours, maintain order, enforce the rules, impose fines, etc., under the direction of the Committee of Arrangements.[4] He is not allowed personally to buy or sell securities upon the floor of the Exchange.[5]

The Assistant Chairman is appointed by and acts under the direction of the Committee of Arrangements.[6]

The Governing Committee may for any good cause remove officers by two-thirds vote of its members.[7]

Committees.

There are twelve standing Committees:

First: A Committee of Arrangements, consisting of seven members, to which is entrusted the general care and supervision of the Exchange, the enforcement

[1] Art. V.
[2] Art. VI.
[3] Art. VII.
[4] Art. VIII, Sec. 1.
[5] Art. VIII, Sec. 2.
[6] Art. VIII, Sec. 3.
[7] Art. X, Sec. 3.

of the rules for conduct of business, etc.; the control and regulation of quotation service and telephone and telegraph connection with the Exchange, the appointment of employees, etc.[1]

Second: A Committee on Admissions, consisting of fifteen members, whose duty it is to consider applications for membership and reinstatements. Re-admission or reinstatement may be had upon the consent of two-thirds of the members of the Governing Committee present when the application therefor is considered.[2]

Third: An Arbitration Committee of nine members. They investigate and decide all claims and differences arising from contracts subject to the rules of the Exchange, between members or at the instance of a non-member between members and non-members. Their decision is final, unless an appeal is taken by a member of the committee, or the case involves $2,500 or more, in which case either party may appeal within ten days to the Governing Committee. A non-member, making a claim, must execute an agreement to abide by the rules of the Exchange, and execute a full release of his claims, the latter to be delivered to the defendant or cancelled and returned according to the result of the proceedings.[3]

[1] Art. XI.

[2] The Committee on Admissions is a court of special or inferior jurisdiction. Its jurisdiction must be shown. It is not presumed.

Matter of Seymour, Johnson & Co., 37 Misc. 264, 274.

[3] "All claims" here referred to are only those which invoke Stock Exchange transactions.

Bernheim v. Keppler, 34 Misc. 321, 325.

The real parties to an arbitration are entitled to notice and hearing.

Morris v. Grant, 34 Hun, 377.

In Heath v. President of Gold Exchange, 7 Abb. Pr. N. S. 251, it was held that the most that could possibly be claimed for the arbitra-

Fourth: A Committee on Business Conduct, of five members, whose duty it is to consider matters relating to the business conduct of members with respect to customers' accounts, and to keep in touch with the course of prices of securities listed on the Exchange, with the

---

tion clause was that it should have the same force and effect as an agreement in writing, made by persons, to submit to the decision of one or more arbitrators any controversy existing between them. Such agreements, until an award has been made, are not binding on the parties. The N. Y. Rev. St. (2 Rev. St. 544, Sec. 23) permitted a party to revoke the powers of the arbitrators at any time before the cause is finally submitted to them for their decision. The court, citing cases, said the section seemed to apply to all cases of submission.

A by-law, providing for arbitration of business disputes, provided for suspension for refusal to submit them after due notification, and for expulsion after a hearing, if the gravity of the offense was deemed to merit it. The by-law was held valid.

Evans v. Chamber of Commerce, 86 Minn. 448.

Where a board provides a tribunal, a member cannot invoke a court of equity without first having recourse to the tribunal, unless, by fraud or otherwise, it refuses to move to a determination.

Pacaud v. Waite, 218 Ill. 138.

Aside from the question of validity of such a rule a member who voluntarily submits claims against him to the arbitration committee of an association and takes two successive appeals from the decision against him assents to the jurisdiction and cannot afterwards question it in a court of law.

Nat. League of Com. Merchts. v. Hornung, 148 App. Div. 355.

The award of arbitrators, within their jurisdiction, is binding upon the parties. The courts will not disturb it for errors of judgment merely, though they will for exceeding the jurisdiction.

Bartlett v. Bartlett & Son Co., 116 Wis. 450.

The decision of an arbitration committee composed of interested persons should not be allowed to stand. In such a case the members should be sent to the courts to determine the controversy.

Moffatt v. Board of Trade (Mo.) 111 S. W. 894.

The omission of arbitrators to be sworn (N. Y. Prod. Exch.) may be waived by appearing before them and arguing the case without interposing objections.

Sonneborn v. Lavarello, 2 Hun, 201.

An exchange has a right to try and discipline a member for action inconsistent with just and equitable principles of trade in failing to comply with a contract made by him outside of and not upon the floor of the exchange.

view of determining when improper transactions are being resorted to.[1]

Fifth: A Committee on Clearing-House, of five members, which has general charge of the Clearing-House of the Exchange and its business, and designates the securities to be cleared.

Sixth: A Committee on Commissions, of five members, which enforces the rules relating to commissions, partnerships and branch offices, and reports to the Governing Committee violations thereof or any undesirable partnership or branch office.

Seventh: A Committee on Constitution, of five members, which considers all additions, alterations or amendments to the constitution.

Eighth: A Finance Committee, of seven members, which acts as a Board of Audit and examines the condition of the Gratuity Fund.

Ninth: A Committee on Insolvencies, of three members selected from the Committee on Admissions, which investigates every case of insolvency immediately after

---

In re Haebler v. N. Y. Prod. Exch. 149 N. Y. 414.

The fact that the board of managers of an exchange has power only to discipline when the member refuses to arbitrate or conciliate does not make the by-law unreasonable,coercive or contrary to public policy.

In re Haebler v. N. Y. Prod. Exch. 149 N. Y. 414.

An offer to arbitrate before another Exchange or before non-members is not sufficient to prevent trial and discipline.

In re Haebler v. N. Y. Prod. Exch. 149 N. Y. 414.

[1]Resolution of March 5, 1913. This is entirely new and seems to be the last word in control of members by the Governing Committee of the Exchange. The most rigid and searching inquiry has been made by this committee into various transactions of members, with instant beneficial results. Because of its activities it has been dubbed "The Police Committee."

its announcement, and reports to the Committee on Admissions.

Tenth: A Law Committee, of five members, which considers all questions of law affecting the interests of the Exchange, and is empowered to examine into the dealings of any member.

Eleventh: A Committee on Securities, of five members, which makes rules defining the requirements for regularity in the delivery of securities dealt in on the Exchange, and decides all questions relating to the settlement of contracts, subject to the rules of the Exchange, or to deliveries thereof, and all questions relating to reclamations therefor.[1]

Twelfth: A Committee on Stock-List, of five members, which considers applications for placing securities upon the Exchange list and reports to the Governing Committee, giving a full statement as to the organization, capitalization, resources, and indebtedness of the applicant. It is empowered to place upon and remove from the list, without report, Government and State or City obligations and subscription receipts. It has charge of the arrangement and revision of the list of securities. It is one of the most important committees of the Exchange,

[1]The committee's jurisdiction of all questions "as to the regularity of stock certificates, bonds, etc. . . . dealt in at the Exchange" embraces questions as to the regularity of the form of bonds; regularity of issue, which includes genuineness; regularity as to being within the list of admissions to the board, and questions of that nature; but the committee has nothing to do with the legality of a tender or delivery of bonds conceded to be regular in all those respects, but refused or objected to on some ground not available against a bona fide holder for value.

Morris v. Grant, 34 Hun, 377.

and exercises its power in a most wholesome and beneficial way. It is constantly obtaining details and report of corporations whose shares find a market on the Exchange and is thus in a position to keep all persons informed as to the general character, conditions and perhaps dealings of any of the companies whose names appear on the stock list.[1]

Appeals.

The constitution also provides for appeals from the decision of standing committees to the Governing Committee.[2]

Admission to Membership.

Every applicant for membership in the Exchange must be twenty-one years of age and a citizen of the United States.[3]

There is no constitutional limit as to the number of members, but it can only be increased by the action of the Governing Committee, which must prescribe the number and terms of admission. This action must be submitted to the Exchange in the same way as an amendment to the constitution.[4]

The initiation fee on a transfer of membership is $2,000,[5] payable on the day of applicant's election.[6]

[1]In England, the Companies (Consolidation) Act of 1908 provides by statute for the collection of the information gathered by this committee.

[2]Art. XII.

[3]Art. XIII, Sec. 1.

[4]Art. XIII, Sec. 2.
The present limit of membership is eleven hundred. Of these only about six hundred are active upon the floor of the Exchange.

[5]Art. XIII, Sec. 3.

[6]Art. XIII, Sec. 4.

Before admission to the privileges of membership, the person elected must sign the constitution. By such signature he pledges himself to abide by the same and by all subsequent amendments.[1]

Dues and Fines.

The Exchange is supported by dues of $100 per year, payable semi-annually.[2]

If in arrears for three months a member may be suspended. If dues are not paid at the end of one year, the Committee on Admissions is authorized to dispose of the membership.[3]

Transfer of Membership.

Transfer of membership is made on approval of two-thirds of the Committee on Admissions. Notice of the proposed transfer must be posted on the bulletin ten days prior to transfer.[4]

---

[1] Art. XIII, Sec. 5.

[2] Art. XIV, Sec. 1.

[3] Art. XIV, Sec. 2.

A member of a voluntary unincorporated exchange, who was illegally expelled for failing to pay dues, is bound, within a reasonable time after obtaining knowledge of his expulsion, to assert his rights; otherwise, he will be deemed to have assented to the expulsion.

Konta v. St. Louis Stock Exchange, 189 Mo. 26 (where a member of the St. Louis St. Exch. was expelled when memberships therein were worthless. He waited over a year, when a membership was worth $7,500, before attempting to assert his rights).

[4] Art. XV, Sec. 1.

A seat on the N. Y. Stock Exchange is property within the meaning of the Tax Law (then L. 1896, ch. 908, Art. 10), and subject to the inheritance transfer tax prescribed by Article 10 of the Tax Law, upon the death of the owner and its devolution to his personal representatives.

Matter of Hellman, 174 N. Y. 254.

All contracts subject to the rules of the Exchange made by a member proposing to transfer his seat mature on

But it is not personal property within Sec. 2, subd. 4, of that Tax Law, and is not subject to the annual tax thereunder.

People v. Feitner, 167 N. Y. 1.

A seat is not a "personal privilege" merely.

In re Hurlbutt, Hatch & Co., 135 Fed. 504, 507, following Sparhawk v. Yerkes, 142 U. S. 1.

The Stock Exchange cannot be compelled to admit to membership the purchaser of a seat, and a purchaser who is admitted takes the seat subject to the constitution and rules of the Exchange.

Hyde v. Woods, 94 U. S. 523 (San Francisco St. Exch.); Page v. Edmunds, 187 U. S. 596; People v. Feitner, 167 N. Y. 1; In re Hayes, 75 N. Y. Supp. 312, 321.

A membership in the N. Y. Stock Exchange can only be transferred under the rules of the Exchange and by consent of the Committee on Admissions.

O'Dell v. Boyden (C. C. A.), 150 Fed. 731.

A seat cannot be transferred without the consent of the association, and a forced sale of the seat would not give the purchaser the right to occupy the seat.

Shannon v. Cheny, 156 Cal. 567.

There can be no sale of a seat except in subordination to the rules of the Exchange. The privilege of transacting business on the Exchange has been defined as "a personal privilege of being and remaining a member of a voluntary association with the assent of the association."

Lowenberg v. Greenbaum, 99 Cal. 162.

Shannon v. Cheney, 156 Cal. 567.

On the insolvency of a firm one of whose partners is a member of the Exchange, the membership passes to the assignee in bankruptcy. The fact that the Stock Exchange continues to regard the insolvent member as a member in no way injures the assignee, and an action by him to restrain the insolvent member from using the seat and to compel him to assign and transfer it to the plaintiff is unnecessary.

Platt v. Jones, 96 N. Y. 24.

McCabe v. Lawrence, 51 N. Y. Super. Ct. 219.

In re Hurlbutt, Hatch & Co. (C. C. A.), 135 Fed. 504.

Similarly, a purchaser from the trustee is in a position to apply to the Exchange to have his rights recognized, either in his own person, or he may apply to have another person accepted as a member. The recognition of another person by the Exchange as a member entitled to the seat through transfer by the insolvent member after his assignment is no bar to his application, which is his first step, and injunctive relief before wrongful refusal of the Exchange to admit him will be denied him.

McCabe v. Emmons, 51 N. Y. Super. Ct. 219.

A right of transfer of the seat of a bankrupt member of the Philadelphia Stock Exchange passes to his trustee in bankruptcy, the bankrupt

the tenth day of posting of notice; no further contracts may be made by him pending approval by the committee. This rule also applies to cases where a

---

having no unsettled accounts with members of the exchange at the time of filing his petition in bankruptcy; and the trustee is entitled to sell the seat as part of the bankrupt's assets. This right is subject to the approval by the proper authorities of the Exchange to the transfer to any given person.

In re Page (C. C. A.), 107 Fed. 89.

The bankruptcy court may compel the member to execute a transfer of the seat to his firm's assignee in bankruptcy.

In re Hurlbutt, Hatch & Co. (C. C. A.), 135 Fed. 504.

A membership in the Exchange has a pecuniary value, constituting property, to which an equitable right may be given by an assignment. But it cannot in fact be transferred except by the substitution of a new member in accordance with the rules of the Exchange. Therefore, on the bankruptcy of a member, his membership passes into the possession of his trustee as assets of his estate, notwithstanding any previous assignment, although it may be subject to the equities of the assignee and its transfer and conversion into money can then only be effected pursuant to orders of the bankruptcy court.

O'Dell v. Boyden (C. C. A), 150 Fed. 731.

"There may be property belonging to this body, derived from the payment of dues or fines, or consisting of the furniture of the room where the board meets; but the possession of it is a mere incident, and not the main purpose or object of the association. A member has no proprietary interest in it, or a right to any proportionable part of it upon withdrawing. He has merely the enjoyment and use of it while he is a member, but the property remains with and belongs to the body while it continues to exist."

White v. Brownell, 2 Daly, 329, 356.

A seat or membership in the N. Y. Stock Exchange undoubtedly is property for certain purposes, but even then it is property of a peculiar nature.

McCabe v. Emmons, 51 N. Y. Super. Ct. 219, 225.

A seat in the Philadelphia Board of Brokers is not property in the eye of the law, and cannot be seized in execution for debts of the members.

Thompson v. Adams, 93 Pa. St. 55.

A membership in the N. Y. Stock Exchange is personal to the holder, and is evidenced by no certificate.

O'Dell v. Boyden, (C. C. A.) 150 Fed. 731.

A seat on the Boston Stock Exchange may be pledged for indebtedness.

Nashua Savings Bank v. Abbott, 181 Mass. 531.

This is due to a specific rule to that effect, and in this regard the Boston Stock Exchange differs from the N. Y. Stock Exchange.

membership is disposed of by the Committee on Admissions.[1]

Upon transfer voluntarily or by disposition of the Governing Committee or the Committee on Admissions, the proceeds thereof are applied in the following order:

1. Payment of all fines, dues, assessments, and charges of the Exchange against the transferor.

2. Payment of creditors, members of the Exchange, or firms registered thereon, of all filed claims arising from contracts subject to the rules of the Exchange, as allowed by the Committee on Admissions. If insufficient to pay claims allowed in full, the proceeds are applied *pro rata*.

3. The surplus, if any, is paid to the transferor or to his legal representatives on the execution of a release.[2]

All unmatured debts or other obligations, arising out of contracts subject to the rules of the Exchange, become due and payable, immediately prior to the transfer.[3]

A Stock Exchange seat is not such a collateral as may be sold by the pledgee. The way in which it could be accomplished would be to report the failure of the member to meet his obligations to the Stock Exchange, whereupon he might be suspended for a year and for such further time as the governing board in its discretion might give. The seat cannot be sold by individuals. It is not transferable like a stock or bond; membership in the Exchange is the right to participate as a member in a voluntary private organization. The courts cannot force a person upon the Exchange.

Ketcham v. Provost, 141 N. Y. Supp. 437.

[1]Art. XV, Sec. 2.

[2]Art. XV, Sec. 3.

[3]Art. XV, Sec. 4.

"All contracts, debts, etc., *shall become due and payable*," means current contracts, debts, or obligations between members, and originating between them in their membership capacity. Claims long since accrued would not, first, have to be declared due and payable.

A member forfeits all right to share in the proceeds of a membership by failing to file claim prior to the transfer, subject to his right to be paid out of any sur-

Bernheim v. Keppler, 34 Misc. 321, 324.

Cochran v. Adams, 180 Pa. St. 289, is to the same effect.

Construing this article it was held that the present Article XV, Sec. 7, relating to the disposition by the Committee on Admissions of a seat on death, and Article XV, Sec. 3, relating to the disposition of the proceeds of a seat whether transferred voluntarily or by the Exchange, appear to cover the former Section 4 of Article 13.

Claims of members of the Exchange mean claims arising from transactions between members as such, and do not include a claim arising out of a transaction between the claimant and the deceased member prior to the latter's admission to membership in the Exchange.

Bernheim v. Keppler, 34 Misc. 321.

See also Cochran v. Adams, 180 Pa. St. 289.

A general assignment by an insolvent member does not affect the contractual rights of members of the Exchange in the seat. Dividends paid them out of the sale of the seat are not to be deducted in estimating their right to dividends out of the assigned estate.

In re Hayes, 75 N. Y. Supp. 312.

A member suspended for insolvency transferred his membership in blank to the Committee on Admissions, who sold it. The proceeds of the seat, notwithstanding the prior general assignment made by the member's firm, were primarily liable for the payment of the debts contracted by him and it to members of the Exchange, and also for such debts due to the firms of members of the Exchange.

In re Hayes, 75 N. Y. Supp. 312.

The court observed that in respect of the facts of the case, the constitution was ambiguous in not expressly providing for the distribution of the proceeds of the membership of a member suspended for insolvency, who voluntarily agreed to transfer his membership (p. 316). It was held that usage might be proven to give the effect intended, where a debt was due to a *member's firm*.

In re Hayes, 75 N. Y. Supp. 312.

A rule of an Exchange providing that claims due to members from a defaulting member may be collected by an Exchange and applied to debts due other members is invalid, as in violation of the bankruptcy law.

Cohen v. Budd, 52 Misc. 217. (Consol. St. Exch.)

A., not a member, furnished the money with which R. became a member of the Philadelphia Board of Brokers. R. died. A. claimed that he was the equitable owner of the seat and entitled to the proceeds in preference to debts due by R. to other members of the Exchange. A.'s claim was denied, he being an entire stranger, unknown to the board.

Thompson v. Adams, 93 Pa. St. 55.

plus after all other claims allowed have been paid in full.[1]

Claims between partners, members of the Exchange, do not share in the proceeds of the membership of one of the partners until after all other claims allowed are paid in full.[2]

The membership of a deceased member is disposed of by the Committee on Admissions.[3]

A member suspended for insolvency, who did not settle within one year, voluntarily transferred his membership, in blank, to the Committee on Admissions, which sold it. Notwithstanding a prior assignment by the member's firm the proceeds were held primarily applicable to the payment of debts to members and their firms arising from transactions within the Exchange.

Matter of Seymour, Johnson & Co., 37 Misc. 264.

[1]Art. XV, Sec. 5.

[2]Art. XV, Sec. 6.

[3]Art. XV, Sec. 7.

The claims of members that are to be satisfied out of proceeds of the sale of a decedent's seat are claims between members arising on the floor of the Exchange, and do not include a claim arising out of transactions had with a non-member who afterwards became a member.

Bernheim v. Keppler, 34 Misc. 321.

A creditor member is entitled, besides the receipt of dividends out of the sale of a membership, to prove, as against mere general creditors, for the whole of his original claim, provided he does not receive more than his full claim.

Matter of Seymour, Johnson & Co., 37 Misc. 264.

Persons having claims against a member or ex-member of the Exchange who might submit the same to the Committee on Admissions pursuant to the constitution may be precluded from doing so by their own acts or omissions, and may be enjoined from so doing by a court of competent jurisdiction.

In re Currie (C. C. A.), 185 Fed. 263.

O'Dell v. Boyden (C. C. A.), 150 Fed. 731.

Bankruptcy proceedings were instituted in Michigan against a member of the New York Stock Exchange. The bankrupt was indebted to Hayden, Stone & Co. in an amount secured by pledged collateral. How much of the collateral would be available to them was doubtful. The trustee in bankruptcy took proceedings to compel the Stock Exchange to pay over to him the proceeds of the sale of the seat. Hayden, Stone & Co. had propounded their demand to as much of the

The membership of a member expelled or becoming ineligible for reinstatement may be disposed of by the Committee on Admissions.[1]

The expulsion or suspension of a member does not affect the rights of creditors who are members of the Exchange or of firms registered thereon.[2]

When a member is in debt to another member, the death of the latter or the transfer of his membership does not affect his right, or that of his firm or estate to share in the proceeds of the membership of the debtor member.[3]

Insolvency.

A member who fails to comply with his contracts, or is insolvent, or who is a partner of a registered firm in such a position, must immediately inform the President in writing and prompt notice must be given to the Exchange. He thereby becomes suspended until, after settlement with his creditors, he is reinstated.[4]

When the President ascertains that a member or his firm has failed to meet engagements or is insolvent

---

collateral as they could get in the Michigan courts, and contemporaneously asserted their right to the whole or part of the proceeds of the sale of the seat before the Committee on Admissions. It was held that they had a right to do so and the trustee's application was denied.

In re Currie (C. C. A.), 185 Fed. 263.

[1]Art. XV, Sec. 8.

[2]Art. XV, Sec. 9.

[3]Art. XV, Sec. 10.

[4]Art. XVI, Sec. 1.

A rule requiring a broker to report his default in complying with his stock contracts has been held to apply only to contracts for the purchase or sale of stocks on the board.

Rorke v. San Francisco Stock Exch. Bd. 99 Cal. 196.

and has neglected to comply with these provisions he announces to the Exchange the insolvency of such person or firm.[1]

On the failure of a suspended member to settle with his creditors and apply for reinstatement within one year from the time of suspension, his membership is disposed of by the Committee on Admissions. The time of settlement may be extended by the Governing Committee, by a two-thirds vote of members present, for periods not exceeding one year each.[2]

When a suspended member applies for reinstatement he must furnish a list of his creditors, a statement of the amounts originally owing, and the nature of the settlement made in each case. After notice of the proposed consideration of his application posted for three days, and his presenting satisfactory proof of settlement, the Committee on Admissions ballots for him. Failing an approving vote of two-thirds of the entire committee, the applicant is entitled to be balloted for at any five subsequent meetings within one year of suspension, or such extended time as is granted by the Governing Committee. If rejected on the sixth ballot, the applicant may appeal to the Governing Committee, who may reinstate him on an affirmative vote of not less than twenty-five members. On a member's failure to make such applications, or if rejected by the Governing Committee, his membership may be disposed of.[3]

[1]Art. XVI, Sec. 2.

[2]Art. XVI, Sec. 3.

[3]Art. XVI, Sec. 4.

Under these sections, when a member is suspended, the rights of other

Whenever the Governing Committee determines that a member's or a firm's failure is due to reckless or unbusinesslike dealing, such member or partner or partners may, by two-thirds vote of existing members of the Governing Committee, be declared ineligible for reinstatement.[1]

A complete list of creditors and amounts due must be filed with the Secretary by every suspended member within thirty days after suspension.[2]

Expulsion and Suspension.

The penalty of expulsion may be inflicted, and the period of suspension determined, by a vote of a majority of the members of the Governing Committee; and the penalty of expulsion or of ineligibility of a suspended

---

members in the proceeds of his seat do not become fixed immediately, unless the seat is then sold. If the period of settlement is extended for successive yearly periods until the member's death, the Committee on Admissions are to determine the rights of creditors in accordance with the provisions of the constitution relating to the distribution of the proceeds of sale after the death of a member, and not as these provisions stood at the time of his suspension.

Haight v. Dickerman, 18 N. Y. Supp. 312.

"Debts" means debts contracted among members as such.

Bernheim v. Keppler, 34 Misc. 321, 324.

[1]Art. XVI, Sec. 5.

[2]Art. XVI, Sec. 6.

The right of a voluntary association to provide, in its constitution or by-laws, expulsion as a penalty for an infraction or disobedience of its laws is well settled.

Nat. League of Com. Merchts. v. Hornung, 148 App. Div. 355.

Expulsion for indictable offenses can take place only after a conviction by a jury, but where the offense is against the member's duty as a member he may be expelled on trial and conviction by the corporation.

Leech v. Harris, 2 Brewst. (Pa.) 571.

The court will not examine upon the merits the question decided by the Governing Committee and resulting in a member's expulsion. It will only reverse the committee's decision when there is a total absence

member for readmission may be inflicted by a vote of two-thirds of said members.[1] A member adjudged guilty of fraud or of fraudulent acts shall be expelled.[2] Expulsion is the penalty for making a misstatement on a material point upon a member's application either for membership or reinstatement or extension of time.[3] Suspension for not more than one year or expulsion is the penalty for being connected with any organization in the city of New York permitting dealings in securities, etc., dealt in on the Exchange.[4] Suspension for not more than one year is the penalty for making a transaction with a non-member in the rooms of the Exchange in such securities, etc.[5] Suspension or expulsion is the penalty for wilful violation of the Constitution or of a resolution of the Governing Committee regarding conduct or business, or conduct inconsistent with just and equitable principles of trade.[6] The Governing Committee may require production of such portion of a member's books or papers as are material or relevant

of evidence warranting it, or when the proceedings before the committee were contrary to natural justice.

Young v. Eames, 78 App. Div. 229, affirmed 181 N. Y. 542.
Nat. League v. Hornung, 148 App. Div. 355.
Baum v. N. Y. Cotton Exch., 4 N. Y. Supp. 207.
Neukirch v. Keppler, 56 App. Div. 225, affirmed 174 N. Y. 509.
People v. N. Y. Produce Exch., 149 N. Y. 401
People v. Board of Trade, 80 Ill. 134.
Board of Trade v. Riordan, 94 Ill. App. 298.

[1]Art. XVII, Sec. 1.

[2]Art. XVII, Sec. 2

[3]Art. XVII, Sec. 3.

[4]Art. XVII, Sec. 4.

[5]Art. XVII, Sec. 5.

[6]Art. XVII, Sec. 6.

to any matter under investigation by said Committee or any Standing or Special Committee. A member refusing or neglecting to make such production may be adjudged guilty of an act detrimental to the interest or welfare of the Exchange.[1] A member adjudged guilty of such an act may be suspended for not more than one year.[2] An accusation charging a member with the commission of an offense or a violation of the laws or regulations of the Exchange shall be in writing, specifying the charge or charges with reasonable detail, and signed by the person or persons making the charge or charges. A copy thereof shall be served upon the accused member, who shall have ten days or such further time as the Governing Committee may deem proper within which to answer. The answer shall be in writing signed by the accused member, and filed with the Secretary. Upon filing or refusal to answer, the Governing Committee shall, at a regular or special meeting,

---

Pitcher v. Board of Trade, 121 Ill. 412.
Nelson v. Board of Trade, 58 Ill. App. 399.
Ryan v. Lamson, 44 Ill. App. 204.

The principle whereby a court of equity may interfere and restore a member of a corporation who has been expelled does not apply to a voluntary unincorporated body like the Stock Exchange. The privilege of membership in the latter is not a franchise. It is derived exclusively from the body which bestows it, and may be conferred or withheld at its pleasure.

White v. Brownell, 2 Daly, 329, 357.

The judgment of the Governing Committee, made after regular proceedings, hearing and full investigation, as to certain transactions alleged to have been fraudulently conducted by the member, cannot be reviewed on the merits by the courts.

Neukirch v. Keppler, 56 App. Div. 225.

All the member could require was that the investigation should be

[1] Art. XVII, Sec. 7.

[2] Art. XVII, Sec. 8.

proceed to consider the charge or charges; if the meeting be a special meeting, notice of its object shall be sent to the members of the Committee and to the accused, who shall be entitled to be personally present and to examine and cross-examine the witnesses produced and to present any defense, testimony or explanation. If the accused member is adjudged guilty the Committee shall expel or suspend such member, as the case may be; the President shall announce the result to the Exchange, and a written notice shall be served upon the member. The finding of the Committee shall be final and conclusive.[1] The Committee may proceed summarily in the case of misconduct, or the commission of an offense for which the penalty is limited to suspension for a period not exceeding sixty days. If adjudged guilty, the accused may be suspended for such period as the Constitution provides.[2] Announcement of suspension shall be made to the Exchange, and the member deprived of all rights and privileges of membership, except those pertaining to the Gratuity Fund.[3] Professional

conducted *bona fide* upon notice to him and an opportunity to be heard, and that the decision made should be within the scope of the jurisdiction conferred on the committee.

id. citing
Bigelow v. Benedict, 70 N. Y. 204.
Lewis v. Wilson, 121 N. Y. 288.
White v. Brownell, 2 Daly, 329.
Lambert v. Addison, 46 L. T. Rep. 20.

Where a member is expelled in conformity with the rules, and the proceedings are regular and in good faith, it is final, and no judicial tribunal can interfere.

White v. Brownell, 2 Daly, 329, 359.

[1]Art. XVII, Sec. 9.
[2]Art. XVII, Sec. 10.
[3]Art. XVII, Sec. 11.

counsel are excluded from any investigation or hearing before the Governing Committee or any Standing or Special Committee.[1]

Rules for the Conduct of Business.

A large number of rules regulate the conduct of business upon the Exchange. All contracts are subject to these rules.[2]

Hours are prescribed within which the Exchange must remain open, except by order of the Governing Committee,[3] and a fine is imposed for dealing in other than the official hours.[4] Dealing upon any other Exchange

---

But a court of equity may interfere for the purpose of holding the association to a fair and honest administration of its rules.

Hutchinson v. Lawrence, 67 How. Pr. 38.

The courts will not interfere with the rules on the motion of a non-member.

Heim v. N. Y. Stock Exch., 64 Misc. 529, aff'd 138 App. Div. 96.

An expulsion, if regularly made, is conclusive, and cannot be inquired into collaterally, by mandamus or otherwise. The court can give no relief, except in case of irregularity of the proceedings.

Leech v. Harris, 2 Brewst. (Pa.) 571.

But a broker cannot be irregularly expelled, and injunction will lie to restrain an illegal expulsion, even before the report of the committee.

Leech v. Harris, 2 Brewst. (Pa.) 571.
Moffatt v. Board of Trade (Mo.), 111 S. W. 894.

Right to expel for "bad faith and dishonorable conduct" does not give a board the right to expel members at its pleasure, without reference to the deeds it considers bad faith and dishonorable conduct.

Nelson v. Board of Trade, 58 Ill. 399.

Mandamus will not lie for the reinstatement of an expelled member, nor suit for an injunction.

Matter of Weidenfeld v. Keppler, 84 App. Div. 235.
Baum v. N. Y. Cotton Exch., 4 N. Y. Supp. 207.
People v. Board of Trade, 80 Ill. 134.

[1] Art. XVII, Sec. 12.

[2] Art. XXII.

[3] Art. XX, Secs. 1 and 2.

[4] Art. XX, Sec. 3.

in the city of New York or publicly outside the Stock Exchange in securities listed or quoted on the Exchange is prohibited.[1]

The manner of making and accepting bids and offers for stock is regulated, and these rules must be observed under penalty of fine and suspension.[2] Briefly stated, all

Bostedo v. Board of Trade, 227 Ill. 90.
Baster v. Board of Trade, 83 Ill. 146.
Pitcher v. Board of Trade, 121 Ill. 412.
Board of Trade v. Weare, 105 Ill. 289.

A member in resisting the unlawful authority of the Exchange, commits no offense against his duty as a member.

Leech v. Harris, 2 Brewst. (Pa.) 571.

Action was brought against the board of managers of an Exchange for damages for unlawful suspension, after the member had been reinstated by the courts. It was held that in the absence of malice, the board, acting in a *quasi* judicial capacity, was not liable for errors of judgment determining matters within its jurisdiction.

Lurman v. Jarvie, 82 App. Div. 37.

A member of a Board of Trade was under charges for alleged violation of its rules and by-laws. He urged that he had sold his membership prior to the preferring of the charges. It was held that as the transfer of the seat had not been consented to by the board he had not ceased to be a member, and the board did not lose jurisdiction to try him on the charges.

Bostedo v. Board of Trade, 227 Ill. 90.

In trials of a member by a committee the laws of the association limit the jurisdiction of the tribunal.

Bartlett v. Bartlett & Son Co., 116 Wis. 450.

Voluntary submission by a member to a trial before a committee estops him from denying its jurisdiction.

Ryan v. Cudahy, 157 Ill. 108.

A by-law should state the causes of suspension and expulsion with such reasonable degree of certainty that a member may know the transgressions which will subject him to the penalty.

People v. N. Y. Produce Exch., 149 N. Y. 401.

An accused member is entitled to proper notice of proceedings for his expulsion, so that he may be heard.

People v. East Buffalo Live Stock Assn., 88 App. Div. 619.
State v. Milwaukee Chamber of Commerce, 47 Wis. 670.

A strict compliance with the Constitution and by-laws in this respect is essential.

[1]Art. XX, Sec. 4.

[2]Art. XXIII.

bids and offers must be made either (a) "Cash," i. e., for delivery upon the day of contract; (b) "Regular Way," i. e., for delivery upon the business day following the contract; (c) "At three days," i. e., for delivery upon the third day following the contract; (d) "Buyer's" or "Seller's" options for not less than four days nor more than sixty days.[1] These bids or offers must not be

---

Quentell v. N. Y. Cotton Exchange, 56 Misc. 150.

"The principle to be deduced from all the cases is that in every proceeding before a club, society or association, having for its object the expulsion of a member, the member is entitled to be fully and fairly informed of the charge and to be fully and fairly heard."

Hutchinson v. Lawrence, 67 How. Pr. 38, 55.

Charges against members are not to be tested by the strict rules of criminal pleading. It is sufficient if the member is notified of what the alleged violation consists.

Board of Trade v. Nelson, 162 Ill. 431.

The decision of a committee may be avoided on account of its refusal to hear competent evidence.

Ryan v. Cudahy, 157 Ill. 108.

A member of an Exchange like the New York Cotton Exchange, against whom proceedings are instituted under its by-laws, must first exhaust his remedies within the association before he may invoke redress from the courts.

Moyse v. New York Cotton Exchange, 143 App. Div. 265. (Proceedings for expulsion for violation of by-laws.)

Hurst v. N. Y. Produce Exchange, 100 N. Y. 605.

Lewis v. Wilson, 50 Hun. 166.

The rule that a member must first exhaust his remedy within the association applies only when the proceedings are conducted in accordance with the constitution and by-laws.

Quentell v. N. Y. Cotton Exch., 56 Misc. 150.

A member is not bound by a judgment of the board if not conducted in accordance with the by-laws.

Board of Trade v. Riordan, 94 Ill. App. 298.

The law does not require resort to higher authority within the organization when it appears that such action would be futile.

Quentell v. N. Y. Cotton Exchange, 56 Misc. 150, where the highest power, the board of managers, had approved in advance of the illegal methods pursued by the supervisory committee in proceeding against the plaintiff.

[1] Art. XXIII, Sec. 3.

made at a less variation than one-eighth of one per cent.[1]

Fictitious transactions are forbidden under penalty of suspension for not more than one year.[2]

A customer is entitled to the return of the money deposited by him where there has been no genuine transaction.[3]

By a resolution of February 5, 1913, no member or his firm shall give or knowingly execute orders for the purchase or sale of securities which would involve no change of ownership, under the same penalty. Dealing in privileges to receive or deliver securities is punishable by a fine.[4]

By resolution of December 14, 1898, members having orders to buy and sell the same security must offer it at one-eighth per cent. higher than their bid before making transactions with themselves.

"Specialists" are forbidden to deal in the stocks entrusted to them, to buy or sell directly or indirectly for their own account, for account of a partner, or for

---

[1] Art. XXIII, Sec. 5.

[2] Art. XXIII, Sec. 8.
See Laws 1913, ch. 476. Penal Law sec. 951, infra p. 207.
Laws 1913, ch. 253. Penal Law sec. 953, infra p. 208.
Laws 1913, ch. 595. Penal Law sec. 957, as to delivery of memoranda of transactions to customer, infra p. 212.
Where a transaction may from one point of view be regarded as a fictitious sale, and from another as fraudulent sale of stock, the Governing Committee may treat it as a fraudulent one.
Young v. Eames, 78 App. Div. 229.

[3] Fuller v. Mun. Tel. & St. Co. 117 App. Div. 352.
Haight v. Haight & Freese Co., 46 Misc. 501; 102 App. Div. 475; aff'd 190 N. Y. 540.

[4] Art. XXIII, Sec. 9.

any account in which they have an interest.[1] The rule does not apply where the member, having neglected to execute an order, is compelled to take or supply the securities on his own account. In such a case he is not acting as a broker and can charge no commission.

Members are forbidden to deal in any listed security, anywhere outside of the Exchange, except at a legitimate auction. This rule has been emphasized by a resolution declaring that *this practice in any form* is detrimental to the interest and welfare of the Exchange.[2]

Transactions with or for "bucket-shops" are forbidden,[3] as well as speculative transactions for clerks of members or of banks, trust companies, bankers or insurance companies, without the written consent of their employers.[4]

Members are required to use diligence to learn the essential facts relating to all accounts accepted by them, and to the possible use of a name for the account other than that of the party interested.[5]

All wire or other connection with the Consolidated Stock Exchange or the offices of its members is pro-

NOTE

The prohibition of all wire or other connection with the Consolidated Stock Exchange, etc., as stated on pages 27 and 28, was rescinded by a resolution of the Governing Committee of the New York Stock Exchange on June 25, 1913.

[5] id.

hibited, as well as the transaction of business, directly or indirectly, with the members of that Exchange.[1]

No telephonic or telegraphic connection may be made between the office of a member or his firm and the office of any firm or individual not a member without the approval of the Committee of Arrangements. Where such connection is allowed, the member making it is not permitted to pay the expense of telegraph opertors or any other expense connected with it except that of the wire connection. Only the wires of companies approved by the Committee of Arrangements may be used.[2]

Telephonic communication between the offices of members and the Exchange is no longer a matter of right, but is in the discretion of the Committee of Arrangements. A member aggrieved by its decision may appeal to the Governing Committee. If the privilege is withdrawn from a member no other member may, after the decision is posted, furnish the member or his

[1]Resolution of May 19, 1909.

Since the adoption of this Resolution chapter 477, Laws of 1913 was enacted. This Law makes discrimination against other Exchanges and brokers a misdemeanor. See summary of laws, infra p. 52.

See Heim v N. Y. Stock Ex., 64 Misc. 529, aff'd 138 App. Div. 96.

[2]Resolution of May 9, 1900.

Outsiders have no status, it appears, to restrain an Exchange from prohibiting all its members from doing business on the floor for the outsiders. The Exchange's action appearing to be regular, the outsiders cannot undertake to regulate its manner of conducting business.

Russell v. N. Y. Produce Exch. 27 Misc. 381.

The resolution of May 19, 1909, prohibiting business with members of the Consolidated Exchange, not being adopted through any bad motives but to protect its own interests,is not an "illegal combination in restraint of trade" in violation of Laws 1890, p. 1514, c. 690.

Heim v. N. Y. Stock Exch. 64 Misc. 529, aff'd 138 App. Div. 96.

firm with any such telephonic facilities under penalty of suspension for two months.[1]

A member must report his transactions as promptly as possible at his office, where opportunity must be offered for prompt comparison.[2] The seller must compare, or endeavor to compare, each transaction at the office of the buyer, not later than one hour after the closing of the Exchange.[3] The buyer must investigate, before 10 A. M. of the day after the purchase, each

[1]Resolution of Nov. 8, 1911.

In Illinois the sending out of quotations to encourage speculation in futures is held by its Supreme Court to be in violation of the State statutes. The Federal Court, eighth circuit (Missouri), therefore holds that the Chicago Board of Trade cannot assert its claimed property right in such quotations in a court of equity.

Christie Grain & Stock Co. v. Board of Trade (C. C. A.), 125 Fed. 161, reversing 116 Fed. 944.

But the seventh circuit seems to hold an entirely different opinion. Even supposing, it holds, that a large proportion of the contracts made on the Exchange were gambling transactions, that did not deprive the Board of Trade of its property right in the price quotations. These quotations were the same for the lawful as for the unlawful transactions, and the right of property therein was not affected by the fact that they might be used for unlawful purposes. The court felt unable to concur in the Christie Grain & Stock Co. case and other cases cited.

Board of Trade of City of Chicago v. L. A. Kinsey Co. (C. C. A.), 130 Fed. 507.

The U. S. Supreme Court took the view of the seventh circuit.

Board of Trade v. L. A. Kinsey, 198 U. S. 236.

The N. Y. Stock Exchange may, as a condition of furnishing a telegraph company with its quotations, require transmission to approved persons only; a rejected applicant is not entitled to mandamus to compel the telegraph company to instal a ticker in his office and furnish him with quotations.

Matter of Renville, 46 App. Div. 37.

The right is not surrendered by allowing its subscribers to post the quotations upon blackboards in their places of business for the advantage of the subscribers and not of the public.

McDearmott Commission Co. v. Board of Trade (C. C. A.), 146 Fed. 961.

[2]Art. XXIV, Sec. 1.

[3]Art. XXIV, Sec. 2.

transaction not compared by the seller.[1] Neglect of either to do so is punishable by fine.[2]

Various rules regulate the mode of making comparisons.[3] Comparisons are made by an exchange of an original and a duplicate comparison ticket. An exchange of Clearing-House tickets constitutes a comparison.[4] When written contracts have been exchanged the signers thereof only are liable.[5]

The party delivering securities may require payment upon delivery; if delivery is made upon transfer, at the time and place of transfer.[6] The receiver has the option of requiring delivery either in certificates or by transfer, except where personal liability attaches to ownership, where the seller has the right to make delivery by transfer.[7] Payment must be made not later than 2:15 P. M. for all stock tendered in lots of one hundred shares or multiples thereof; the buyer may buy in the undelivered portion "under the rule" as hereinafter described.[8]

All deliveries must be made before 2:15 P. M., failing which the contract may be closed "under the rule." (See page 31.) The party in default is liable for any damage caused thereby, provided claim for such damage is

---

[1]Art. XXIV, Sec. 3.
[2]Art. XXIV, Sec. 4.
[3]Art. XXIV, Secs. 5–9.
[4]Art. XXIV, Sec. 5.
[5]Art. XXIV, Sec. 10.
[6]Art XXV, Sec. 1.
[7]Art. XXV, Sec. 2.
[8]Art. XXV, Sec. 4.

made before 3 P. M. on the business day following the default.[1] The neglect or failure of a member or firm to exchange Clearing-House tickets constitutes a default, and the contract may then be closed "under the rule," except that the time limit for delivery of notice of intention to close is 10:30 A. M. of the following business day and the time for closing is not before 10 A. M.[2] Rules regulate delivery on half-holidays.[3]

The Stock Exchange Clearing-House acts as the common agent of the members in receiving and delivering the securities designated by the Clearing-House Committee.[4]

To constitute a good delivery all deliveries on sales of stock must be accompanied by a stamped sales ticket.[5]

An important regulation is that governing the closing of contracts "under the rule." When the insolvency of a member or firm is announced, members having contracts subject to the rules of the Exchange with such member or firm must proceed to close them without unnecessary delay. If the securities involved are quoted on the Exchange the closing must be on the Exchange, either officially by the Chairman, or by personal purchase or sale. If they are not dealt in on the Exchange

[1]Art. XXVI, Sec. 1.

[2]Art. XXVI, Sec. 2.

[3]Art. XXVI, Secs. 4, 5.

[4]Art. XXVII.

[5]Resolution of November 9, 1910.
See also Laws 1909, Chap. 61, Penal Law, sec. 270, as amended, providing for stamp taxes, infra p. 236.

they must be purchased or sold in the best available market. If the contract is not so closed, the price of settlement is the price current when it should have been closed.[1]

A contract not fulfilled according to its terms may be officially closed "under the rule" by the Chairman.[2] Written notice of intention must be given the defaulting party before 2:30 P.M., and the contract cannot be closed before 2:35 P. M.[3] When a loan of money is not paid before 2:15 P. M. of the day it becomes due, the borrower is considered as in default, and the lender may sell "under the rule" so much of the pledged securities as may be necessary to liquidate the loan.[4]

Mutual cash deposits not exceeding ten per cent. may be required by either party to a contract at any time,[5] and the holder of a due-bill issued for the dividend on stock contracted for may require the maker of the due-bill to deposit the full amount in a trust company, payable to the joint order of the parties.[6] Failure to

---

[1]Art. XXVIII, Sec. 1.

A brokerage firm sold stock for an undisclosed principal and soon after notified the Exchange of its insolvency. The buying broker closed his contracts under the rule, settling by the payment to the receiver of differences on this and other contracts. The owner of the stock demanded that they take and pay for it. It was held that the owner could not recover the purchase price in an action against the purchasing broker, the announcement of the failure being a request to the defendant to close his contract. (Kent v. De Coppet, 149 App. Div. 589.)

[2]Art. XXVIII, Sec. 2.

[3]Art. XXVIII, Secs. 2, 3.

[4]Art. XXVIII, Sec. 10.

[5]Art. XXXI, Sec. 1.

[6]Art. XXXI, Sec. 2.

comply with a demand for a deposit constitutes a default, and the other party may have the contract reëstablished "under the rule."[1]

The time when a security becomes "ex-dividend" and "ex-rights" is regulated.[2]

A charge of one per cent. may be made for collecting dividends; but no charge may be made for collecting dividends accruing on securities deliverable on a contract.[3] Offers to buy or sell dividends may not be made publicly on the Exchange under penalty of a fine.[4]

Corporations whose shares are listed must maintain a transfer agency and a registry office in the Borough of Manhattan acceptable to the Committee on Stock List.[5] Thirty days notice must be given of a proposed increase of capital stock before it can be listed.[6] Shares may be registered on the conversion of convertible bonds, and listed on notice to the Exchange.[7] The Governing Committee may suspend dealings in any securities quoted on the Exchange, or summarily remove any securities from the list.[8] After admission of a security no change

[1]Art. XXXI, Sec. 4.

[2]Art. XXXII, Secs. 1, 2.

[3]Art. XXXII, Sec. 3.

[4]Art. XXXII, Sec. 4.

[5]Art. XXXIII, Sec. 1.

Under this article, the transfer and registry offices must be maintained separately. This is insisted upon by the Exchange in order that every precaution may be taken against fraud.

[6]Art. XXXIII, Sec. 2.

[7]Art. XXXIII, Sec. 3.

[8]Art. XXXIII, Sec. 4.

in the form of certificate, or of the transfer agency or the registrar of shares or of the trustee of bonds may be made without the approval of the Committee on Stock List.[1]

When the Committee on Stock List is of opinion that the outstanding amount of any listed security has become so reduced as to make further dealings inadvisable it may direct it to be taken from the list.[2]

Commissions must be charged on all purchases and sales of securities. These must be absolutely net, without any rebatement, direct or indirect; and no bonus or share of commission may be given directly or indirectly for business procured for a member.[3] The employment of clerks in nominal positions because of the business obtained by them for their employers is a violation of this rule.[4] The custom of "bunching" orders and not charging any commission to an associate in the sale is prohibited.[5] The rates of commission which may be charged members and non-members are fixed by the rules.[6] Transacting business in commodities without commission, or for a nominal commission, for a customer dealing in securities is a method for rebatement of commissions

[1]Art. XXXIII, Sec. 5.

[2]Resolution of March 27, 1895.

[3]Art. XXXIV, Sec. 1.

[4]Resolution of January 23, 1901.

[5]Resolution of June 12, 1912.

[6]Resolutions of November 23, 1881; October 24, 1894; April 13, 1910; April 12, 1911; June 12, 1907; December 28, 1911, and January 24, 1912.

and a violation of the commission rule. And giving reciprocal business in commodities dependent on the amount of Stock Exchange business received is also a violation.[1] A proposition for the transaction of business at less than the minimum rates of commission provided by the rules is a violation of the commission rule.[2] A suspended member is not entitled to have his business transacted at members' rates of commission, except in the case of a member suspended by reason of insolvency.[3] The penalty for violation of the commission rule is, for the first offense, suspension for from one to five years; for the second offense, the penalty is expulsion.[4] Arbitrage trading with cities in the United States based upon quotations from the Exchange, and arbitrage business by joint account, or account designed to produce the same result, having been found to nullify the commission rule, is forbidden.[5]

An arrangement with a customer for special or unusual rates of interest, or money-advances upon unusual terms to give the customer special advantages is a violation of the commission rule.[6]

The Governing Committee is of opinion that a member who relieves a customer from any part of the Stamp Tax violates the commission rule.[7]

[1]Resolution of April 14, 1897.
[2]Art. XXXIV, Sec. 4.
[3]Art. XXXIV, Sec. 5.
[4]Art. XXXIV, Sec. 6.
[5]Resolution of January 26, 1898; resolution of April 20, 1911.
[6]Resolution of March 26, 1902.
[7]Resolution of May 24, 1905.
See Tax Law secs. 270-277 infra p. 236.

The addresses of members and their partnerships and dissolutions must be registered with the Secretary.[1] No member can be a general or special partner in more than one registered firm at one time,[2] except in the case of foreign partnerships.[3] Members may not form partnerships with suspended or expelled members, nor with an insolvent person, nor with a former member against whom a member holds an unsettled claim. A member who is a special partner does not confer any of the privileges of the Exchange on his firm.[4] A general partner is liable for the acts and omissions of his firm; but he may be relieved from liability in the discretion of the Governing Committee.[5] Branch offices may be established by members, the managing clerk and other employees of which must be paid by fixed salaries, not varying with the business; and no agents for the solicitation of business shall be employed on any other basis.[6] If the Governing Committee disapproves of any partnership, branch office or interest in a foreign partnership, it may require the dissolution of the partnership, or the discontinuance of the branch office or the interest in the foreign partnership.[7] The penalty for violation of the rules as to partnership is suspension for one year.[8]

[1]Art. XXXV, Sec. 1.
[2]Art. XXXV, Sec. 2.
[3]Art. XXXV, Sec. 3.
[4]Art. XXXV, Sec. 4.
[5]Art. XXXV. Sec. 5.
[6]Art. XXXV, Sec. 6.
[7]Art. XXXV, Sec. 7.
[8]Art. XXXV, Sec. 8.

The publication of an advertisement of other than a strictly legitimate business character is prohibited.[1]

Rules as to irregularity in securities,[2] disagreement in terms of contracts,[3] disorderly conduct,[4] minutes, visitors, the reading of communications to the Exchange,[5] responsibility for losses made by comparison,[6] will be found in the Appendix.

Additions, alterations and amendments to the constitution may be made by the Governing Committee after consideration by the Committee on Constitution. When adopted by the Governing Committee they are submitted to the Exchange, and become law if not disapproved within one week by majority vote of the entire membership.[7] No amendment of Article XVIII as to the gratuity fund may be made impairing the obligation of members to contribute to that fund.[8]

The payment of interest by a proposing borrower of money on collateral after 3 P. M., without actually effecting the loan, is prohibited.[9]

---

[1]Resolution of February 9, 1898.
See Laws 1913, ch. 475. Penal Law Sec. 952 infra p. 208.

[2]Art. XXIX.

[3]Art. XXX.

[4]Art. XXXVI.

[5]Art. XXXVII.

[6]Resolution of November 9, 1904.

[7]Art. XXXVIII.

[8]id.

An unauthorized amendment of by-laws by the directors of an exchange is not binding on the members.
Moffatt v. Board of Trade (Mo.) iii S.W. 894.

[9]Resolution of October 25, 1889.

The following important resolutions were passed by the Governing Committee on February 13, 1913:

1. Against the carrying of an account either for a member or non-member, without proper and adequate margin. Penalty, suspension for one year.

2. Against the improper use of a customer's securities by a member or his firm. Penalty, suspension or expulsion.[1]

3. Against reckless or unbusinesslike dealing.[2] Penalty, suspension or expulsion, or, if suspended, ineligibility for reinstatement.

Gratuity Fund.

The gratuity fund in connection with the Exchange is supported by an original assessment of $10 from each member on admission[3] and an assessment of $10 on each member upon the death of a member,[4] until the date of transfer of membership.[5]

The sum of $10,000 is paid to the beneficiaries of a deceased member within one year of his death.[6] These are, in their order,

(a) the widow, if no descendants;
(b) the widow and descendants, one-half to each;
(c) the descendants, if no widow; no adopted child to share if the member leaves a widow or descendants;

[1]In reference to this see also Chap. 500, Laws 1913, Summary of Laws infra p. 44.

[2]In reference to this see also Laws 1913, ch. 500. Penal Law sec. 956 infra p. 211.

[3]Art. XVII, Sec. 1.

[4]Art. XVII, Sec. 2.

[5]Art. XVII, Sec. 3.

[6]Art. XVII, Sec. 4.

(d) if no widow or descendants, an adopted child or children.[1]

The gratuity cannot be mortgaged or pledged.[2]

The privilege does not continue after transfer of membership, whether voluntary or involuntary, nor after expulsion, but is extended to suspended members.[3] The management of the gratuity fund is in the hands of seven trustees chosen for a term of five years.[4] Vȧrious rules regulate their powers and duties and the election of officers.[5]

[1]Art. XVII, Sec. 5.

[2]Art. XVII, Sec. 7.

Under a similar by-law of the New York Produce Exchange the interests of beneficiaries are assignable as security for the repayment of such moneys as may be paid by another to keep alive such interests and without which they would have been absolutely destroyed. (Holmes v. Seaman, 184 N. Y. 486, reversing 99 App. Div. 624.)

[3]Art. XVII, Sec. 9.

[4]Art. XIX, Sec. 1.

[5]Art. XIX, Secs. 2-13.

With loss of full membership by failure to pay dues and assessments for the gratuity fund a member's right to the fund fell during his life, and he had nothing to transmit to his representatives.

MacDowell v. Ackley, 93 Pa. St. 277 (Phila. St. Exch.).

A rule of a gratuity fund provided that the payment should be deemed to be an absolute donation to the payee designated by the deceased member, free from all other claim or control. Such donation formed no part of the deceased member's estate, and his personal representatives had no right of action for it.

Swift v. San Francisco St. & Exchange Board, 67 Cal. 567.

The gratuity fund by-laws may be altered by any reasonable amendment, which means one that does not impair the member's vested rights thereunder.

Parish v. N. Y. Produce Exch., 169 N. Y. 34.

A suspended member cannot question the validity of amendments of the gratuity fund rules validly made.

MacDowell v. Ackley, 93 Pa. St. 277 (Phila. St. Exch.).

A rule giving the association power to suspend a member, without notice, for non-payment of his assessment, is not against public policy nor unreasonable.

People v. Board of Trade, 224 Ill. 370.

PART II

SUMMARY OF LAWS AND DECISIONS

PART II

SUMMARY OF LAWS AND DECISIONS

THERE have always been laws upon the statute books by which the legislature has endeavored either to control the conduct of stockbrokers or to throw around the pursuit of their calling such safeguards for the public as would ensure fair dealing.

Some of these laws are of long standing. Quite a few of them were enacted undoubtedly in response to an agitation which arose recently. While some of more recent date are mere declarations, as it were, of the common law, as it has heretofore existed, a few of them by supposedly creating new crimes, place upon the stockbroker additional burdens and responsibilities which are expected to secure a customer, and the public, perhaps, against loss in its dealings, not so much with the stockbrokers themselves, as in the general pursuit of investment or even speculation in corporate shares.

Whatever view one may have as to the necessity of this legislation, the merest inquiry will disclose that loss through misconduct of stockbrokers occurs in a very small percentage of cases. In five years, during which time there were on an average eleven hundred members on the New York Stock Exchange, the small number of nineteen failures occurred; and in the majority of these cases the creditors, including the customers, were either paid in full, or received compromises to their own satisfaction, and so rehabilitated the broker that he was fairly entitled to reinstatement.

The laws referred to are numerous and some of them lengthy and couched in such legal phraseology that it is deemed best that the more important of them should be summarized so that they may be read by the broker and his customer. For the purpose of making clear, if possible, what these laws have been held by the courts to mean, references have been made to decisions where same were obtainable.

No scheme or order could be devised for the presentation of these laws; they do not appear here in the order of their importance; they have been grouped where any relation existed between them, and the authorities have been cited wherever possible.

Unauthorized Pledging (Hypothecation) or Other Disposition of Customers' Securities.

Laws 1913, ch. 500. Penal Law, Sec. 956. In effect May 8, 1913.[1]

A broker who,

1. Having in his possession, for safekeeping or otherwise, securities belonging to a customer, without having any lien thereon or any special property therein, pledges or disposes thereof without the customer's consent; or,

[1]For full text see infra p. 211.

2. Having in his possession securities on which he has a lien for indebtedness, pledges them for more than the amount due to him thereon, or otherwise disposes of them without his customer's consent, and without having in his possession or under his control the equivalent of such securities, whereby the customer loses such securities or the value thereof, in whole or in part, is guilty of a felony, punishable by a fine of not more than $5,000 or imprisonment for not more than two years, or by both.

Every member of a firm of brokers, who either does or consents or assents to the doing of such an act, is guilty as above.[1]

The first clause of this section deals with the unauthorized pledge or other disposition of a customer's stocks held by the broker on which he has no lien. The second makes a felony what the law previously regarded as a conversion only,[2] i.e., the pledging of margined stock for more than the amount of the broker's advances. Even before the enactment of the statute, if the conversion had been made with intent to steal, it would have constituted larceny. The pledgor is still, of course, entitled to his civil remedy.[3]

A broker who has purchased stock on margin for a customer may pledge the stock for his advances.[4] All

[1]See The Exchange and its Constitution, supra p. 37.

[2]Hardy v. Jaudon, 1 Rob. 261
Strickland v. Magoun, 119 App. Div. 113.
In re Tracy, 191 Fed. 810

[3]See infra. p. 46.

[4]Rothschild v. Allen, 90 App. Div. 233, affirmed 180 N. Y. 561.

that is required of him is to have on hand the equivalent in kind and quantity of the margined stock.[1] He may, it has been held, sub-pledge and borrow money on margined stock en bloc.[2]

It is not conversion to transfer pledged stock certificates under an arrangement whereby the pledgee retains control over them.[3] It is not conversion for the broker to register in his own name.[4]

It is conversion if the broker, holding stock certificates as margin for his own benefit, rehypothecates the customer's securities for a greater amount than the customer's indebtedness to him, not having in his possession a like amount of similar securities,[5] or if he rehypothecates them to secure a different or larger debt than that for which they were pledged.[6]

An unauthorized pledge may be ratified by the owner of stock by his approval after the transaction is brought to his notice.[7]

A broker holding stock as marginal security pledged it for his own debt, without his pledgor's knowledge, and could not redeem the stock. The broker's pledgee

[1] Rothschild v. Allen, 90 App. Div. 233, aff'd 180 N.Y. 561.
Austin v. Hayden (Mich.) 137 N. W. 317.

[2] Skiff v. Stoddard, 63 Conn. 198.
Austin v. Hayden (Mich.) 137 N. W. 317.
But see infra p. 95.

[3] Heath v. Griswold, 5 Fed. 573.

[4] Ritchie v. Burke, 109 Fed. 16.

[5] Douglas v. Carpenter, 17 App. Div. 329.

[6] Smith v. Savin, 141 N. Y. 315.
Lawrence v. Maxwell, 53 N. Y. 19.
But see Mayer v. Monzo, cited infra p. 97.

[7] Curtis v. Leavitt, 15 N. Y. 9.

was held to have a good title to the stock as against the owner, though the broker had been guilty of conversion.[1]

Trading by Brokers Against Customers' Orders.

Laws 1913, ch. 592. Penal Law, Sec. 954. In effect May 17, 1913.[2]

A broker who trades against the orders of a customer, who has employed him to buy and carry stocks, bonds, etc., on margin, is guilty of a felony, punishable by a fine of not more than $5,000 or imprisonment for not more than one year. Every member of a firm who does or consents to such an act is guilty under this section.[3]

A custom creating in the broker an interest adverse to that of his customer has been disapproved.[4]

It has been held that a broker cannot act as principal and agent in the same transaction without his customer's consent.[5] Such dealings are held to be contrary to public policy, and the question of fraud or injury to the customer is immaterial.[6]

Delivery of Memoranda of Transactions.

Laws 1913, ch. 595. Penal Law, Sec. 957. In effect Sept. 1, 1913.[7]

A broker must deliver to his customer a statement or

[1]Whitlock v. Seaboard Nat. Bank, 29 Misc. 84.

[2]For full text see infra p. 209.

[3]See The Exchange and its Constitution, supra p. 37.

[4]Day v. Holmes, 103 Mass. 306.

[5]Porter v. Wormser, 94 N. Y. 431.
Pickering v. Demerritt, 100 Mass. 416.

[6]Mayre v. Strouse, 5 Fed. 483.

[7]For full text see infra p. 212.

memorandum of each purchase or sale made for him, containing a description of the securities purchased or sold, the name of the person, firm or corporation from whom they were purchased, or to whom they were sold, and the day, and the hours between which the transaction took place. Refusal to deliver such a statement or memorandum within twenty-four hours after written demand therefor by the customer, or delivery of a statement or memorandum which is false in any material respect, is a misdemeanor, punishable by a fine of not more than $500 or imprisonment for not more than one year or both.

This statute is entirely new. It has always been the custom of brokers to deliver to their customers a memorandum of transactions giving the above required particulars, excepting the time of execution. It is doubtful whether this provides any added security, though in case of fraud (bucketing), the burden of proving execution of the order is more easily shifted when it is shown that the notice erroneously specifies the time.

Manipulation of Prices of Securities. "Rigging the Market."

Laws 1913, ch. 253. Penal Law, Sec. 953. In effect April 10, 1913.[1]

Any person who influences or attempts to influence the market prices of securities by means of fictitious purchases, sales, or other transactions or devices, is

[1]For full text see infra p. 208.

guilty of a felony punishable by a fine of not more than $5,000, or imprisonment for not more than two years, or by both.[1]

The Anti-Bucket-Shop Law.

Penal Law, Sec. 390.[2]

(1.) One who makes or assists in making any contract for the purchase or sale of securities with the intention that the contract shall be settled upon the basis of the market quotations on any exchange, and without intending a *bona fide* sale; or

(2.) when such market quotations shall reach a certain figure without intending a *bona fide* purchase or sale; or

(3.) based upon the differences in such market quotations at which such securities are bought or sold; or,

(4.) who, as proprietor or person in charge, conducts any bucket-shop, or knowingly allows therein any contravention of the preceding three sections, is guilty of a felony.

Every broker must furnish to a customer upon written demand therefor, a written statement containing the names of the persons from whom the securities have been purchased or to whom they have been sold, and the time and place of the transaction, and the amount and price thereof. Refusal or neglect to do so within

[1]See The Exchange and its Constitution supra p. 25.

[2]For full text see infra p. 199.

forty-eight hours after the demand is *prima facie* evidence of violation of the statute.[1]

On conviction of a domestic corporation of a second offense, the Supreme Court may, upon an action by the Attorney-General, dissolve the corporation; in the case of a foreign corporation, it may restrain it from doing business in this state.[2]

"Bucket-shop" is defined as "any building, or any room, apartment, booth, office, or store therein, or any other place where any contract prohibited by" the statute "is made or offered to be made."[3] Keeping a bucket-shop has been made an offense by statute in Illinois,[4] where it is unnecessary to prove the intention of the keeper to keep such a place.[5]

A customer is entitled to the balance of his account with a "bucket-shop" as shown upon the trial in an action for accounting.

Printed agreements on the back of bought and sold notes, for the protection of the broker against his liability to furnish the names of customers whose orders were offset against the plaintiff's were held to be unreasonable, against public policy, and void.[6]

---

[1]Penal Law, Sec. 392.

[2]Penal Law, Sec. 393.

[3]Penal Law, Sec. 394.
See the Exchange and its Constitution supra p. 26.
See also infra p. 179.

[4]Weare Commission Co. v. People, 209 Ill. 528.
See also Peller v. Leiter, 189 N. Y. 361.

[5]Soby v. People, 134 Ill. 66.
Caldwell v. People, 67 Ill. App. 367.

[6]Haight v. Haight & Freese Co., 46 Misc. 501.

Transactions by Brokers After Insolvency.

Laws 1913, ch. 500. Penal Law, Sec. 955. In effect May 8, 1913.[1]

A broker who, knowing that he is insolvent, accepts or receives from a customer ignorant of his insolvency, money, or securities otherwise than in liquidation of, or as security for, an existing indebtedness, whereby the customer loses such money, etc., in whole or in part, is guilty of a felony punishable by a fine of not more than $5,000, or imprisonment for not more than two years, or by both. A person is insolvent within the meaning of the statute whenever the aggregate of his property shall not, at a fair valuation, be sufficient in amount to pay his debts.

This law is new. It is analogous to and was no doubt adapted from the provisions of the Penal Law which provide that an officer or employee of a bank or an individual or private banker who receives a deposit knowing that such bank or banker is insolvent, is guilty of a misdemeanor, if the amount or value of the deposit is less than $25; and of a felony if it is $25 or over that sum.

A broker who knows that another broker is insolvent and imposing on his customers, and who continues to coöperate with him and assist him to buy stock on margin, secured by stocks known to belong to the insolvent broker's customers, is liable equally with the insolvent broker to his customers for his acts.[2]

[1]For full text see infra p. 210.

[2]Austin v. Hayden (Mich.) 137 N. W. 317.

For a broker to pledge stock in his hands fully paid for, left with him for safe-keeping, is without color of right, fraudulent and criminal. (There is no statute on this subject in Michigan.)[1]

Discrimination by Exchange or Members.

Laws 1913, ch. 477. Penal Law, Sec. 444. In effect Sept. 1, 1913.[2]

No exchange shall forbid or prevent its members from dealing, at the regular rates of commission, with or for the members of any other exchange, or penalize or discipline any of its members for so doing. Any person or corporation violating the statute, and any member of any exchange refusing to deal with a member of another exchange, is guilty of a misdemeanor.[3]

Under this statute, in order to be guilty of a misdemeanor, the member must refuse to trade with a member of some other exchange *on the ground* that he is a member of such exchange. Presumably he might legally refuse for any other reason he chose.[4]

---

[1]Austin v. Hayden (Mich.) 137 N. W. 317, 323.

[2]For full text see infra p. 203.

[3]See The Exchange and its Constitution supra p. 27.

[4]The question arose before the statute was passed and it was held that a resolution of the Governing Committee of the Exchange prohibiting business with members of the Consolidated Exchange, not being adopted through any bad motives, but to protect its own interest, was not an illegal combination in restraint of trade, in violation of Laws of 1890, p. 1514, chap. 690.

Heim v. N. Y. Stock Exchange, 64 Misc. 529, aff'd 138 App. Div. 96.

Validity of Certain Agreements Made Without Consideration.

Personal Property Law, Sec. 33.[1]

An agreement for the purchase, sale, transfer or delivery of a certificate of stock or other evidence of municipal or corporate debt, is not void or voidable for want of consideration, or because the vendor, at the time of making the contract, is not the owner or purchaser of the certificate or other evidence of debt.[2]

A contract in futures is not illegal, even if it takes the form of a short sale or an option contract, except where there is no intention on either side to deliver or receive the stock, but the contract is merely one in differences. Short selling has been held valid in New York in numerous cases, and the statute of 1856 authorizing it is still in force.[3] If it was understood by both parties that there was to be no transfer of stock, but a mere

[1]For full text see infra p. 213.

[2](Former Pers. Prop. L. Sec. 22; originally revised from L. 1858, ch. 134.)

[3]Pers. Prop. Law. Sec. 33.
McIlvaine v. Egerton, 2 Rob. 422.
Tyler v. Barrows, 6 Rob. 104.
Stanton v. Small, 3 Sandf. 230.
Cassard v. Hinman, 1 Bosw. 207.
Fletcher v. Dold Packing Co., 169 N. Y. 571.
Kingsbury v. Kirwan, 43 Super. Ct. 451, affirmed 77 N. Y. 612.
Zeller v. Leiter, 114 App. Div. 148.
Springs v. James, 137 App. Div. 110.
White v. Smith, 54 N. Y. 522.
Barber v. Ellingwood, 144 App. Div. 512.
Campbell v. Wright, 8 N. Y. St. Rep. 471.
Sterling v. Jaudon, 48 Barb. 459.
Lazare v. Allen, 20 App. Div. 616.

gambling in differences, the transaction is a wager and invalid.[1]

Options in futures were held lawful, provided there was a bona fide intention to make a sale.[2]

In Illinois and other states there are statutes prohibiting options absolutely.[3] Such statutes have been held valid as an exercise of the police power.[4]

A broker knowing the transaction to be a gambling one and illegal, cannot recover for his commissions and advances;[5] and margin deposited on such an illegal transaction cannot be recovered back,[6] although in some states, as in Illinois, this is permitted by statute.[7]

In the absence of a statute, unlawful intention on the part of one only of the parties does not make the transaction illegal.[8]

---

[1]Bigelow v. Benedict, 70 N. Y. 202.
West v. Wright, 86 Hun, 436.
Peck v. Doran etc. Co., 46 Hun, 454.
La Gar v. Carey, 12 N. Y. St. Rep. 171.
Hurd v. Taylor, 181 N. Y. 231.
Weld v. Cable Co., 199 N. Y. 88.

[2]Story v. Salomon, 71 N. Y. 420.
Bigelow v. Benedict, 70 N. Y. 202.
Brown v. Hall, 5 Lans. 177.
Kingsbury v. Kirwan, 77 N. Y. 612.

[3]Minnesota Lumber Co. v. Whitebreast Coal Co., 160 Ill. 85.
Pearce v. Foote, 113 Ill. 228.

[4]Logan v. Tel. etc. Co., 157 Fed. 570.

[5]Dwight v. Badgley, 75 Hun, 174.
Fuller v. Tel. etc. Co., 117 App. Div. 352.

[6]Staples v. Gould, 9 N. Y. 520.
Crummey v. Mills, 40 Hun, 370.

[7]Kruse v. Kennett, 181 Ill. 199.

[8]Hentz v. Minor, 18 N. Y. Supp. 880.
Kingsbury v. Kirwan, 43 N. Y. Super. Ct., 451, aff'd 77 N. Y. 612.

Dealing in futures where there is no intention on either side of delivery or acceptance of the stock was made an offense by Laws 1889, c. 428.[1]

Prior to that time it was held that though such a contract was one of wager, and not binding upon the parties, it did not violate the provisions of Sec. 343 (now Sec. 973) of the Penal Law providing that the keeping of a room, etc., for gambling or any purpose or in any manner forbidden by the article, was a misdemeanor.[2]

Brokerage on Loans.

General Business Law, Sec. 380.[3]

Brokerage on procuring of loans is limited to the rate of fifty cents per $100, except loans on real estate security; and to thirty-eight cents for making or renewing any bond, bill, note or other security given for or concerning the same.

Any excess paid may be sued for and recovered by the payer within one year after payment, failing which the overseers of the poor of the city or town where the offense was committed may, within one year, sue for and recover the same.[4] The repayment and return of the excess with payment of the costs of such suit is a bar to further penalties.[5]

---

[1]People v. Wade, 59 N. Y. Supp. 846.
[2]People v. Todd, 51 Hun, 446.
[3]For full text see infra p. 234.
[4]Gen. Bus. Law, Sec. 381.
[5]Gen. Bus. Law, Sec. 382.
Buchanan v. Tilden, 18 App. Div. 123.
Corp. v. Brown, 2 Sand. 293.

The statute is not limited to loan brokers.[1] The statute applies to all loans without regard to time.[2]

Compensation for other services should be separated from the brokerage fee, so that it may be seen that it is not merely a cover for demanding unlawful commission.[3]

Advances on Collateral Security. (Usury.)

Laws 1882, ch. 237. General Business Law, Sec. 379.[4]

It is lawful to receive or contract for any sum to be agreed upon in writing by the parties as compensation for advances of money, payable on demand, of $5,000 or more, upon warehouse receipts, bills of lading, certificates of stock, certificates of deposit, bills of exchange, bonds or other negotiable instruments, pledged as collateral security.[5]

A demand note for $5,500, of which $500 was compensation for the loan, secured by the pledge of certificates of stock, was held to be within the statute, and not void for usury.[6]

Broad v. Hoffman, 6 Barb. 177.
Cook v. Phillips, 56 N. Y. 310.
Brown v. Post, 6 Robt. 111.
Vanderpool v. Kearns, 2 E. D. Smith, 170.
Woodward v. Stearns, 10 Abb. Pr. N. S. 395.

1 Buchanan v. Tilden, 18 App. Div. 123.

2 Cook v. Phillips, 56 N. Y. 310.
Broad v. Hoffman, 6 Barb. 177.

3 Cook v. Phillips, 56 N. Y. 310.

4 For full text see infra p. 233.

5 In the following cases loans were held not usurious under this statute:
Wright v. Toomey, 137 App. Div. 401.
Hawley v. Kountze, 6 App. Div. 217.
Frost v. Stokes, 55 N. Y. Super. Ct. 76.
In re Wilde, 133 Fed. 562.

6 Wright v. Toomey, 137 App. Div. 401.

A borrower gave his demand note for $15,000, with interest at six per cent. and pledged 14 shares of stock as collateral, also giving an agreement to sell to the lender, at the latter's option, 4 shares of the stock at $2,000 a share, which it was claimed was less than its actual value. It was held to be within the statute and not usurious.[1]

Frauds in Organization of Corporations.

Penal Law, Sec. 660.[2]

A person who,

(1.) Without authority subscribes the name of another to or inserts the name of another in any prospectus, circular or other advertisement or announcement of any corporation, etc., with intent to permit the same to be published and so to lead persons to believe that such person whose name is used is an officer, agent, member or promoter of such corporation; or,

(2.) Signs the name of a fictitious person to any subscription for or agreement to take stock in any corporation, existing or proposed; or,

(3.) Signs to any such subscription or agreement the name of any person, knowing that such person does not intend to comply therewith, or under any understanding or agreement that its terms are not to be enforced; is guilty of a misdemeanor.

It has been held in England to be a gross fraud upon the public for company promoters to induce men of character

[1]Hawley v. Kountze, 6 App. Div. 217.

[2]For full text see infra p. 204.

and financial standing to lend the use of their names as directors on a promise of indemnity from responsibility.[1]

It has frequently been held that subscriptions privately agreed to be for collateral purposes only, such as to make up a deficiency to enable the company to obtain its charter, or subscriptions made to induce others to subscribe or to give credit to the concern, the subscriber to be released from payment, are absolute and binding subscriptions.[2] The reason has been given that to release the subscription of the particular subscriber would be a fraud on the other subscribers.[3] And for the very reason that the subscriber is held not released, such a decoy subscription is held not available as a defense to any of the other subscribers.[4]

Fraudulent Issue of Stocks and Bonds.

Penal Law, Sec. 662.[5]

Any officer or other servant of a corporation, who wilfully, with intent to defraud,

---

[1]Re Life Assn. of England, 34 Beav. 639, 643, 11 Jur. N. S. 359, 34 L. J. Ch. 278, where Sir John Romilly, M. R. said: "It is obvious that a more gross misrepresentation can hardly be made than holding out to the world that responsible persons, who have nothing at all to do with the company, are directors of it."

[2]Mangles v. Grand Collier Dock Co., 10 Sim. 519, 16 Eng. Ch. 519.
In re Gen. Prov. Assur. Co., L. R. 9 Eq. 74.
Matter of Marylebone Banking Co., 3 De G. & S. 21.
White Mountains R. Co. v. Eastman, 34 N. H. 124.
Litchfield Bank v. Church, 29 Conn. 137.
Pickering v. Templeton, 2 Mo. App. 424.
Blodgett v. Morrill, 20 Vt. 509.
Downie v. White, 12 Wis. 176.

[3]LaGrange etc. Plank Road Co. v. Mays, 29 Mo. 64.

[4]Bach v. Tuch, 126 N. Y. 53.
Armstrong v. Danahy, 75 Hun. 405.

[5]For full text see infra p. 204.

(1.) sells, pledges or issues, or signs or executes for such purpose, any certificate of stock, etc., without prior authority from the corporation, or contrary to its charter or laws, or in excess of its power; or,

(2.) re-issues, sells, pledges, or disposes of any surrendered or cancelled certificates or other evidence of transfer or ownership of such shares, is punishable by imprisonment for not more than seven years, or by a fine not exceeding $3,000, or by both.

An innocent purchaser of shares which are part of an over-issue of stock may recover damages from the directors guilty of the fraud. The rule applies whether the plaintiff purchased directly from the company or from the directors or in the open market.[1] The corporation itself has remedies, both at law and in equity, against its officers or agents for damages caused by the illegal issue or over-issue of stock.[2]

Reporting or Publishing Fictitious Transactions.

Laws 1913, ch. 476. Penal Law, Sec. 951.[3]

The reporting or publishing of fictitious transactions in stocks, etc., or causing it to be done, with intent to deceive, is a felony punishable by a fine of not more than $5,000, or by imprisonment for not more than two

[1]Bruff v. Mali, 36 N. Y. 200.
Shotwell v. Mali, 38 Barb. 445.
Cazeaux v. Mali, 25 Barb. 578.

[2]Rutland R. Co. v. Haven, 62 Vt. 39.
Commonwealth Bank v. Schuylkill Bank, 1 Pars. Eq. Cas. (Pa.) 180.
American Ins. Co. v. Fisk, 1 Paige, 90.
Boyce v. Grundy, 3 Pet. 210.

[3]For full text see infra p. 207.

years, or both.[1] Brokers who, after receiving money and securities from a customer as margin, did not obey his instructions by making actual purchases and sales, but reported to him fictitious transactions, were held guilty of fraud and the customer was entitled to recover his money and securities, regardless of whether he had suffered any loss. The continuous failure of the transactions to be either cleared or reported at the Stock Exchange raised a presumption that the transactions did not occur.[2]

False Statement or Advertisement as to Securities.

Penal Law, Sec. 952. Laws 1913, ch. 475. In effect May 9th, 1913.[3]

Any person who, with intent to deceive, makes, issues, or publishes, any false statement or advertisement as to the value or as to facts affecting the value of any securities, or as to the financial condition of any corporation issuing, or about to issue securities, is guilty of a felony, punishable by a fine of not more than $5,000, or by imprisonment for not more than three years, or both.[4]

This law is very sweeping, more so than it looks at first sight. Formerly the well-settled rule of law was, and of course remains, that if a duly authorized agent of any corporation induces any person to become a

[1] See The Exchange and its Constitution, supra p. 28.

[2] Prout v. Chisholm, 21 App. Div. 54.

[3] For full text see infra p. 208.

[4] See The Exchange and its Constitution, supra. p. 36.

subscriber to its stock by fraudulent misrepresentations or concealments, the person deceived can obtain the rescission of the contract to take the shares.[1] This is a matter between the person defrauded and the corporation, and the reasonableness of the rule is apparent. It has various exceptions, chief of which are that it is not applicable where the rights of innocent third parties have intervened owing to the negligence of the subscriber, or where the subscriber could and ought to have informed himself as to the facts.[2] It is to be noticed that the fraud must have been committed by an *agent* of the corporation, and by an *authorized* agent, i. e., he must have been at the time acting within his authority.[3] The statute strikes at "any person" with intent to deceive. The subscriber may waive his right to rescind the contract.[4]

Under the statute the making of the statement, or causing it to be made, is a felony. Action by the subscriber is unnecessary and recourse against the corporation is left to the common law. The fraud, to ground a rescission, must be material.[5] The statute does not extend to the suppression of material facts in an advertisement. Under the statute intent to deceive is necessary. To obtain rescission it is not necessary. The statute strikes at *making* statements; therefore

---

[1]Willets v. Poor, 141 App. Div. 743.
Custar v. Titusville Gas etc. Co. 63 Pa. St. 381.

[2]In re Furniture Co., 170 Fed. 485.

[3]Robinson v. Pittsburgh etc. R. Co., 32 Pa. St. 334.

[4]Ruggles v. Brock, 6 Hun, 164.

[5]Willets v. Poor, 141 App. Div. 743.

oral statements are included. It has been expressly decided by several cases that mere puffing or *exaggeration as to the value* of the company's property or prospects will not ground a rescission if there is no misstatement of *material existing facts.*[1] The statute covers "any statement or advertisement as to the value or as to facts affecting the value" of the stock containing any material representation, prediction or promise knowing or having reasonable ground to believe the same to be false. The false statement must still be *material.*

Inserting advertisements in newspapers for the purpose of depressing the market value of the stock of a corporation is punishable as a misdemeanor under Section 435 of the Penal Code.[2]

Transfers of Certificates and Shares of Stock.

Personal Property Law, Art. VI.

Sec. 162. *How title to certificates and shares may be transferred.* (a.) By delivery of the certificate indorsed either in blank or to a specified person by the person appearing by the certificate to be the owner of the shares, or (b) by delivery of the certificate and a separate written assignment by such person.

Sec. 163. The powers of those lacking full legal capacity and of fiduciaries are not enlarged.

[1]Union Nat. Bank v. Hunt, 76 Mo. 439.
Denton v. Macneil, L. R., 2 Eq. 352.
Kisch v. Venezuela Cent. R. Co., 34 L. J. Ch. 545.
Thornburgh v. Newcastle etc. R. Co., 14 Ind. 499.
[2]People v. Goslin, 67 App. Div. 16, affirmed 171 N. Y. 627.

Sec. 164. Corporations are not prevented from treating the registered holder of shares as owner in regard to dividends, voting, calls and assessments.

Sec. 165. The certificate delivered endorsed or with a separate transfer extinguishes the title of a transferee under power of attorney or assignment not written on the certificate.

Sec. 166. The delivery is effectual although by one having no right of possession or authority from the owner of the certificate.

Sec. 167. The endorsement is effectual in spite of fraud, duress, mistake, revocation, death, incapacity, or lack of consideration or authority.

Sec. 168. Rescission of transfer may be made for the reasons mentioned in Sec. 167 unless the certificate has been transferred to a purchaser for value without notice, or in the case of waiver or laches by the injured party.

Sec. 169. Rescission of the transfer of a certificate does not invalidate subsequent transfer by transferee in possession to purchaser for value, who takes in good faith, and the latter obtains good title to the certificates and the shares represented thereby.

Sec. 170. Delivery of an unendorsed certificate, with intent to transfer it, imposes an obligation to indorse it upon the person making the delivery.

Sec. 171. An ineffectual attempt to transfer amounts to a promise to transfer.

Sec. 172. Warranties — On the transfer of stock the law implies certain warranties. They are (a) that the certificate is genuine, (b) that the transferor has a legal right to transfer it, and (c) that he does not know of any fact impairing its validity.

Sec. 173. The holder for security of a certificate demanding payment of the debt for which it is security does not warrant its genuineness or value.

Sec. 174. No attachment or levy upon shares shall be valid unless the certificate is seized or surrendered or transfer enjoined by the holder.

Sec. 175. A creditor is entitled to the same aid from the courts in reaching certificate owned by his debtor as in the case of property not readily attached or levied upon by ordinary process.

Sec. 176. No corporation shall have a lien upon shares of stock represented by a certificate, nor restrict the transfer of its stock by any by-law or otherwise, unless corporation's right to such lien or restriction is stated upon the certificate.

Sec. 177. The alteration of the certificate whether fraudulent or not does not divest the owner's title to the shares, originally held, and he can transfer good title to the certificate and the shares originally represented thereby.

Sec. 178. The court, in a proceeding brought for that purpose, may order a corporation to issue a new certificate, in place of one lost or destroyed, upon the giving of a proper bond. The corporation is not released from liability to a purchaser for value and in good faith of original certificate, who had no notice of the proceedings.

Secs. 179-180. Unimportant.

Secs. 181-182-183. Definitions of "endorsement," "person appearing to be the owner" of a certificate, "certificate," "delivery," etc.

Sec. 184. Article applies only to certificates issued after its taking effect, Sept. 1, 1913.

This statute is new. It is substantially in the form prepared by the commissioners for the promotion of uniformity of legislation in the United States. It is the result of the recognized necessity of having uniform laws affecting the transfer of stocks sold and otherwise disposed of throughout the country and of having uniformity in the warranties to be implied against persons making transfers and in the presumptions arising in connection with such transfers.

Stock Transfer Tax Law.

Tax Law, Article XII.[1]

A tax is imposed on all sales, or agreements to sell, or memoranda of sales of stock, and upon all deliveries or transfers of shares, or certificates of stock, whether made upon the books of the company or by an assignment in blank, or by delivery, or by any paper, intermediate or final, whether transferring the beneficial or legal title to or merely the possession or use of the stock, of two cents per $100 or fraction thereof. The transferor must affix the stamps and pay the tax. Agreements evidencing the deposit of stock certificate collateral for loans are exempt, as well as the certifi-

[1]For full text see infra p. 236.

cates themselves. If the transaction is shown by the company's books the stamp must be placed upon the books by the company, on its being furnished by the transferor; if made by delivery or transfer of a certificate the surrendered certificate must be stamped; in cases of agreement to sell, or delivery of the certificate assigned in blank the seller must deliver to the buyer a duly stamped bill or memorandum of the sale. Every bill or memorandum of sale or agreement to sell must show the date of the transaction, the seller's name, the stock concerned, and the number of shares.[1]

Adhesive stamps are prepared and sold by the State Comptroller.[2] Failure to affix or furnish the stamps by the persons described in Section 270 is a misdemeanor punishable by a fine of $500 to $1,000, or imprisonment for not more than six months, or by both.[3] The stamp must be cancelled by the person affixing it by writing or stamping the initials of his name and the date of using, and cutting or perforating the stamp so that it cannot be used again. Failure to cancel the stamp is a misdemeanor punishable by a fine of $200 to $500, or imprisonment for not less than six months, or both.[4]

The wilful removal or alteration of the cancelling marks on a stamp, or permitting that to be done, with intent to use the stamp again, or the buying, preparing

[1]Sec. 270.
[2]Sec. 271.
[3]Sec. 272.
[4]Sec. 273.

for use, using, possessing or suffering to be used any washed, restored or counterfeit stamp, or intentionally removing, or causing or knowingly permitting to be removed any affixed stamp is a misdemeanor, punishable by a fine of $500 to $1,000, or imprisonment for not more than a year, or both.[1]

Brokers must keep at some accessible place within the state a book of account to contain the dates of every sale, agreement to sell, delivery or transfer of shares or certificates of stock, the name of the stock, the names of the transferor and the transferee and the number and face value of the adhesive stamps affixed. Companies must keep stock certificate books, books of account, and transfer ledgers or registers for the entry of similar details of transfers and stamps. They must also retain all their books of account, transfer ledgers, registers, and stock certificate books, and all surrendered or cancelled shares or stock certificates, and all memoranda relating to sales or transfers thereof for at least two years. These must be open to examination by the Comptroller or his representative at all times between 10 A. M. and 3 P. M. except Saturdays, Sundays and holidays. The Comptroller may bring action for any unpaid tax and penalties. Failure to keep such records, or the alteration, cancellation, obliteration or destruction of any part of them, or the making of false entries therein, or the refusal to allow examination thereof by the Comptroller, is a misdemeanor, pun-

[1]Sec. 275.

ishable by a fine of $500 to $1,000, or imprisonment for from three months to two years, or both.[1]

Violation of Sections 270 and 272 entails, in addition to the penalties therein, a civil penalty of $10 for each share sold or transferred. Violation of the other provisions entails a civil penalty of $500 for each violation.[2]

The Stock Transfer Tax Act (L. 1906, Ch. 414, Sec. 1) purported to amend the prior Stock Transfer Tax Act of 1905 by imposing a tax of two cents "on each share of one hundred dollars of face value or fraction thereof" instead of "on each hundred dollars of face value or fraction thereof." It was declared invalid on account of arbitrary discrimination, all members of the class of corporate shares not being treated alike. Being void, it did not repeal the prior statute.[3]

The Stock Transfer Stamp Tax Law of 1905 was held constitutional. It was held that the state has power to tax the sale of stock of foreign corporations by citizens of the state if the sale is made within this state. Ingraham J., in a dissenting opinion, pointed out (p. 835) that "Shares of stock of incorporated companies are selected, and upon a sale of such stock there is imposed a tax, not based upon the value of the property or the amount for which it was actually sold, but upon what is called the face value of the stock, a

[1]Sec. 276.

[2]Sec. 277.
See The Exchange and its Constitution, supra pp. 30, 31 and infra p. 186.

[3]People ex. rel. Farrington v. Mensching, 187 N. Y. 8.

value which rarely, if ever, represents its true selling value."[1]

The tax is payable where shares of stock covered by a mortgage issued to secure bonds are sold on foreclosure.[2]

The act does not impose a tax on the original issuance of stock.[3]

A provision authorizing the Comptroller to secure evidence of violation of the statute from private books and papers of the party under investigation violates Sec. 6 of Art. I of the State Constitution, providing that no person shall be compelled "in any criminal case to be a witness against himself."[4] The effect of the section is that any sale *or gift* of stock cannot be enforced, whenever the defense is properly pleaded that no tax stamp was affixed at the time of delivery of the certificate of stock.[5] The section does not deprive the vendor of his property, therefore is not unconstitutional.[6]

Trust certificates issued by a voting trustee are taxable under Section 270.[7]

Failure by a vendor to pay the tax *at the time of the transfer* by placing stamps upon the stock certificates will preclude him from recovering from the vendee the purchase price, even if his failure to pay it was inad-

[1]People ex rel. Hatch v. Reardon, 110 App. Div. 821, affirmed 184 N. Y. 431, affirmed 204 U. S. 152.

[2]Glynn v. Conklin, 127 App. Div. 473.

[3]People v. Duffy-McInnerney Co., 122 App. Div. 336.

[4]People v. Reardon, 197 N. Y. 236.

[5]Matter of Raleigh, 75 Misc. 55.

[6]Sheridan v. Tucker, 145 App. Div. 145.

[7]U. S. Radiator Corp. v. State of N. Y., 151 App. Div. 367, aff'd 208 N. Y. 144.

vertent, if the vendee, when sued, properly pleads the failure to pay the tax as a defense.[1]

[1]Bean v. Flint, 204 N. Y. 153, affirming 138 App. Div. 846. Sheridan v. Tucker, 145 App. Div. 145.

PART III

THE BROKER AND HIS CUSTOMER

PART III

THE BROKER AND HIS CUSTOMER

THE relation between the broker and his customer has been the subject of numerous decisions by the Courts in this country and in England. The cases that have arisen deal largely with either the effort on the part of the broker to recover the balance of his account for stock-brokerage as against his customer, or with the effort on the part of the customer either to recover from the broker securities purchased or deposited for margin, or to obtain their value, upon the theory that the broker dealt with them without complying with the law in regard to notice and time and place of sale.

In reading these decisions, it is apparent, that while a considerable measure of natural justice entered largely in determining the issues that arose, the laws seemed to lean altogether in the direction of protecting the customer. This is accomplished by holding the broker to the strictest performance of his duties to his customer and visiting upon him a full measure of responsibility for any dereliction.

Most of the cases arrange themselves under the head of pledgor and pledgee, in which is included those decisions dealing with the right to hypothecation and what amounts to conversion. They are presented here as nearly as possible in the sequence in which the ideas arise when the relation of stockbroker and customer is thought of, and the whole is preceded by definitions of those terms most likely to be encountered in a reading of the reported cases.

Definitions.

Some judicial definitions of terms commonly used by those who deal on the Stock Exchange follow.

"MARGIN" DEFINED.

"Margin" is security nothing more.[1]

"SHORT SALE" DEFINED.

A "short sale" is a sale of stock which the seller does not possess, but which he hopes to buy in at a lower price than that for which he sells.[2]

"BULL" DEFINED.

A "bull" is one who buys stock with the expectation of making a profit through a rise of price; he is then said to be "long of stock."[3]

"OPTION" DEFINED.

An "option" in one sense denotes a future contract,

---

[1] Hopkins v. O'Kane, 167 Pa. St. 478.

[2] Baldwin v. Flagg, 36 N. J. Eq. 57.
White v. Smith, 54 N. Y. 522.
Knowlton v. Fitch, 52 N. Y. 288.
Hess v. Rau, 95 N. Y. 359.

[3] 5 Am. & Eng. Enc. Law 2nd Ed. 18.
Baldwin v. Flagg, 36 N. J. Eq. 56.

in which one side has a right to insist upon compliance with the contract at any time within a given period.

In another sense it means where one side has a right to insist upon such compliance as to cancel the contract at his election, such as a "put" or a "call."[1]

"PUT" DEFINED.

A "put" is judicially defined as the "privilege of delivering or not delivering" the thing sold.[2]

"CALL" DEFINED.

A "call" is defined as the "privilege of calling for or not calling for" the stock bought, or an option to claim stock at a fixed price on a certain day.[3]

"FLY-POWER" DEFINED.

A "fly-power" is a written assignment in the form generally used on the reverse of stock certificates, which when signed and attached to such certificate, is sufficient to transfer the same in like manner as an endorsement thereon.[4]

Good Faith and Care.

The stockbroker is bound to exercise good faith in

---

[1]Jackson v. Foote, 12 Fed. 37.
Bigelow v. Benedict, 70 N. Y. 202
Story v. Salomon, 71 N. Y. 420.

[2]Bigelow v. Benedict, 70 N. Y. 202.
Asgood v. Bander, 75 Iowa, 550.

[3]Pixley v. Boynton, 79 Ill. 353.
Muller v. Bensley, 20 Ill. App. 530.

[4]Carlisle v. Norris, 142 N. Y. Supp. 393, 396.

his dealings with his customer,[1] and reasonable skill and diligence,[2] but he is liable only for the reasonable care and diligence which an ordinarily prudent purchaser would exercise.[3]

Secret Profits.

He may not make secret profits for himself out of the transaction.[4] But as the broker is not obliged to retain the identical stock purchased, the purchaser cannot, if he orders a subsequent delivery of the stock, and pays for it at the contract price, recover a profit the brokers have made through being able to secure the stock actually delivered at a lower figure owing to a fall in the market.[5]

Notice of Transactions.

He must notify his customer of the transactions made.[6]

Broker Bound by Manager's Acts.

A manager of a stockbroker's office, as between the stockbroker and a customer, is a general agent of the

---

[1]Hoffman v. Livingston, 46 N. Y. Super. Ct., 552.
Levy v. Loeb, 85 N. Y. 365.
Bate v. McDowell, 49 N. Y. Super. Ct. 106.

[2]Boyle v. Henning, 121 Fed. 376.
Harris v. Turnbridge, 83 N. Y. 92.

[3]Peckham v. Ketchum, 5 Bosw. 506.
Gheen v. Johnson, 90 Pa. St. 38.

[4]Illingworth v. De Mott, 59 N. J. Eq. 8.
The customer may ratify the taking of secret profits by failing to object.
Sprague v. Currie, 133 App. Div. 18.

[5]Helm v. Ennis, 109 App. Div. 42.

[6]Hoffman v. Livingston, 46 N. Y. Super. Ct. 552.
Tuell v. Paine, 39 Misc. 712.

broker, who is bound by the manager's acts done in the course of business though he violates some private instruction not known to the customer.[1]

Payment before Delivery.

A customer cannot demand delivery of stock purchased by his order until he has paid or tendered the price paid.[2]

Prior Indebtedness.

A broker cannot apply the margin put up on a transaction upon a prior indebtedness which is disputed by the customer. If he does so, and exhaustion of margin results in a sale, the sale is unauthorized.[3]

Broker Must Obey Definite Order.

A broker who fails to carry out a definite order by his customer to buy or sell is, in ordinary circumstances, liable for any consequent loss.[4] Brokers who have been told that a special account in a customer's name is for another, are not entitled to sell the stock to make up

[1]Newman v. Lee, 87 App. Div. 116.
For liability of broker for acts of employee of lower grade see Reichard v Hutton, 158 App. Div. 122.

[2]Weir v. Dwyer, 114 N. Y. Supp. 528, 532.

[3]Hurt v. Miller, 120 App. Div. 833.

[4]Zimmerman v. Heil, 156 N. Y. 703.
Allen v. McConihe, 124 N. Y. 342.
Taylor v. Ketchum, 5 Rob. 507.
Galigher v. Jones, 129 U. S. 193.
Kilmer v. Hutton, 131 App. Div. 625.
Picard v. Beers, 195 Mass. 419.
King v. Zell, 105 Ind. 435.
Cochran v. Ellis, 107 Ill. 413.
Silence on receiving a communication is not a direction to sell.
Lynch v. Simmonds, 87 N. Y. Supp. 420.

deficiency in the customer's own account.[1] A "stop order" does not impose an obligation upon the broker to hold the stock until it reaches the price named in the order. It is a measure of protection which the purchaser provides for himself against loss beyond a certain point in a fluctuating market.[2]

Broker May Buy Smaller Quantity than Ordered.

An ordinary order to purchase mining stock is not an entire contract. The broker may buy a smaller quantity than is ordered.[3]

Keeping Proper Accounts.

It is a broker's duty to keep proper accounts showing the names of the persons with whom he deals for his customer.[4] Failing this, presumptions of value will be against him.[5]

Authorization to Sell Distinguished from Order.

A customer in New York dealt with brokers in Chicago, but the transactions were all made by their representatives in New York, V. &. A., on the plaintiff's direct orders. The customer telegraphed the brokers, "I will have to let my stocks go," whereupon they instructed V. &. A. to sell the stocks. The customer also instructed V. &. A. to do so, so that the order was duplicated. It

[1] Conklin v. Raymond, 127 App. Div. 663.

[2] Richter v. Poe (Md.), 71 Atl. 420, 424.

[3] Marye v. Strouse, 5 Fed. 483.

[4] Prout v. Chisholm, 89 Hun, 108.

[5] Bate v. McDowell, 49 N. Y. Super. Ct. 106.

was held that the customer's telegram was an *authorization* to sell, not an *order*, and until the broker had notified him of their election to exercise the authority, the customer was at liberty to instruct V. &. A. directly; and the brokers' order was held for their own account.[1]

Manner of Sale.

A customer gave a stop order containing no directions as to the manner of sale of the bonds his brokers were carrying for him. They were sold between the calls at the Stock Exchange at private sale as government bonds usually are. It was held that the manner of sale was not open to objection in the absence of evidence to impeach its fairness.[2]

Proof of Receipt of Order.

A customer's evidence that he mailed a letter ordering a purchase at the opening market price is insufficient without proof that the broker received it in time to execute the order.[3]

Pooled Stock.

In a suit against brokers for refusing to sell certain stocks purchased for the plaintiff as a member of a pool, the plaintiff testified to an agreement that as a member of the pool he might sell his stock at any time on order, but he admitted that the right of members of the pool to sell would render it ineffective. It was shown that he was a financial writer and perfectly familiar with the operation

[1]Evans v. Wrenn, 93 App. Div. 346.
[2]Porter v. Wormser, 94 N. Y. 431.
[3]Birnbaum v. May, 58 App. Div. 76.

of pools and syndicates. It was held that his testimony that his contract entitled him to sell his holdings was so inconsistent with the necessities of a successful pool agreement that a verdict in his favor was against the weight of evidence.[1] A pool member who causes the pool account to be transferred to an account of his own, acts as agent of the other members, closes the pool account, and becomes individually liable thereon.[2]

Order to Sell at Discretion.

A broker may have authority from his customer to sell at his discretion. In such a case the customer cannot, without showing fraud, hold him liable for selling at a lower price than the stock touches at other times.[3]

When Broker Not Compelled to Sell.

When the customer is a speculator, in debt to the broker and in poor credit, the broker is not liable for refusing to obey his order to sell and buy with the proceeds other stocks which the broker thinks less safe even though these go up afterwards.[4] Where discretionary authority is given a broker to sell he has a reasonable time within which to do so. Seven or eight days has been held reasonable.[5]

Brokers are not obliged to sell stock on the exhaustion of margin. They may hold it and depend upon the custo-

[1] Ridgely v. Taylor & Co., 118 App. Div. 10.

[2] Post v. Thomas, 153 App. Div. 865.

[3] Wronkow v. Clews, 52 N. Y. Super. Ct. 176.

[4] Jones v. Gallagher, 3 Utah 54.

[5] Davis v. Gwynne, 57 N. Y. 676.

mer's liability without security, if there is no agreement that it is to be sold when the margin is exhausted.[1]

Ratification of Unauthorized Transaction.

An unauthorized purchase or sale may be ratified by the customer.[2] But where the customer was not apprized of all the facts, such as omitting to state the selling price, a delay of twelve days in repudiating the transaction did not amount to a ratification.[3] A purchaser may ratify an unauthorized purchase by agreeing to pay the balance shown by statements to be due by him, by depositing stock to secure the indebtedness, and by actually paying it.[4] A customer may ratify acts of his brokers amounting to a taking of secret profits by accepting their account stated and paying the balance shown, without objection.[5]

If a customer ratifies a sale in ignorance of the facts and the brokers send him a second statement to the effect that the price mentioned in the first is due to a clerical error, the customer may disaffirm his ratification, but if he elects to continue the ratification he can only recover the price actually received.[6]

[1]Little v. McClain, 134 App. Div. 197.
[2]Ramsay v. Miller, 202 N. Y. 72.
Burhorn v. Lockwood, 71 App. Div. 301, affirmed 177 N. Y. 539, 554.
Rock v. Carpenter, 110 N. Y. Supp. 261.
[3]Burnham v. Lawson, 118 App. Div. 389.
[4]Buck v. Houghtaling, 110 App. Div. 52.
[5]Sprague v. Currie, 133 App. Div. 18.
[6]Stewart v. Harris, 101 App. Div. 181.

Failure to Execute Orders.

The customer's acceptance of a check in settlement of the stockbroker's account stated will not ratify the broker's unauthorized failure to purchase where the broker represented he had done so.[1]

Waiver or Revocation of Order.

Circumstances may show a waiver or revocation of the order. The question whether a telegram to the broker, two or three months after an order to sell, which he had not executed, "Have you sold? Will they go lower?" was a waiver, has been held to be one of fact for the jury.[2]

Customs and Usages and Rules of Stock Exchange.

Customers are presumed to have authorized the broker to carry through the transaction in accordance with the usages and customs of the particular Exchange, so far as these concern the manner of performing the contract, although these are not known to the customer; and this applies to the rules of the Stock Exchange themselves.[3] This has been held to apply to the following customs; to sell stocks deposited as collateral security for call loans at the board on the borrower's failure to pay on the day demand is made,[4] of brokers to purchase

[1]Des Jardins v. Hotchkin, 142 App. Div. 845.
[2]Stone v. Lothrop, 109 Mass. 63.
[3]Horton v. Morgan, 19 N. Y. 170.
Spring v. James, 137 App. Div. 110.
[4]Colket v. Ellis, 10 Phila. (Pa.) 375.

stock in their own names, without disclosing their principals,[1] to close out a transaction on the customer's default,[2] to settle claims against defaulting customers,[3] to accept certain stocks as collateral for additional margin, imposing upon the broker the duty to accept them.[4] But apparently the transaction must have been on the Exchange.[5]

Customs Disapproved.

The following customs have been disapproved: to make fictitious transactions;[6] to sell stock deposited with them as collateral;[7] to disregard statutory enactments as to the manner of conducting transactions;[8] a custom altering, contradicting or adding to the express contract;[9] a custom creating in the broker an interest adverse to that of the customer.[10]

A customer is of course bound where the contract is expressly made subject to the customs prevailing on the

[1]Horton v. Morgan, 19 N. Y. 170.

[2]Greely v. Doran-Wright Co., 148 Mass. 116.
Van Dusen-Harrington Co., v. Jungeblut, 75 Minn. 298.
"There is a well-established custom that, if a stock touches margin, it is to be sold for the highest it will bring."
Potter v. Malcolm (1907), 104 N. Y. Supp. 760.

[3]Lehman v. Feld, 37 Fed. 852.

[4]Ling v. Malcolm, 77 Conn. 517.

[5]Ayer v. Mead, 13 Ill. App. 625.

[6]Rosenstock v. Tormey, 32 Md. 169.

[7]Lawrence v. Maxwell, 53 N. Y. 19.

[8]Neilson v. James, 9 Q. B. D. 546.

[9]Markham v. Jaudon, 41 N. Y. 235.
Spear v. Hart, 3 Robt. 420.

[10]Day v. Holmes, 103 Mass. 306.

Exchange.[1] The customer is entitled to presume that the broker will act within the rules of the Exchange.[2]

The Broker Cannot Act for Buyer and Seller.

A broker cannot act for both buyer and seller.[3]

The Broker Cannot Buy Customer's Stocks.

He cannot act as principal and agent in the same transaction without his customer's consent.[4] But headings of notices of sale indicating that he has done so do not prevent him showing that the sales were actually made to others.[5] The question of actual fraud or injury done his customer is immaterial if he so acts, such dealings being held contrary to public policy.[6]

Buying on Margin.

A speculative contract for the purchase and sale of stocks on margin is valid.[7]

Broker Must Purchase Margined Stock, and Cannot Purchase It on Margin Himself.

A broker must purchase, obtain possession of, and hold margined stocks, subject to his right to pledge them for

[1]Baker v. Drake, 66 N. Y. 518.

[2]Newman v. Lee, 87 App. Div. 116.

[3]Levy v. Loeb, 85 N. Y. 365.
Rice v. Davis, 136 Pa. St. 439.

[4]Porter v. Wormser, 94 N. Y. 431.
Pickering v. Demeritt, 100 Mass. 416.

[5]Porter v. Wormser, 94 N. Y. 431.

[6]Marye v. Strouse, 5 Fed. 483.

[7]Richter v. Poe (Md.) 71 Atl. 420.

his advances in excess of the customer's margin. He cannot buy them on margin from another broker, because in such a case the securities would be subject to that broker's right to pledge them for advances to him.[1] A broker who has bought on margin for a customer cannot sell without the customer's authority while he holds sufficient margin.[2]

A contract between broker and customer with reference to margined transactions authorized the broker to close when the margin was "exhausted." It was held that this meant "depleted" or "impaired," and the broker was not required to wait for a loss before closing. "A margin," the court said, "is intended for the protection of the broker, but if he be compelled to postpone the sale of the property which he is carrying for the customer until he has no margin left, it is difficult to perceive upon what theory any adequate protection is afforded."[3]

A cotton broker was instructed, when the customer had $9,600 to his credit on his books, "to hedge when margin about exhausted." The customer subsequently drew down $6,000, and the broker allowed cotton to go down until the remaining margin of $3,600 was exhausted, and $4,000 in addition. It was held that his instructions covered, not only the particular margin at the time, but

[1]Des Jardins v. Hotchkin, 142 App. Div. 845.
Mayer v. Monzo, 151 App. Div. 866.

[2]Taylor vs. Ketchum, 35 How. Pr. 289, holding such an unauthorized sale to be a conversion, regardless of whether or not notice of it is given to the customer.
See also Denton v. Jackson, 106 Ill. 433.

[3]Foster v. Murphy & Co. (C. C. A.), 135 Fed. 47.

any margin in the hands of the brokers at any time before the close of the trades.[1]

Demand for Margin.

Before closing a transaction on failure of margin, either where stock has been bought or sold short, the broker must first make a demand on his customer for additional margin.[2]

Demand Must Be Specific.

Such demands for margin must be specific, definite, and certain. To constitute a sufficiently specific demand it must either mention a particular sum or state facts from which a particular sum may be ascertained with certainty.[3] An alternative demand calling for an answer from the customer has been held insufficient.[4]

Notice of Exhaustion.

The New York rule as to notice of exhaustion of margin in the case of stocks bought is different from that held in Massachusetts and possibly in some other jurisdictions. In New York notice of the sale must be given to the customer, notwithstanding that the broker may have already demanded additional margin and the customer has not complied with the demand.[5]

[1] Winston v. F. A. Longshore & Co., 116 La. 21.

[2] Markham v. Jaudon, 41 N. Y. 235.
Stenton v. Jerome, 54 N. Y. 480.
Ritter v. Cushman, 35 How. Pr. 284.
Rogers v. Wiley, 14 N. Y. Supp. 622, affirmed 131 N. Y. 527.

[3] Boyle v. Henning, 121 Fed. 376.

[4] Esser v. Linderman, 71 Pa. St. 76.

[5] Gruman v. Smith, 81 N. Y. 25.
See also,

"The object to be attained by giving the notice is to afford the debtor an opportunity to redeem, and to be present at the sale to see and know that it is fairly conducted and the property disposed of to the best advantage."[1] In other words, the notice must be reasonable in time, and definite as to the place and manner of the sale.

But the rule is a general one which must be applied to an infinite variety of circumstances. In a very recent case[2] the conditions were exceptional. "It was a time of tense excitement, of sudden and violent fluctuations in prices, of veritable panic in which individual judgment was torn from its moorings by the impact of popular frenzy. Notwithstanding these conditions, it was still the duty of the defendants to give the plaintiff reasonable notice."[3]

Brokers called, for margin, at the office of a customer who was away on his vacation. They did not attempt to get his address, which they could have gotten from his partner. An employee of the brokers, through whom the customer did business with them, had told the customer before he started that his account was all right, and that if anything happened the employee would take care of it. The brokers closed out the stocks without

Taylor v. Ketchum, 35 How. Pr. 289.
Baker v. Drake, 66 N. Y. 518.
Fairchild v. Flowerfelt, 79 Misc. 42.
[1]Wheeler v. Newbould, 16 N. Y. 392, 401.
[2]Small v. Housman, 208 N. Y. 115.
[3]id. p. 125.

notice to the customer of the sale. They were held liable for conversion.[1]

Reasonable Time to Make Good.

The customer is entitled to reasonable time to furnish the additional margin demanded.[2] One hour's notice is not ordinarily sufficient;[3] one day's notice has been held sufficient,[4] and two days' notice has been held sufficient.[5] Where the customer was in Texas and the broker in New York deposit of margin within two hours after notice was held good, even though made after 12 noon on Saturday.[6]

Before selling for lack of margin a broker must give notice of *time* of sale.[7]

If brokers exercise ordinary care and reasonable efforts to give the customer notice and are unable to do so through the customer's neglect, they are not obliged at their peril to find him and give him *actual* notice and a reasonable time to make the margins good before selling the contracts.[8]

Actual notice of the time and place of sale is only necessary when the broker holds property in pledge for the customer.[9]

---

[1]Rosenbaum v. Stiebel (1910), 122 N. Y. Supp. 131.

[2]Boyle v. Henning, 121 Fed. 376.

[3]Lazare v. Allen, 20 App. Div. 616.

[4]Harris v. Pryor, 18 N. Y. Supp. 128.

[5]Stewart v. Drake, 46 N. Y. 449.

[6]Langer v. Price, 114 App. Div. 78. (Cotton Exchange case.)

[7]Fairchild v. Flowerfelt, 79 Misc. 42.

[8]Smith v. Craig, 151 App. Div. 648.

[9]Smith v. Craig, 151 App. Div. 648, 654.
Leiter v. Thomas, 110 App. Div. 879.

A contract provided that the customer should keep a margin of five per cent. and reserved to the brokers the right to sell at their discretion at any time when in their opinion the condition of the account warranted it. The customer's margin dropped below one per cent. to his knowledge. It was held that the brokers were entitled to sell without notice.[1]

A broker may waive a provision in his contract reserving the right to close transactions without further notice whenever margins were running out, either in express terms or by a course of dealing giving the customer the right to believe that this would not be done.[2]

Sufficiency of Notice of Time and Place of Sale.

Where the broker advanced the whole amount instead of requiring margin a written notice to take up the securities or supply sufficient margin to carry them stated that unless the customer made suitable arrangements "before Wednesday next (August 13) we shall sell this stock and hold you responsible for the loss." It was held the notice was defective because it contained no statement as to the time or place of sale; and, in the absence of any agreement dispensing with such notice, a sale "on the curb," the customer having failed to respond on the day specified, constituted a conversion.[3]

On a purchaser's failure to pay for a stock purchased,

[1]Estes v. Perkins, 137 App. Div. 367.

[2]Miller & Co. v. Lyons (Va.), 74 S. E. 194, where the broker was held estopped from closing without notice by failing to exercise or claim the right during a period of four years.

[3]Content v. Banner, 184 N. Y. 121.

"the sale should be made at some place where all the parties interested may have an opportunity to attend and see that it is fairly conducted." Ordinarily it is the place where transactions of the same description are customarily made, and by employing a stockbroker a customer impliedly authorizes him to perform the business in the manner and at the place established by custom. So, where the customer has requested the stock to be bought on the curb it is a fair inference that it was the intention of the parties that the stock, if sold, should be sold on the curb.[1]

A pledged stock was sold upon the curb and the pledgees purchased it themselves. The agreement for pledge gave them the right to become purchasers only in case the sale was made "at brokers' board or at public auction." The sale was held to be at neither, the curb not constituting a "brokers' board."[2]

In another case the jury, on conflicting evidence, was held warranted in finding that brokers had assented to their customer having the whole day in which to put up margin or arrange for taking care of the shares, but they sold the customer out before one o'clock and thus violated the agreement they had made. They were therefore held liable for damages for the unauthorized sale.[3]

A sale of stock took place at two o'clock in the afternoon of October 24th, following two conversations on the

[1]Weir v. Dwyer, 114 N.Y. Supp. 528, 531. (Chicago Subway stock.)
[2]Manning v. Heidelbach, 153 App. Div. 790.
[3]Blaine v. Thomas, 103 App. Div. 600, 153 App. Div. 790.

same day between the customer's agent and a member of the firm of brokers. Sales took place on October 25th, apparently immediately after a similar conversation between the same persons at 10 o'clock in the forenoon of that day. The New York Court of Appeals held that the sufficiency of these notices should have been submitted to the jury, and was not a question of law for the court.[1]

Special Agreement.

A defense to an action for damages for the alleged unauthorized sale of stock was that the stock was purchased under a special agreement by which the customer was to keep on deposit with the brokers at all times a margin of $25,000, and that in the event that the market price depreciated and the customer failed to keep such margin unimpaired they were to be at liberty to sell the stock "without other notice than notice that said margin had been reduced," and that they gave the customer every notice to which he was entitled by virtue of the special agreement or by custom. The principal question was whether such a special agreement had been made. The jury found for the customer, but the Appellate Division held that their verdict was against the weight of evidence, and reversed the judgment.[2]

In a very recent case it was contended for the customer that after certain transfers of stock had been

[1]Small v. Housman, 208 N. Y. 115.

[2]Leiter v. Thomas, 110 App. Div. 879.

made, the brokers gave a promise to the agent of the customer (the latter being abroad) that what remained of the customer's account would be carried by the brokers until the customer's return. It was held that though this promise, if made, was probably not an irrevocable contract, it could not be ignored to the prejudice of the customer. If the brokers by their promise did lead the customer's agent to believe that he had nothing further to fear until his principal's return, they were bound at least to give reasonable notice of their intention to retract this promise. Whether such an arrangement was really made was not a question of law for the court, but one of fact for the jury.[1]

Brokers may agree to buy and carry stock on a nominal margin.[2]

Notice to Customer's Agent.

Notice given to the customer's agent may be sufficient.

A customer's son was employed by the stockbrokers who handled her account, which was entirely operated by the son; the customer never came in contact with the brokers. The customer went to Europe, leaving her account in charge of her son, and her securities in a safe deposit box, in charge of a friend, who from time to time took securities from the box and gave them to the customer's son, who delivered them to the brokers in response to calls for margins. In an action for damages for the conversion of certain of the stocks and bonds by the brokers, it was held that the son was his mother's

[1]Small v. Housman, 208 N. Y. 115.

[2]Keller v. Halsey, 202 N. Y. 588

general agent to transact business with reference to the account, and that a demand on the son for further margins was notice to him and to the customer that, if they were not furnished, securities already pledged with the brokers would be sold.[1]

Waiver of Customer's Default in Complying with Demand for Additional Margin.

The broker's waiver of his customer's default in complying with a demand for additional margin will prevent him from being entitled to close the transaction until a new demand is made.[2]

Tender of Stock.

In addition to demand for additional margin and notice of intention to sell, it appears that the broker must also, before sale, tender the certificates of the stock and demand payment of the balance due, if there has been no waiver by the customer of one or other of these requirements.[3]

Sale Without Demand and Notice a Conversion.

The relation between the broker and his customer in a transaction where stock is bought for the latter on margin is that of pledgee and pledgor, and the sale by a broker

[1]Small v. Housman, 208 N. Y. 215.

[2]McGinnis v. Smythe, 101 N. Y. 646.
Rogers v. Wiley, 14 N. Y. Supp. 622, affirmed 131 N. Y. 527.
Morgan v. Jaudon, 40 How. Pr. 366.
In Harris v. Pryor, 18 N. Y. Supp. 128, it was held that the default there was not waived.

[3]Stenton v. Jerome, 54 N. Y. 480.
Quell v. Paine, 39 Misc. 712.

of pledged stock without demand and notice is a conversion.[1]

"Under the contract, arising by operation of law, out of the relation between the parties, a sale of the stock by the brokers without notice of the time and place of sale, constituted a conversion, in the absence of an agreement dispensing with such notice or providing for otherwise disposing of the pledged property."[2]

Notice Not Necessary When Direct Authorization to Sell.

On a request for margin over the telephone the customer replied, "If you have to sell, sell out." It was held that this authorization relieved the broker from the necessity of giving further or written notice to put up more margin or of the time and place of sale.[3]

Duty as to Retaining Stock Purchased.

Brokers need not keep on hand the identical securities purchased for their customer. Their duty is to keep on hand, or under their control, either these securities or a like kind and amount of securities.[4]

[1]Clappe v. Taylor, 125 App. Div. 605.
Markham v. Jaudon, 41 N. Y. 235.
Baker v. Drake, 66 N. Y. 518.
Gruman v. Smith, 81 N. Y. 25.
Gillett v. Whiting, 120 N. Y. 402.
Austin v. Hayden (Mich.), 137 N. W. 317.
Tomkins v. Morton Trust Co., 91 App. Div. 274.

[2]Content v. Banner, 184 N. Y. 121, 124.

[3]Pierson v. Frenkel, 103 N. Y. Supp. 49.

[4]Sprague v. Currie, 133 App. Div. 18.
Shiel v. Stoneham, 77 Misc. 125.
Tomkins v. Morton Trust Co., 91 App. Div. 274.
Austin v. Hayden (Mich.), 137 N. W. 317.
Carlisle v. Norris, 142 N. Y. Supp. 393.

Broker's Right to Pledge Margined Stock.

A stockbroker who has purchased stocks on margin for a customer may pledge the stock, and his pledgee will obtain a good lien thereon, which he may enforce by a sale of the stock without notice to the customer, and without incurring liability to him or to the broker. A broker who so pledges the stock is bound at all times to keep himself in readiness to deliver the particular shares or an equivalent number of similar shares to the customer whenever the latter offers to pay the unpaid portion of the purchase price of the stock. If the pledge made by the broker secures to the customer the right to obtain the stock from the pledgee upon payment of the balance of the purchase price, the pledge by the broker does not operate as a conversion of the stock, although he neglects to keep on hand an equivalent number of shares of similar stock. But if the broker's pledgee sells the stock without giving the customer notice of the time or place of the sale, or an opportunity to protect his interest by depositing more margin (to which he was entitled under his contract with the broker) and thereafter the broker refuses to comply with the customer's demand for delivery of the stock upon payment of the balance of the purchase price, the broker is guilty of a conversion.[1]

Right to Pledge Stocks En Bloc.

In other jurisdictions it has been held that a broker

[1]Rothschild v. Allen, 90 App. Div. 233, affirmed 180 N. Y. 561. See Summary of laws, supra p. 44.

may sub-pledge and borrow money on margined stocks en bloc.[1]

In New York it has been held that a broker cannot mingle his customer's margined stock with other securities and pledge the whole for a larger amount than the customer's indebtedness on that stock, and that to do so is a conversion. The basis of this decision is shown in the words of the opinion: "It would not do to say that the plaintiffs (the brokers) might go into the market and buy other securities of a like kind and amount on payment or tender being made by defendant, because the plaintiffs might not have the funds to purchase the new securities," and all the customer would have to rely upon would be the personal financial responsibility of the brokers.[2]

This doctrine has been much criticised. In a concurring opinion in the same case, Patterson J. says that all the broker is required to do is to have shares *under his control*, so that when, in due course of business, he is called upon, he can deliver without going into the market to buy. But he continues that the broker may pledge and repledge *even in bulk* so long as he has shares under his control.[3] The Appellate Division has recently refused to adopt the doctrine that it is a conversion ipso facto to commingle stocks belonging to different

---

[1]Skiff v. Stoddard, 63 Conn. 198.
Austin v. Hayden (Mich.), 137 N. W. 317.

[2]Douglas v. Carpenter, 17 App. Div. 328, 332.
This case was followed in Strickland v. Magoun, 119 App. Div. 113.
See also Rothschild v. Allen, 90 App. Div. 233.

[3]Douglas v. Carpenter, 17 App. Div. 335.

customers and to obtain a loan on all, in excess of the amount due from any one of the customers whose stocks are thus commingled.[1] It has been pointed out by legal writers that if the decision in Douglas v. Carpenter were strictly followed it would be difficult for brokers to conduct their business conveniently, if at all.[2]

Pledging Stock.

A pledgor of collateral security has not a right, without tender of payment, to demand a return of the collateral. The holder of the collateral has an election. He may sue without regard to the collateral upon the original indebtedness, or he may apply the collateral without attempt to collect from the original debtor. The pledgor must dispose of the debt before he can dispose of the lien and get back his collateral.[3]

The unauthorized rehypothecation of a customer's stock purchased upon margin as collateral for a loan to the broker is a conversion for which he is liable.[4]

A claim was made against a pledgee of a certificate of stock with the right to rehypothecate it for not more than the indebtedness of the pledgor. The claim was based on the pledgee's rehypothecating the stock for an amount in excess of the pledgor's indebtedness a month before the pledgee was adjudged a bankrupt, and refusing to deliver the certificate in possession of the receiver

[1] Mayer v. Monzo, 151 App. Div. 866, Clarke J. dis.

[2] "The right to pledge securities carried on a margin," by E. Norton in "The American Lawyer," Vol. 5, p. 573.

[3] Ketcham v. Provost, 156 App. Div. 477

[4] Strickland v. Magoun, 119 App. Div. 113.

in bankruptcy to the pledgor on tender of his debt. It was held that it was predicated on the pledgee's breach of contract and not for conversion and was provable in bankruptcy.[1]

A pledgee of stock who gives up possession to the pledgor without any qualification waives his lien. And if he accepts in return, as security, certificates standing in the name of a third person as trustee for the pledgor, he holds the stock subject to the trust.[2]

Certificates of stock are not the stock itself, and the latter may be validly pledged without delivery of the scrip. Stock pledged with delivery of the scrip may be subsequently pledged to another party subject to the prior lien. The possession of the first pledgee will be regarded as that of the second through the agency of the former.[3]

A pledgor of stock with a broker did not sign the blank power of attorney on the assignment attached to the certificate, but only wrote his name as owner in the first blank space. He therefore did not part with the title. The broker sold it, without notice, at private sale. It was larceny and conferred no title on the transferee. The pledgee was entitled to sell the stock only at public auction on notice.[4] Had the assignment been executed in blank it would have been payable to bearer and an innocent purchaser for value without notice, at a

[1] Wood v. Fisk, 141 N. Y. Supp. 342.
[2] Hickok v. Cowperthwait, 137 App. Div. 94.
[3] First Nat. Bank of Waterloo v. Bacon, 113 App. Div. 612.
[4] Treadwell v. Clark, 114 App. Div. 493, affirmed 190 N. Y. 51.

private sale without notice to the owner would have obtained a good title.[1]

In an action for conversion of securities (here pledged with the defendant) the plaintiff must show an existing right to immediate possession at the time of the alleged conversion.[2]

Pledge of securities deposited as margin is a wrongful conversion where the broker's transactions are purely fictitious and he is never liable to a loss on the customer's account.[3]

Bonds were purchased by brokers for various customers whom they treated as the common owners thereof. On the insolvency of the brokers the customers were held entitled to the surplus proceeds of the bonds which had been, without authority, pledged as collateral and sold by the pledgee for the debt of the brokers.[4]

Unauthorized rehypothecation as collateral is conversion for which the broker is liable, but the pledgee may obtain a good title to the stock if he acts in good faith upon present and valuable considerations and without knowledge of the true owner's claims.[5]

Right of Pledgee from Broker.

The rights of a bona fide purchaser or pledgee from a broker are based upon the estoppel of the owner of the stock in so acting as to preclude him from disputing,

[1]Treadwell v. Clark, 114 App. Div. 493, affirmed 190 N. Y. 51.
[2]Byrne v. Weinfeld, 113 App. Div. 451.
[3]In re Tracy, 191 Fed. 810.
[4]Hunt v. Marquand, 109 App. Div. 729.
[5]Strickland v. Magoun, 119 App. Div. 113.

as against the pledgee, the existence or the powers of his bailee, the broker.[1]

Agreement to Carry Customer's Account for a Definite Period.

A broker may agree to carry a customer's account for a certain period or until the happening of a certain event without calling for additional margin. The closing of the transaction before the expiration of the time or happening of the event renders him liable in damages.[2]

A court will not readily infer an agreement by a broker to carry stock until it should decline to a certain price.[3]

Stockbrokers had sold a stock short for a customer. It began to rise and the customer wished to cover the sale and go long of the stock. The stockbrokers advised him not to do so. The customer took the advice on the stockbrokers' promise to carry the account without additional margin until the customer could get out without loss, if the stock went up to a price specified, which would have exhausted the margin. The stock continued to advance, but did not go above the price named. The stockbrokers bought in at a price which about exhausted the margin, without notice to the customer. Upon receiving notice of the purchase the latter repudiated it. The market subsequently declined and the customer directed the stockbrokers to buy to cover the short sale,

---

[1]Matter of Mills, 125 App. Div. 730.

[2]Michael v. Hart (1901), 2 K. B. 867, 85 L. T. Rep. (N. S.) 548.

In Harris v. Pryor, 18 N. Y. Supp. 128, it was found that there was no agreement to hold the stock.

[3]Richter v. Poe (Md.), 71 Atl. 420, 424.

to sell the securities he had desposited as margin, and to account. This they declined to do. In an action by the customer to recover damages, it was held that the defendant's promise to carry the account without further margin gave a right to recover, whether considered as an agreement with a sufficient consideration or as a waiver of notice to furnish more margin, or as an estoppel. In either case the purchase was unauthorized and the customer was entitled to recover the difference between the amount paid on such purchase and what the stock might have been bought for when he gave directions to purchase.[1]

A broker who purchased July wheat on margin for a customer agreed to carry the wheat until July 1st without additional margin, and that the deal should not be closed until the customer so ordered. This agreement was held to mean that the deal should not be closed before July 1st unless so ordered.[2]

A contract to carry stock does not oblige the broker to carry it indefinitely where it does not prescribe a period. Where a stock was carried more than five years, it was held a reasonable time had elapsed before tender.[3]

Sale at the Market.

In an action for the balance of an account due to a loss on 100 shares of Steel common which the plaintiffs

[1]Rogers v. Wiley, 131 N. Y. 527, affirming 14 N. Y. Supp. 622.

[2]Amsden v. Jacobs, 75 Hun, 311.
See Gould v. Trask, 10 N. Y. Supp. 619, as to the effect of the deposit of a note as "temporary collateral."

[3]Kridel v. Bloomingdale, 149 App. Div. 605.

were carrying for their customer the plaintiffs alleged that the customer, on being asked for additional margin, directed them to sell at the market. The defendant alleged that she directed them to sell at 45, and at that time the stock stood at $45\frac{1}{2}$. The case turned on the question of fact as to the directions given by the purchaser. The market, it was held, meant the best price that could be obtained for the stock at the time the sale was made, not the price at which the stock was quoted at that time. (The market was panicky, and the stock was sold at 28.)[1]

An order to sell at the market means at the best price obtainable at the time the order is executed, and not at the price quoted at the time the order is given.[2]

Customer's Death.

A broker had sold stock short for a customer, borrowing the stock for delivery according to custom, from time to time as required. While the transaction was so kept alive the customer died. The broker continued to keep the speculation alive until the appointment of an executrix, upon whom the proper notice could be served in order to close it. It was held that the broker was authorized to do so, provided he acted in good faith. Being himself obligated for the return of the borrowed stock, he had such an interest in the transaction on account of this personal obligation as entitled him to continue it until a representative should be appointed. But it was

[1]Fairbairn v. Rausch, 104 App. Div. 259.

[2]Fairbairn v. Rausch, 104 App. Div. 259.

not meant that a broker might not be justified in closing a stock transaction immediately after the death of the principal.[1]

Broker's Correspondent His Agent.

A broker's correspondent is the agent of the broker, and not of the customer, even though the latter instructs him directly.[2]

Short Sales.

Short selling (sale for future delivery) is valid, as distinguished from gambling in differences.[3]

A broker is bound to carry the customer's account to sell short for a reasonable time as long as the margin deposited remains good.[4] Without demand for additional margin he cannot cover the sale without instructions from the customer.[5] On an unauthorized buying in of stock to cover the sale the customer may repudiate the transaction and recover the margin deposited.[6] If the margin is not kept good, the broker may, on demand and notice, close the transaction by buying to cover the sale.[7] He must show that there was occasion to call for further margin, and that the customer failed

---

[1]Hess v. Rau, 95 N. Y. 359.
[2]Evans v. Wrenn, 93 App. Div. 346.
Gheen v. Johnson, 90 Pa. St. 38.
[3]Richter v. Poe (Md.), 71 Atl. 420.
[4]White v. Smith, 54 N. Y. 522.
[5]Barber v. Ellingwood, 144 App. Div. 512.
[6]Campbell v. Wright, 8 N. Y. St. Rep. 471.
[7]White v. Smith, 54 N. Y. 522.
Sterling v. Jaudon, 48 Barb. 459.

to furnish it after receiving reasonable notice prior to the purchase.[1]

In closing out a short sale account the broker is not required to give notice to the customer of the time and place at which he proposes to purchase. Such a notice is only required where stocks are pledged for the payment of a debt.[2] But if the broker elects to close the transaction for reasons other than a shortage of security he must give the customer reasonable notice.[3]

Where a broker has "sold short" for a customer he may, in a rapidly rising market, and after the customer has refused to put up more margin, buy in the stock and charge the loss to the customer's account. He is not obliged to take into consideration rumors communicated by the customer that the stock may be bought lower next day; nor to hunt him up and repeat to him every rumor or piece of information before protecting himself.[4]

Coöperating with Insolvent Broker.

A broker who knows that another broker is insolvent and imposing on his customers, and who continues to coöperate with him and assist him to buy stock on margin, secured by stocks known to belong to the insolvent broker's customers, is liable equally with the insolvent broker to his customers for his acts.[5]

---

[1]Lazare v. Allen, 20 App. Div. 616.
See Boyle v. Henning, 121 Fed. 376.

[2]Sterling v. Jaudon, 48 Barb. 459.

[3]Barber v. Ellingwood, 144 App. Div. 512.

[4]Armstrong v. Bickel, 217 Pa. 173 (where Northern Pac. shares rose from $60 to $600).

[5]Austin v. Hayden (Mich.), 137 N. W. 317.

Conversion of Stock.

Every unauthorized taking of personal property, and all intermeddling with it, beyond the extent of the authority conferred, in case a limited authority is given, with intent so to apply and dispose of it as to alter its condition or interfere with the owner's dominion, is a conversion.[1]

So, where stock certificates were endorsed and delivered to a broker's clerk for transfer to the transferee on the corporate books, and he dealt with the stock as his own through a speculative account with the brokers in his brother's name, resulting in the transfer of the certificates to the brokers, it was held that the brokers had constructive notice of the clerk's conversion of the certificate, and were themselves guilty of constructive conversion.[2] A transfer of stock may be a conversion, although it is not a strict sale, the effect being the same.[3]

Where it is not the custom of brokers to sell their customers' stock, purchased on margin, without notice, and they have made no call for margins and given no notice of intention to sell, or of the time and place of sale, the sale of the stock by the broker is a conversion,[4] in the absence of an agreement dispensing with such notice, or a provision that otherwise disposes of the pledged property.[5]

---

[1]Kilmer v. Hutton, 131 App. Div. 625

[2]Kilmer v. Hutton, 131 App. Div. 625

[3]Reichland v. Hutton, 148 App. Div. 813.

[4]Gillett v. Whiting, 120 N.Y. 402; rev'g 55 N. Y. Super. Ct. 187.

[5]Moore v. Rodewald, 142 App. Div. 741, 749.

An unauthorized sale by the broker while he holds sufficient margin has been held a conversion, whether he has given notice of the sale to the customer or not.[1]

An unauthorized sale of pledged stock at a place not public, which is not ratified by the pledgor, is a conversion.[2]

A mere allegation in an action that brokers sold or converted to their own use certain securities which they had bought on margin for their customer is too vague and indefinite.[3]

Collateral stock was transferred on the books to the names of the broker's employee, who knew the facts. There was no conversion until a tender of the amount of the debt had been made and a demand for the collateral made and refused.[4]

A claim for conversion of a certificate of stock is predicated on a wrongful assumption of ownership or interference with the owner's right to possession, and a tender by a pledgor of the amount due, and a demand of the return of the pledge, made when the pledgor knows that the law renders it impossible for the pledgee to accept the tender or comply with the demand do not show a conversion.[5]

When Hypothecation Is Larceny.

The hypothecation by brokers for their own obligations of stock entrusted to them for safekeeping is larceny.[6]

[1]Taylor v. Ketchum, 35 How. Pr. 289; 5 Rob. 507.
[2]Manning v. Heidelbach, 153 App. Div. 790
[3]Sprague v. Currie, 133 App. Div. 18.
[4]Jones v. Seaman, 133 App. Div. 127.
[5]Wood v. Fisk, 141 N. Y. Supp. 342.
[6]Matter of Mills, 125 App. Div. 730.

As to every one except a pledgee from the broker, who has actually in good faith advanced money upon the apparent title conferred by the owner of the securities upon the broker as his bailee or agent, the owner is entitled to stock deposited with a broker for safe-keeping.[1]

Measure of Damages — Sale of Stock.

If a broker unjustifiably closes out a short sale transaction, the customer may recover the profit he would have made had the broker given him reasonable notice of his intention,[2] i. e., the difference between the price at which the short stock was bought in and the lowest market price of the stock, within a reasonable time, not from the date of the sale, but from *the time the customer learns of the conversion of the stock.*[3]

The highest market prices, varying from a few days to within two months of the conversion have been held within the rule.[4]

All the customer is entitled to is a reasonable time necessary to enable him to determine upon his line of action. He cannot speculate at the expense of his brokers.[5]

Brokers made an unauthorized sale of a customer's stocks while he was away in the country. The "rea-

[1]Matter of Mills, 125 App. Div. 730.

[2]Barber v. Ellingwood, 144 App. Div. 512.

[3]Barber v. Ellingwood, No. 2, 137 App. Div. 704, 144 App. Div. 512.
Burnham v. Lawson, 118 App. Div. 389.
But see Wolff v. Lockwood, 70 App. Div. 569.

[4]Mullen v. Quinlan & Co., 195 N. Y. 109.
Hurt v. Miller, 120 App. Div. 833.

sonable time" in computing damages was not when he threatened them with criminal proceedings, while still away, on receiving notice of the sale, but two weeks later, when he returned and spent a full day in the city and wrote them threatening proceedings.[1]

Broker's Insolvency — Stock Goes to Customer.

On a broker's insolvency, stock which he has been carrying for a customer goes to the customer, not to the broker's assignee.[2]

Rights of the Defrauded Customer of an Insolvent Broker.

The conflict between various claimants against an insolvent broker arises when various customers have delivered money or securities to the broker either for or upon the execution of orders or for safekeeping or otherwise. Assuming that the relation of customer and broker has arisen, the broker becoming insolvent throws upon the court the burden of deciding how the moneys in bank or elsewhere, the securities in actual possession of the broker and the securities hypothecated with the banks or bankers shall be distributed. Ordinarily all creditors of the bankrupt broker would share on an equal basis, pro rata, in the latter's estate, but circumstances sometimes give one customer a superior claim or equity over other customers. The most common instance is where the customer has given the broker the money in full to purchase outright the securities ordered.

[1]Rosenbaum v. Stiebel, 122 N. Y. Supp. 131.

[2]Willard v. White, 56 Hun, 581.
Le Marchant v. Moore, 79 Hun, 352.

If the securities have been purchased and the certificate is in the hands of the broker at the time of failure, the customer is entitled to its immediate delivery to him, upon its being properly identified. If the securities have not been purchased, and it can be shown that the funds were deposited in bank and there remained at the time of failure, the customer is entitled to have such fund repaid to him; that is, he is entitled to the bank account itself.[1] The same is true where the customer has given securities to the broker and the latter has appropriated them and put the proceeds of the unauthorized sale in his bank account. Following a leading English case,[2] if the broker mingles the customer's funds with his own, the court will presume that the money he withdraws is his own and that the remaining funds belong to his customer.[3] This upon the familiar doctrine of tracing trust funds.

The situation here prescribed is of course entirely independent of the criminality involved in the broker's conduct either in misappropriating moneys given to him by his customer for the purchase of stock or in misappropriating stock delivered to him for a specific purpose. In such cases he is guilty of embezzlement.[4] This became material in deciding the superiority of equities that arises when the broker mingles stock and hypothecates them all en bloc, some rightfully and

[1] In re Mulligan, 116 Fed. 715.
[2] In re Halletts Estate, L. R. 13 Ch. D. 696.
[3] In re Mulligan, 116 Fed. 715.
[4] People v. Meadows 199 N. Y. 1.

some wrongfully, when it is held that the customer whose stock is wrongfully hypothecated has the superior equity and is entitled to have prior payment to make good his losses, providing his stock or its proceeds can be traced.[1]

Briefly, therefore, it is necessary first to trace the property of the customer, either money or securities. But having done so, another difficulty arises, namely, other customers may have been similarly defrauded and their securities or money similarly misappropriated or converted. Those whose property or money cannot be traced under the circumstances remain the unfortunates, and the conflict of equities lies only between those who have been successful in so doing. As between the latter the court will divide the claimants into two classes, those whose money has been misappropriated or "whose securities have been wrongfully hypothecated" and "those whose securities have been rightfully pledged." "Superior rights" are granted the first class of claimants, and the securities of the second class, whose rights are "clearly inferior," can secure satisfaction of their claims only after those in the first class are made whole so far as the specific securities or money traced will allow.[2]

[1]West v. McLaughlin, 162 Fed. 124.
In re Ennis, Ex parte Bramford, 187 Fed. 720.
In re Brown, Ex parte Horrocks, 185 Fed. 766.
In re Brown, Ex parte Bank of Princeton, 175 Fed. 769.

[2]In re Ennis, Ex parte Bramford, 187 Fed. 720, 722.
In re McIntyre, Ex parte Pippey, Ex parte Hudson, 181 Fed. 955.
In Matter of Mills, 125 App. Div. 730, claimants were denied the right to participate in the superior class. The case is interesting as illustrating the distinctions indulged in determining to which class a claimant belongs. A very interesting article covering numerous phases of this branch of the subject will be found in the Columbia Law Review for May 1912.

Cornering the Market Illegal.

It is well settled that it is illegal to attempt to corner the market. As it is the intention to force the parties who may sell to those making the attempt to settle differences, it is a gambling transaction, and the contracts are unenforceable. Some courts hold corners to be illegal as in restraint of trade.[1]

Guaranteeing Stock.

A broker does not guarantee the genuineness of the stock purchased for a customer.[2] Nor has he any implied authority to warrant stock sold for his customer.[3]

Unauthorized Sale — Right to Advances, etc.

Whether an action is for conversion of securities bought on margin or on the contract, the broker is entitled to counterclaim for advances, interest, and commissions, if these have not been covered by the proceeds of the unauthorized sale.[4]

In an action for the balance of the customer's account after selling his stock, the brokers must show a sale in good faith and to a person authorized to purchase.[5]

Broker's Lien.

A wife allowed her husband to pledge her securities as margin on his own stock transactions. Although the

---

[1] Arnott v. Pittston etc. Coal Co., 68 N. Y. 558.
Livermore v. Bushnell, 5 Hun, 285.

[2] Peckham v. Ketchum, 5 Bosw. 506.

[3] Smith v. Tracy, 36 N. Y. 79.

[4] Barber v. Ellingwood, No. 2, 137 App. Div. 704.
McIntyre v. Whitney, 139 App. Div. 557.

[5] Camman v. Huntington, 89 App. Div. 99.

brokers knew that these securities belonged to the wife, they had nevertheless a valid lien on them, and could sell them to satisfy it, after notice to the wife.[1]

In an action by exchange brokers against curb brokers the defense was that the owners were guilty of fraud in inducing the sale. It was held that the defense was available, the relationship between Stock Exchange broker and customer not being exempt from the ordinary rules of principal and agent.[2] But if the broker was not a party to his principal's fraud, he had a lien on the stock to the amount of his advances thereon.[3]

An Account Stated.

An account stated requires the acts of two parties, the debtor and the creditor. Stockbrokers cannot recover upon an account stated where it is shown that the customer repudiated the account rendered.[4]

When a customer retained an account rendered to him by his brokers' assignee for more than a month without objection, it was a question for the jury whether he assented to it so as to make it an account stated.[5]

Broker's Clerk as Customer's Agent.

The clerk of a broker may be constituted the agent of a customer to receive from the broker the return of

[1] Moore v. Rodewald, 142 App. Div. 741.
[2] Leo v. McCormack, 186 N. Y. 330.
[3] id.
[4] Schultheis v. Caughey, 146 App. Div. 102.
[5] Little v. McClain, 134 App. Div. 197.

stock certificates given as security for a margin account, or their equivalent.[1]

Stock Certificate Not a Negotiable Instrument.

A certificate of stock is not a negotiable instrument. An assignment of a certificate of stock with a P/A endorsed on the certificate, although in blank, except as to signatures and witness, presents such indicia of title that an innocent holder obtains a good title.[2]

Undisclosed Principal.

A broker who sells stock though acting for another without disclosing his principal is himself liable as principal.[3] A broker selling worthless bonds in this way is personally liable to the purchaser.[4]

Joint Account.

When two parties open a joint account the broker is not obliged at the request of one of them to cancel the joint account and accept in lieu thereof the separate liability of each for one-half of the joint liability.[5]

Demand for Money Deposited.

A customer must make a demand for money deposited with his broker before bringing an action.[6]

[1] Carlisle v. Norris, 142 N. Y. Supp. 393.
[2] Talcott v. Standard Oil Co., 149 App. Div. 694.
[3] Bassett v. Perkins, 65 Misc. 103.
[4] Pugh v. Moore, 44 La. Ann. 209.
[5] Levy v. Potter, 104 App. Div. 457.
[6] Ennis v. Ross, 37 Misc. 160.

PART IV

CONSTITUTION, BY-LAWS AND RULES OF THE NEW YORK STOCK EXCHANGE

PART IV

Constitution, By-laws and Rules of the New York Stock Exchange

Constitution — Rules for the Government of the Exchange as amended to January 1, 1914

ARTICLE I.

Title — Objects.

The title of this Association shall be the "NEW YORK STOCK EXCHANGE."

Its object shall be to furnish exchange rooms and other facilities for the convenient transaction of their business by its members, as brokers; to maintain high standards of commercial honor and integrity among its members; and to promote and inculcate just and equitable principles of trade and business.

ARTICLE II.

Government.

The government of the Exchange shall be vested in a Governing Committee, composed of the President and the Treasurer of the Exchange, and of forty Members, elected in the manner hereinafter provided. The members of the Governing Committee, and the Secretary, shall be the officers of the Exchange.

ARTICLE III.

Governing Committee.

Sec. 1. The Members of the Governing Committee shall be divided into four classes, each class consisting of ten members, as follows: first class, to hold office for one year; second class, for two years; third class for three years; fourth class, for four years.

Sec. 2. The Governing Committee shall determine the manner and form by which its proceedings shall be conducted; appoint and dissolve all Standing or other Committees, define, alter and regulate their jurisdiction as stated in this instrument; have original and supervisory jurisdiction over any and all subjects and matters referred to said Committees; it may direct and control their actions or proceedings at any stage thereof, and shall try all charges against members of the Exchange and punish such as may be found guilty. It shall have entire control of the finances of the Exchange and fix the amount of fees and compensation to be paid to members of Committees, to Officers of the Exchange and to appointees of the Governing Committee. It may require of all officers or appointees of the Exchange a good and sufficient bond to secure the faithful performance of their duties. The Governing Committee shall be vested with all other powers necessary for the government of the Exchange, the regulation of the business conduct of its members, and the promotion of its welfare, objects and purposes.

SEC. 3. A Member, who shall be absent from three consecutive regular meetings of the Governing Committee, without having been excused by the President, may be declared by a two-thirds vote of the existing members of the Committee to be no longer a Member.

SEC. 4. All vacancies occurring in the Governing Committee shall be filled by said Committee until the ensuing annual election.

SEC. 5. No member of the Governing Committee shall be disqualified from participating in any meeting, action or proceeding of any kind whatever of said Committee, by reason of being or having been a member of a Standing Committee or Special Committee which has made prior inquiry, examination or investigation of the subject under consideration. Nor shall any member of any Standing or Special Committee be disqualified, by reason of such membership, from acting as a member of the Governing Committee upon any appeal from any decision of such Standing or Special Committee. But no member shall participate in the adjudication of any case in which he is personally interested.

SEC. 6. A majority of all the existing members of the Governing Committee shall be necessary to constitute a quorum.

SEC. 7. Any hearing or trial may be adjourned, from time to time, by the Governing Committee in its discretion; but no member thereof, who shall not have been present at every meeting of said Committee at which evidence is taken, or at which an accused member, or a member whose conduct is involved in the hearing, is heard, shall participate in the final decision.

SEC. 8. In the absence of both the President and Vice-President, any ten members of the Governing Committee may call a meeting thereof by written announcement from the rostrum.

SEC. 9. In the case of the temporary absence, or inability to act, of both the President and Vice-President, the Governing Committee may choose an Acting President of the Exchange *pro tem.*

SEC. 10. The Governing Committee shall at its first regular meeting in June of each year, designate counsel for the Exchange; such counsel to be employed at the pleasure of said Committee.

ARTICLE IV.

President.

SEC. 1. The executive power of the Exchange shall be vested in the President, who shall direct the enforcement of the rules and regulations and have the care of all its interests. He may preside over the Exchange whenever he shall so elect, and shall be the presiding officer of the Governing Committee.

SEC. 2. The President may call special meetings of the Exchange, and of the Governing Committee. He shall call special meetings of the Exchange, upon the written request of one hundred members, and special meetings of the Governing Committee, upon the written request of ten members of said Committee.

SEC. 3. Should special exigencies require, the President may appoint committees *ad interim*, to act until the regular appointments are made.

ARTICLE V.

Vice-President.

SEC. 1. The Governing Committee, at its first meeting after every annual election, shall choose from its Members a Vice-President of the Exchange.

SEC. 2. The Vice-President shall, in the absence of the President, assume all the functions and powers, and discharge all the duties of the President.

ARTICLE VI.

Treasurer.

SEC. 1. It shall be the duty of the Treasurer to receive and, acting under instructions from the Finance Committee, to take charge of and disburse moneys of the Exchange. He shall present to the Governing Committee at its first regular meeting in May of each year a report of the finances of the Exchange for the twelve months ending April 30 preceding. He shall be a member of the Finance Committee, and a Trustee of the Gratuity Fund.

SEC. 2. In the event of failure, neglect or inability of the Treasurer, for any reason, to execute the duties of his office the Finance Committee shall appoint one of its members, who, together with either the President or Vice-President, shall act as Treasurer *pro tem.*

ARTICLE VII.

Secretary.

SEC. 1. The Secretary shall be appointed by a majority vote of the Governing Committee and shall hold his position subject to the pleasure of the Governing Committee. It shall be the duty of the Secretary to record in a book of minutes the proceedings of the Exchange and take charge of the books and papers of the association. He shall be the Secretary of the Governing Committee and of the Standing Committees. He shall conduct the correspondence of the Exchange and shall keep a ledger containing the names of all the members, with dates of their admission and transfer of membership. He shall be the accountant of the Exchange, and shall perform such other duties as the Governing Committee may direct.

ARTICLE VIII.

Chairman and Assistant Chairman.

SEC. 1. The Governing Committee may appoint a Chairman, who shall hold his position subject to the pleasure of said Committee. It shall be his duty to preside over the Exchange during business hours, maintain order, enforce the rules, impose fines, and perform such other duties as the Committee of Arrangements may direct.

SEC. 2. The Chairman shall not be permitted personally to buy or sell securities upon the floor of the Exchange.

SEC. 3. The Committee of Arrangements may appoint an Assistant Chairman, who shall hold his position subject to the pleasure of said Committee, and perform such duties as said Committee may direct.

ARTICLE IX

Elections.

SEC. 1. The annual election of the Exchange shall be held on the second Monday of May; at which time there shall be elected by ballot a President, and a Treasurer, each for the term of one year; a Trustee of the Gratuity Fund for the term of five years; and ten Members of the Governing Committee for the term of four years; also members to fill any vacancies which may have occurred during the preceding year either in the Trustees of the Gratuity Fund or in the Governing Committee.

In each case the member receiving the highest number of votes for any office or position shall be declared elected thereto.

SEC. 2. An annual election of the Exchange shall also be held on the second Monday in January, at which time there shall be elected by ballot a Nominating Committee to consist of five members (not officers of the Exchange) who shall serve for a period of one year. Any vacancy during said term shall be filled by the remaining members. The Nominating Committee shall hold at least three meetings in the month of March, due notice of which shall be posted on the bulletin board, and sent to each member of the Exchange, inviting members of the Exchange to attend said meetings for the purpose of suggesting nominees for the offices and positions which are to be filled at the annual election on the second Monday in May following. Said Committee shall report to the Exchange on the second Monday in April, nominees for such offices and positions.

The Nominating Committee shall also hold at least three meetings in the month of November, due notice of which shall be posted on the bulletin board, and sent to each member of the Exchange, inviting members of the Exchange to attend said meetings for the purpose of suggesting nominees for the Nominating Committee for the ensuing year. Said Committee shall report to the Secretary of the Exchange at or before two o'clock P. M. on the third Monday in December, nominations for a Nominating Committee to be balloted for at said annual election on the second Monday in January following.

In addition to the above method, members of the Exchange at large may propose nominees for members of the Nominating Committee *by petition;* a nominee thus nominated must be endorsed by not less than forty members of the Exchange and no member shall endorse more than one nominee. Such petitions shall be filed with the Secretary of the Exchange in sealed envelopes at or before two o'clock P. M. on the third Monday in December. The Nominating Committee and the Secretary of the Exchange shall open said envelopes on said day and the names of the nominees therein proposed shall be arranged alphabetically with those of the five nominees of the Nominating Committee and reported to the Exchange on the following day. The five nominees in this combined list receiving the highest number of votes at the annual election on the second Monday in January, shall constitute the Nominating Committee for the ensuing year. In case of a tie the names of the members involved shall be referred to the retiring Nominating Committee who shall make selection by lot.

SEC. 3. Any member of the Exchange, in good standing, shall be entitled to vote at any election or meeting of the Exchange.

SEC. 4. When the Exchange shall be assembled for the transaction of business other than dealing in securities, a majority of all the members shall constitute a quorum.

ARTICLE X.

Eligibility — Vacancy in Office.

SEC. 1. No person shall be eligible to the office of President, Treasurer, Trustee of the Gratuity Fund, or Member of the Governing Committee, who shall not be, at the time of his election, a member in good standing.

SEC. 2. The expulsion, suspension or transfer of membership of a member holding any office or position, to which he has been either elected or appointed, shall create a vacancy therein which shall be filled as provided in these rules.

SEC. 3. In the event of the refusal, failure, neglect or inability of an officer of the Exchange to discharge the duties of his office, or for any good cause, of the sufficiency of which the Governing Committee shall be the sole judge, said Committee shall have power, by a two-thirds vote of all its existing members, to remove said officer and declare the position held by him to be vacant.

SEC. 4. In case a vacancy shall occur in the office either of President or Treasurer, a new election by ballot shall be held forthwith to fill such vacancy for the unexpired term.

SEC. 5. In case of vacancy in the office of Vice-President, the same shall be filled by the Governing Committee at its next meeting after the vacancy occurs.

SEC. 6. Every appointee, clerk or employee of the Exchange shall hold his office, place or position only during the pleasure of the authority by which he was appointed; and he may be, at any time, removed, dismissed or discharged by a majority vote of the Committee by which he was appointed, or by a like vote of the Governing Committee.

ARTICLE XI.

Standing Committees.

SEC. 1. Promptly after each annual election the Governing Committee shall appoint from its Members the following Standing Committees:

First. — A Committee of Arrangements, to consist

of seven members. It shall have the general care and supervision of the Exchange, enforce all rules and regulations necessary to the conduct of business, to good order and the comfort of the members, and consider all complaints of violation of said rules. It shall control and regulate the quotation service and all telegraph or telephone connection with the Exchange. It shall, except as herein otherwise expressly provided, appoint, dismiss and determine the number, duty and pay of all employees, and provide all supplies for the Exchange and make all necessary repairs to its building.

Second. — A Committee on Admissions, to consist of fifteen members. All applications for membership, and all applications of suspended members for reinstatement to their privileges, shall be referred to this Committee.

The affirmative vote of two-thirds of the entire Committee shall be necessary to elect to membership, or to reinstate a suspended member.

No application for readmission of a person who has ceased to be a member of the Exchange through violation of its Constitution, or for the reinstatement of a member who has been suspended under Sec. 2, Article XVI, shall be considered by this Committee, unless said person has obtained the consent of two-thirds of the members of the Governing Committee present, when such application is considered.

Third. — An Arbitration Committee to consist of nine members. It shall investigate and decide, when properly brought before it, all claims and matters of difference arising from contracts subject to the rules of the Exchange, between members of the Exchange, or at the instance of a non-member between members and non-members. The Committee may dismiss any case and refer the parties to their remedies at law, and it shall so refer them upon the joint request of the contestants. The decision of this Committee shall be final in all cases, unless an appeal be taken by a member of the Committee as in these rules provided, or in cases involving a sum of $2,500 or over, when either party may appeal within ten days to the Governing Committee; said appeal shall be submitted to the Governing Committee by the Secretary of the Exchange upon a printed transcript of the records of the case, together with such printed arguments as the parties to the appeal may desire to make; upon such appeal, the Governing Committee may finally adjudicate the case, relegate the parties to their remedies at law, or direct a rehearing by the Arbitration Committee.

A non-member making a claim shall execute an agreement to abide by the rules of the Exchange, and also a full release of said claim, and shall deliver them to the Chairman of the Arbitration Committee, who shall keep them in trust to abide the result of said arbitration and deliver them to the defendant in any of the following cases:

(*a*) In case the plaintiff shall fail to appear before the Arbitration Committee within such time as said Committee shall designate.

(*b*) In case judgment shall be rendered for said defendant by the Arbitration Committee.

(*c*) In case the defendant shall pay, or offer to pay, to the claimant the amount of judgment rendered in his favor, and shall have filed with the Chairman satisfactory evidence of such payment or proffered payment.

In case judgment shall be rendered against any member of the Exchange, which he neglects to pay, or if the case be dismissed, then such release shall be canceled and returned to the plaintiff.

Fourth. — A Committee on Business Conduct, to consist of five members.

It shall be the duty of this Committee to consider matters relating to the business conduct of members with respect to customers' accounts.

It shall also be the duty of this Committee to keep in touch with the course of prices of securities listed on the Exchange, with the view of determining when improper transactions are being resorted to.

It shall have power to examine into the dealings of any members, with respect to the above subjects, and report its finding to the Governing Committee.

Fifth. — A Committee on Clearing-House, to consist of five members. It shall have general charge of the Clearing-House of the Exchange and the business thereof, and shall from time to time designate the securities to be cleared. It may determine the amount of salary or compensation to be paid to officers and employees of the Clearing-House and make expenditures from its funds for the conduct of its business. It shall make monthly financial reports to the Finance Committee.

Sixth. — A Committee on Commissions, to consist of

five members. It shall enforce the rules relating to commissions, partnerships and branch offices, and shall report to the Governing Committee any undesirable partnership or branch office or any violation of said rules.

Seventh. — A Committee on Constitution to consist of five members, to which shall be referred all additions, alterations, or amendments to the Constitution. It shall report them back to the Governing Committee, but only at regular meetings or at special meetings called solely for the purpose of considering them.

Eighth. — A Finance Committee to consist of seven members. It shall meet prior to the first regular meeting of the Governing Committee in each month and examine the various accounts and vouchers; and, acting as a Board of Audit, the Committee shall report its examination to the Governing Committee. It shall also make examinations of the condition of the Gratuity Fund as provided in Article XIX hereof.

Ninth. — A Committee on Insolvencies to consist of three members selected from the Committee on Admissions. It shall investigate every case of insolvency immediately after the announcement thereof to the Exchange. It shall ascertain the cause of failure and promptly report the result of its examination to the Committee on Admissions.

Tenth. — A Law Committee to consist of five members, to which shall be referred all questions of law affecting the interests of the Exchange.

It shall act in an advisory capacity to the President

when requested, shall represent the Exchange in conferences with other interests, and is authorized and empowered, whenever the Committee shall deem it to be for the interest of the Exchange, to examine into the dealings of any member of the Exchange.

Eleventh. — A Committee on Securities to consist of five members. It shall make rules defining the requirements for regularity in delivery of securities dealt in at the Exchange; and decide all questions relating to the settlement of contracts subject to the rules of the Exchange, of due bills, of irregularities in securities, or in deliveries thereof, and all questions relating to reclamations therefor.

Twelfth. — A Committee on Stock-List to consist of five members. It shall receive and consider all applications for placing securities upon the list of the Exchange, and make report and recommendation thereon to the Governing Committee, giving full statement concerning organization, capitalization, resources and indebtedness.

It shall have power to place upon the list, without report and recommendation to the Governing Committee, any obligations of the Government of the United States or of any state or city thereof, or of a foreign state or city, also temporary receipts issued by any corporation or firm for part or full payment of subscription to bonds, stocks, or other obligations; and it shall have power to direct that any such securities or temporary receipts be taken from the list, and further dealings therein prohibited.

It shall have charge of the arrangement and revision of the list of securities.

Sec. 2. The Standing Committees of the Exchange, and all Special Committees, shall determine the manner and form by which their proceedings shall be conducted; shall make such regulations for their government as they shall deem proper, and may fill any vacancies occurring in their membership, subject always to the control and supervision of the Governing Committee.

Sec. 3. A majority of the members of any Committee shall be necessary to constitute a quorum.

ARTICLE XII.

Appeals.

Sec. 1. An appeal to the Governing Committee, from any decision of a Standing Committee may be taken by a member of the Exchange, interested therein, if made in writing to the President within two days after said decision has been rendered; but nothing herein contained shall authorize an appeal from a decision of the Committee on Admissions, except as provided in Section 4, Article XVI of these Rules, nor from a decision of the Arbitration Committee, except as provided in the third sub-division of Section 1, Article XI, of these Rules.

Sec. 2. A member of a Standing Committee, present at a hearing of a case, may, within two days after the decision has been made thereon, appeal therefrom to the Governing Committee by writing, addressed to the President.

ARTICLE XIII.

Applications for Membership — Eligibility — Initiation Fee.

SEC. 1. Every applicant for membership must be at least twenty-one years of age, and a citizen of the United States.

SEC. 2. The membership of the Exchange shall not be increased except by action of the Governing Committee, which shall prescribe the number of increase and the terms of admission. Such action shall be submitted to the Exchange on the same conditions as those prescribed for amendments to the Constitution.

SEC. 3. Members admitted by transfer shall pay to the Exchange an initiation fee of Two Thousand Dollars.

SEC. 4. If the initiation fee of an applicant for admission to membership is not paid on the day of his election and notification by the Secretary, such election shall be void.

SEC. 5. No person, elected to membership, shall be admitted to the privileges thereof until he shall have signed the Constitution of the Exchange. By such signature he pledges himself to abide by the same and by all subsequent amendments thereto.

ARTICLE XIV.

Dues and Fines — Penalty for Non-Payment.

SEC. 1. The dues of all members of the Exchange shall be payable on May 1st and November 1st of each year, and shall be fifty dollars semi-annually, exclusive of fines, and of assessments under Article XVIII of the Constitution.

SEC. 2. Any member who shall neglect to pay his fines, dues or any assessment for the Gratuity Fund for three months after they become payable, shall be reported by the Treasurer to the President, who shall, after due notice to the delinquent, suspend said delinquent until said dues are paid.

If the fines, dues or assessments of any suspended member are not paid at the end of one year after they become payable, the membership of said suspended member may be disposed of by the Committee on Admissions.

ARTICLE XV.

Transfer of Membership.

SEC. 1. A transfer of membership may be made upon submission of the name of the candidate to the Committee on Admissions, and the approval of the transfer by two-thirds of the entire Committee. Notice of the proposed transfer shall be posted on the bulletin in the Exchange for at least ten days prior to transfer.

SEC. 2. All contracts subject to the rules of the Exchange, made by a member proposing to transfer his membership, shall mature on the tenth day of the posting of notice of the proposed transfer; and said member shall not be permitted thereafter to make any contracts subject to the rules of the Exchange, pending the approval of the proposed transfer by the Committee on Admissions.

This rule shall also apply in cases where a membership is disposed of by the Committee on Admissions.

SEC. 3. Upon any transfer of membership, whether made by a member voluntarily, or by the Governing Committee or the Committee on Admissions in pursuance of the provisions of the Constitution, the proceeds thereof shall be applied to the following purposes and in the following order of priority, viz.:

First. — The payment of all fines, dues, assessments and charges of the Exchange, or any department thereof, against a member whose membership is transferred.

Second. — The payment of creditors, members of the Exchange, or firms registered thereon, of all filed claims arising from contracts subject to the rules of the Exchange, if, and to the extent that, the same shall be allowed by the Committee on Admissions. If said proceeds shall be insufficient to pay said claims, as so allowed, in full, the same shall be applied to the payment thereof *pro rata*.

Third. — The surplus, if any, of said proceeds shall be paid to the person whose membership is transferred, or to his legal representatives, upon the execution by him or them of a release or releases satisfactory to the Committee on Admissions.

The Committee on Admissions shall have power, by rule or otherwise, to secure the observance of the provisions of this Article.

SEC. 4. All unmatured debts or other obligations of a member, arising out of contracts subject to the rules of the Exchange, shall become due and payable immediately prior to the transfer of his membership; and all claims filed with the Committee on Admissions, founded upon contracts subject to the rules of the Exchange, shall, if, and to the extent that the same are allowed by said Committee, be liquidated, and paid, *pro rata*, out of the proceeds of said membership upon consummation of the transfer.

SEC. 5. A member shall forfeit all right to share in the proceeds of a membership, unless he file a statement of his claim with the Committee on Admissions prior to the transfer of such membership; but such claim, as allowed by the Committee on Admissions, may be paid out of any surplus remaining after all other claims, allowed by said Committee, have been paid in full.

SEC. 6. Claims growing out of transactions between partners, who are members of the Exchange, shall not share in the proceeds of the membership of one of such partners, until after all other claims, as allowed by the Committee on Admissions, have been paid in full.

SEC. 7. When a member dies, his membership may be disposed of by the Committee on Admissions.

SEC. 8. When a member is expelled, or becomes ineligible for reinstatement, his membership may be disposed of forthwith by the Committee on Admissions.

SEC. 9. The expulsion or suspension of a member shall not affect the rights of creditors, members of the Exchange or of firms registered thereon.

SEC. 10. When a member is in debt to another member, the death of the creditor member or the transfer of his membership, either by himself voluntarily, or by the Governing Committee, or the Committee on Admissions, shall not affect the rights of said creditor member, his firm, or estate, to share in the proceeds of the membership of the debtor member under this Article, in the same manner and to the same extent as if such creditor member had not died or his membership had not been transferred.

ARTICLE XVI.

Insolvent Members — Suspension — Reinstatement.

SEC. 1. A member who fails to comply with his contracts, or is insolvent, or who is a partner in a firm, registered upon the Exchange, which fails to comply with its contracts, or is insolvent, shall immediately inform the President, in writing, that he or his firm, is unable to meet their engagements, and prompt notice thereof shall be given to the Exchange. He shall thereby become suspended from membership until, after having settled with his creditors, or the creditors of his firm, he has been reinstated by the Committee on Admissions.

SEC. 2. Whenever the President shall ascertain that a member has failed to meet his engagements, or is insolvent, or that a firm registered upon the Exchange has failed to meet its engagements, or is insolvent, and that such member, or such firm, has neglected to comply with the requirements of the preceding section, he shall announce to the Exchange the insolvency and suspension of such member or such firm.

SEC. 3. If a member, suspended under this Article,

fails to settle with his creditors and apply for reinstatement, within one year from the time of his suspension, his membership shall be disposed of by the Committee on Admissions.

The Governing Committee may, by a two-thirds vote of the members present, extend the time of settlement for periods not exceeding one year each. At the expiration of the time granted, the membership of said suspended member shall be disposed of as above provided.

SEC. 4. When a suspended member applies for reinstatement he shall furnish to the Chairman of the Committee on Admissions a list of his creditors, a statement of the amounts originally owing, and the nature of the settlement in each case. Notice of the proposed consideration of the application shall be given through the Chairman of the Exchange on three consecutive days, and said notice shall also be posted upon the bulletin. Upon the applicant presenting satisfactory proof of settlement with all his creditors, the Committee shall proceed to ballot for him in accordance with its rules and regulations. Failing to receive the approving vote of two-thirds of the entire Committee, the applicant shall be entitled to be balloted for at any five subsequent regular meetings of the Committee, to be designated by himself: provided, however, that the six ballotings to which the applicant shall be entitled shall be within one year from the date of his suspension, or within such further extended time for settlement as may have been granted by the Governing Committee.

If on the sixth ballot the applicant be rejected, he may appeal within ten days thereafter to the Governing Committee, who may by an affirmative vote of not less than twenty-five of its members reinstate the applicant.

If he fails to make application to the Committee on Admissions, to be balloted for as above provided, or if rejected by the Governing Committee, his membership shall be disposed of by the Committee on Admissions.

SEC. 5. Whenever the Governing Committee shall determine, upon the report of the Committee on Admissions, that the failure of a member or of a firm registered upon the Exchange has been caused by reckless or unbusinesslike dealing, said member, or the partner or partners in such firm who are members of the Exchange, may, by a two-thirds vote of the existing members of the Governing Committee, be declared ineligible for reinstatement.

SEC. 6. Every suspended member shall file with the secretary of the Exchange, within thirty days after his suspension, a written statement containing a complete list of his creditors and of the amount owing to each.

ARTICLE XVII.

Expulsion and Suspension from Membership.

SEC. 1. Unless otherwise specially provided, the penalty of suspension from membership may be inflicted, and the period of suspension determined, by the vote of a majority of the existing members of the Governing Committee; and the penalty of expulsion from membership or of ineligibility of a suspended member for re-admission may be inflicted by the vote of two-thirds of the existing members of said Committee.

SEC. 2. A member who shall be adjudged, by a two-thirds vote of all the existing members of the Governing Committee, to be guilty of fraud or of fraudulent acts, shall be expelled and the President shall so declare; public announcement of the expulsion shall be made to the Exchange and the membership shall be forthwith disposed of by the Committee on Admissions.

SEC. 3. Whenever it shall appear to a majority of the Committee on Admissions that a misstatement upon a material point has been made to it by a member, upon his application either for membership or reinstatement or extension of time, it shall report the case to the Governing Committee, who by a two-thirds vote of all the existing members of the Committee may expel the member.

SEC. 4. Any member who shall be connected directly, or by a partner, or otherwise, with any organization in the City of New York which permits dealings in any securities or other property admitted to dealing in any department of this Exchange, shall be liable to suspension for a period not exceeding one year, or to expulsion, as the Governing Committee may determine.

SEC. 5. A member making a transaction with a non-member in the rooms of the Exchange, either purchase, sale or loan, in any security or property admitted to dealings in any department of the Exchange, or in money, shall be subject to suspension for such period not exceeding one year as the Governing Committee may deem proper.

SEC. 6. A member who shall have been adjudged, by a majority vote of all the existing members of the Governing Committee, guilty of wilful violation of the Constitution of the Exchange, or of any resolution of the Governing Committee regulating the conduct or business of members, or of any conduct or proceeding inconsistent with just and equitable principles of trade, may be suspended or expelled as the said Committee may determine, unless some other penalty is expressly provided for such offense.

SEC. 7. The Governing Committee may, by a two-thirds vote of its members present, require that a member of the Exchange shall submit to the Governing Committee or any Standing or Special Committee, for examination, such portion of his books or papers as are material and relevant to any matter under investigation by said Committee or by any Standing or Special Committee. Any member who shall refuse or neglect to comply with such requirement, or shall wilfully destroy any such required evidence, or who, being duly summoned, shall refuse or neglect to appear before the Governing Committee or any Standing or Special Committee, as a witness, or refuse to testify before any such Committee, may be adjudged guilty of an act detrimental to the interest or welfare of the Exchange.

SEC. 8. The Governing Committee may, by a vote of a majority of all its existing members, suspend from the Exchange for a period not exceeding one year, any member who may be adjudged guilty of any act which may be determined by said Committee to be detrimental to the interest or welfare of the Exchange.

SEC. 9. An accusation, charging a member before the Governing Committee with having committed an offense, or having violated the laws or regulations of the Exchange, shall be in writing; it shall specify the charge or charges against such member with reasonable detail, and shall be signed by the person or persons making the charge or charges. A copy of such charge or charges shall be served upon the accused member either personally, or by leaving the same at his office address during business hours, or by mailing it to him at his place of residence. He shall have ten days from the date of such service to answer the same, or such further time as the Governing Committee in its discretion may deem proper. The answer shall be in writing, signed by the accused member, and filed with the Secretary of the Exchange. Upon the answer being filed, or if the accused shall refuse or neglect to make answer as hereinbefore required, the Governing Committee shall, at a regular or special meeting thereafter, proceed to consider the charge or charges; if such meeting be a special meeting, notice of the object thereof shall be sent to the members of the Committee. Notice of such meeting shall be sent to the accused; he shall be entitled to be personally present thereat, and shall be permitted in person to examine and cross-examine all the witnesses produced before the Committee, and also to present such testimony, defense or explanation as he may deem proper. After hearing all the witnesses and the member accused, if he desires to be heard, the Governing Committee shall determine whether said member is guilty of the offense or offenses charged. If it determines that the accused is guilty, the Governing Committee shall expel such member, or may suspend him, as the case may be; the result shall be announced to the Exchange by the President, and a written notice thereof served upon said member in the manner hereinbefore provided. The finding of the Governing Committee shall be final and conclusive.

SEC. 10. Should a member be accused before the Governing Committee of misconduct, or of having committed an offense the penalty for which is limited to suspension for a period not exceeding sixty days, said Committee may proceed summarily, and the method of procedure required by the preceding Section shall not apply. The accused shall be summoned before the Committee, informed of the nature of the accusation against him and afforded an opportunity for explanation by personal or other testimony. If the Committee shall determine by a majority vote of all its existing members that the accused is guilty, it may, by a similar vote, suspend him from membership for such period as the Constitution provides.

SEC. 11. Whenever a member is suspended by the Governing Committee, announcement thereof shall be made to the Exchange, and such member shall be deprived during the term of his suspension of all rights and privileges of membership, except those pertaining to the Gratuity Fund.

SEC. 12. No member of the Exchange shall be allowed to be represented by professional counsel in any investigation or hearing before the Governing Committee or any Standing or Special Committee.

The Gratuity Fund and Its Trustees

ARTICLE XVIII.

The Gratuity Fund.

Every member of the Exchange shall be subject to the conditions and entitled to partake of the benefits of the plan providing for the families of deceased members as hereinafter set forth.

SEC. 1. Every person who shall become a member of the Exchange shall pay to the Trustees of the Gratuity Fund the sum of Ten dollars before he shall be admitted to the privilege of membership.

SEC. 2. Upon the death of a member of the Exchange there shall be levied and assessed against every other member the sum of Ten dollars, which shall thereupon become a due from him to the Exchange, and which shall be charged and collected as other dues and fines are or may be then charged and collected.

SEC. 3. Assessments under the provisions of this Article shall be made equally against all members, either living or deceased, until the date of the transfer of their memberships.

SEC. 4. The faith of the Exchange is hereby pledged

to pay, within one year after proof of death of any member, out of the money collected under the provisions of this Article, the sum of Ten thousand dollars, or so much thereof as may have been collected, to the persons named in the next Section, as therein provided, which money shall be paid as a *gratuity* from the other members of the Exchange, free from all debts, charges or demands whatever.

SEC. 5. Should the member die leaving a widow and no descendant, then the whole sum shall be paid to such widow for her own use.

Should the member die leaving a widow and descendants, then one-half shall be paid to the widow for her separate use and one-half to the children for their use, share and share alike, provided that the share of minor children shall be paid to their guardian, and that the issue of any deceased child shall be entitled to receive the share which said child would have received if living, if of age directly, or if minors, through his, her or their guardian or guardians.

Should the member die leaving descendants and no widow, then the whole sum shall be paid to the children as directed in the preceding paragraph to be done with the moiety; but no adopted child shall share in the gratuity if the member leaves a widow or descendants.

Should the member die leaving neither widow nor descendant, but an adopted child or children, then the whole sum shall be paid to such adopted child or children, the issue of any deceased adopted child to take the share which the parent would have taken if living; provided that such adoption shall have been in such manner and form as to be valid under the laws of the State of New York.

Should the member die leaving neither widow, descendant, adopted child nor issue of a deceased adopted child, then the whole sum shall be paid to the same persons who would, under the laws of the State of New York, take the same by reason of relationship to the deceased member had he owned the same at the time of his death; and if there be no such person, then the assessment levied in such case shall be credited to those members of the Exchange against whom it shall have been charged, in reduction of their payments under this Article.

In all cases a certified copy of the proceedings before a Surrogate or Judge of Probate shall be accepted as proof of the rights of the claimants, be deemed ample authority to the Exchange to pay over the money, shall protect the Exchange in so doing, and shall release the Exchange forever from all further claim or liability whatsoever.

Sec. 6. Nothing herein contained shall ever be taken or construed as a joint liability of the Exchange or its members for the payment of any sum whatever; the liability of each member, at law or in equity, being limited to the payment of ten dollars only on the death of any other member, and the liability of the Exchange being limited to the payment of the sum of ten thousand dollars, or such part thereof as may be collected, after it shall have been collected from the members, and not otherwise.

SEC. 7. Nothing herein contained shall be construed as constituting any estate *in esse* which can be mortgaged or pledged for the payment of any debts; but it shall be construed as the solemn agreement of every member of the Exchange to make a voluntary gift to the family of each deceased member, and of the Exchange, to the best of its ability, to collect and pay over to such family the said voluntary gift.

SEC. 8. There shall be credited annually to each member of the Exchange, in reduction of his payments under this Article, his proportion of the surplus income of the Exchange, after setting apart such sum as the Governing Committee shall determine to be necessary for conducting the business of the Exchange.

Whenever the number of deaths of members of the Exchange shall exceed fifteen in any one year, the Trustees of the Gratuity Fund shall pay over to the Treasurer of the Exchange the net income which has been received as interest on the Fund during said year, less the necessary expenses of management and distribution, and each member of the Exchange shall be credited with his proportion of the amount, in reduction of his payments under this Article.

SEC. 9. The provisions of this Article shall not extend to any member whose connection with the Exchange shall have been severed by the transfer of his membership, whether the same is made voluntarily or involuntarily, nor to any member who now is or hereafter may be expelled by the Governing Committee, but shall extend to suspended members.

ARTICLE XIX.

The Trustees of the Gratuity Fund.

SEC. 1. The execution of the provisions of the preceding Article, and the management and distribution of the Fund created thereunder shall be under the charge of a Board of Trustees, to be known as "The Trustees of the Gratuity Fund," and to consist of the President and the Treasurer of the Exchange, and of five other Trustees chosen for the term of five years.

In case of a vacancy occurring among the five chosen Trustees, the Governing Committee, at its next regular meeting thereafter, shall proceed to fill the same until the next annual election of the Exchange.

SEC. 2. It shall be the duty of the Trustees to invest and keep securely invested, in accordance with the laws of the State of New York regulating Trust Funds, all moneys paid to them for the Fund, together with the interest and accretions arising therefrom.

All stock shall be registered in the name of "The Trustees of the Gratuity Fund of the New York Stock Exchange," but without specifying the individual names of such trustees, and may be disposed of and assigned by any four of said Trustees.

SEC. 3. On the first Monday after the annual election of the Exchange, or as soon thereafter as may be practicable, the Trustees of the Gratuity Fund shall organize by electing a Chairman, and a Secretary and Treasurer of the Gratuity Fund, who shall serve for one year or until their successors shall be chosen. The offices of Secretary and Treasurer may be held by the same person.

SEC. 4. There shall be a regular meeting of the Trustees on the third Monday in each month. The Chairman may call a special meeting at any time; he shall call a meeting at the request of two Trustees. At a meeting four Trustees shall constitute a quorum.

SEC. 5. It shall be the duty of the Chairman to preside at meetings; he shall vote on all questions; he shall, on the Monday preceding the annual election of the Exchange, make a report to the President of the Exchange of the condition of the Fund, with a statement by the Treasurer of receipts and disbursements.

SEC. 6. It shall be the duty of the Secretary to keep regular minutes of the proceedings of the Trustees, and to give notice of meetings.

SEC. 7. It shall be the duty of the Treasurer to receive and sign vouchers for all moneys paid to the Trustees, which he shall deposit in such institutions as they may direct, to his credit as "Treasurer of the Gratuity Fund of the New York Stock Exchange."

He shall have the custody of all securities belonging to the Fund, subject to the examination and control of the Trustees.

He shall keep, or cause to be kept, proper books of account.

He shall receive and keep a record of all claims for payment under Article XVIII of the Constitution of the Exchange, and present the same to the Trustees for their action; when allowed and approved by the Trustees, he shall pay the same; but no such payment shall be made until directed by the Trustees.

He shall make such investments for the Fund as may be ordered by the Trustees.

His books shall always be open to the inspection of any Trustee, and he shall make to the Chairman an annual statement of receipts and disbursements.

He shall receive out of the Fund such compensation per annum as may be fixed by the Trustees and approved by the Governing Committee of the Exchange.

SEC. 8. In case any person entitled to any gratuity shall be under age and have no guardian entitled to receive payment at the maturity thereof, the Trustees may, in their discretion, deposit such money with the New York Life Insurance and Trust Company or the United States Trust Company, as the property of, and in trust for, such minor; and in like manner if any person apparently entitled to any payment fails to claim, or has disappeared or cannot be found after reasonable inquiry, the Trustees may deposit the presumptive share of such person in either of said Trust Companies to the credit of "The Trustees of the Gratuity Fund of the New York Stock Exchange, in trust," to the end that it may be paid to such person, if afterwards found, or otherwise to the parties who may subsequently establish their right thereto; a similar discretion shall apply in the case of any dispute between claimants for a gratuity or a portion thereof.

SEC. 9. The Trustees shall have power at their discretion to consult and employ legal counsel; they shall be authorized to make disbursements out of the Fund to defray necessary expenses, but no such disbursements shall be allowed without a resolution specifying the nature and amount of the same, being entered at large upon the Book of Minutes of the Secretary. Each Trustee shall receive from the Fund five dollars for every meeting at which he shall be present.

SEC. 10. In case of a vacancy occurring in the office of Chairman, or Secretary and Treasurer, the Trustees shall forthwith proceed to fill the same for the unexpired term. In case of the temporary absence or inability to act of either the Chairman, or Secretary and Treasurer, the Trustees shall have power to appoint one of their number to act in his stead *pro tem.*

SEC. 11. The Governing Committee of the Exchange shall, at all times, have the right to direct the production before it of the securities belonging to the Fund, the Secretary's Book of Minutes and the Treasurer's books of account.

It shall be the duty of the Finance Committee of the Exchange to make an annual examination of the condition of the Fund; and it shall have the right at any time to make such additional examination thereof as it may deem proper.

SEC. 12. The Governing Committee of the Exchange shall have power to try charges against any Trustee for malfeasance or negligence in office, and by a vote of two-thirds of all its existing members, to suspend him from his functions or to remove him and declare the office vacant.

SEC. 13. It shall be the duty of the Treasurer of the Exchange to pay over, semi-monthly, all assessments collected under Article XVIII of the Constitution, to the Treasurer of the Gratuity Fund.

Rules for Transaction or Conduct of Business

ARTICLE XX.

Hours of Business.

SEC. 1. The Exchange shall be opened for the entrance of members upon every business day at thirty minutes after nine o'clock A. M.

At ten o'clock the Chairman shall announce that the Exchange is open for the transaction of business, and it shall so remain until three o'clock P. M., when he shall announce it to be closed. On half-holidays the closing shall be at twelve o'clock, noon.

SEC. 2. The Exchange shall not be closed at any time between the hours named in the preceding Section, except by order of the Governing Committee.

SEC. 3. Dealings upon the Exchange shall be limited to the interval between the hours above named; and a fine of fifty dollars for each offense shall be imposed by the Chairman, upon any member who shall make any bid, offer or transaction before or after those hours. Loans of money or securities may be made after the official closing of the Exchange.

SEC. 4. Dealing upon any other Exchange in the City of New York or publicly outside of the Exchange, either directly or indirectly, in securities listed or quoted on the Exchange, is forbidden; any violation of this rule shall be deemed to be an act detrimental to the interest or welfare of the Exchange.

ARTICLE XXI.

Calls.

The appointment and arrangement of Calls of Stocks or Bonds shall be under the control and direction of the Committee of Arrangements.

ARTICLE XXII.

Contracts Subject to the Rules of the Exchange.

All contracts of a member of the Exchange, or of a firm having a member of the Exchange as a general partner, with any other member of the Exchange, or with any other firm having a member of the Exchange as a general partner, for the purchase, sale, borrowing, loaning or hypothecation of securities, or for the borrowing, loaning, or payment of money, whether occurring upon the floor of the Exchange or elsewhere, are contracts subject to the rules of the Exchange.

ARTICLE XXIII.

Bids and Offers.

SEC. 1. All bids and offers made and accepted in accordance with these rules shall be binding.

SEC. 2. All offers to buy or sell securities shall be for 100 shares of stock or for $10,000 par value of bonds, unless otherwise stated.

Offers to buy or sell specific amounts, other than as

above stated may be made at the same time and may be independently accepted.

SEC. 3. Bids and offers may be made only as follows:

(*a*) "Cash," *i. e.*, for delivery upon the day of contract;

(*b*) "Regular Way," *i. e.*, for delivery upon the business day following the contract;

(*c*) "At three days," *i. e.*, for delivery upon the third day following the contract;

(*d*) "Buyer's" or "Seller's" options for not less than four days nor more than sixty days.

Bids and offers under each of these specifications may be made simultaneously, as being essentially different propositions, and may be separately accepted without precedence of one over another.

Bids and offers made without stated conditions shall be considered to be in the "Regular Way."

On transactions for more than three days written contracts shall be exchanged on the day following the transaction, and shall carry interest at the legal rate, unless otherwise agreed; on such contracts one day's notice shall be given, at or before 2:15 P. M., before the securities shall be delivered prior to the maturity of the contract.

On offers to buy "Seller's Option" or to sell "Buyer's Option," the longest option shall have precedence. On offers to buy "Buyer's Option" or to sell "Seller's Option," the shortest option shall have precedence.

SEC. 4. All contracts falling due on holidays or half-holidays observed by the Exchange shall be settled on the preceding business day, except that when two or more consecutive days are holidays or half-holidays, contracts falling due on other than the first of such days shall be settled on the next business day.

Loans of money or securities made on the day preceding a holiday or half-holiday observed by the Exchange shall mature on the succeeding business day, unless otherwise specified.

SEC. 5. Bids or offers shall not be made at a less variation than one-eighth of one per cent.

SEC. 6. Bids and offers shall be made on the basis of a percentage of the par value of the securities dealt in, unless otherwise ordered by the Governing Committee.

SEC. 7. Any member violating any of the above provisions of this Article shall be fined by the Chairman in an amount not exceeding twenty dollars; for a repetition of the offense, he shall be liable to suspension for a period not exceeding ten days.

SEC. 8. Fictitious transactions are forbidden. Any member violating this rule shall be liable to suspension for a period not exceeding twelve months.

SEC. 9. No offers to buy or sell privileges to receive or deliver securities shall be made publicly at the Exchange, under penalty of a fine of twenty-five dollars for each offense.

ARTICLE XXIV.

Comparisons — Liability on Contracts.

SEC. 1. It shall be the duty of every member to report each of his transactions as promptly as possible at his office, where he shall furnish opportunity for prompt comparison.

SEC. 2. It shall be the duty of the SELLER to compare, or to endeavor to compare, each transaction at the office of the Buyer, not later than one hour after the closing of the Exchange. Nothing in this Article shall be construed to justify a refusal to compare before the closing of the Exchange.

SEC. 3. It shall be the duty of the BUYER to investigate, before 10 o'clock A. M. of the day after the purchase, each transaction which has not been compared by the Seller.

SEC. 4. Neglect of a member to comply with the provisions of Section 1 or 2 hereof shall render him liable to a fine not exceeding fifty dollars, to be imposed by the Committee of Arrangements.

SEC. 5. Comparison shall be made by an exchange of an original and a duplicate comparison ticket; the party to whom the comparison ticket is presented shall retain the original, if it be correct, and immediately return the duplicate duly signed.

An exchange of Clearing-House tickets shall constitute a comparison.

SEC. 6. Should a difference be discovered in an attempt to compare, the exact liability of the disputants shall be promptly established by purchase, sale or mutual agreement.

SEC. 7. If an original party to a transaction gives up his principal, the latter shall have the same duties in the matter of comparison as the original party.

SEC. 8. No comparison or failure to compare, and no notification or acceptance of notification, shall have the effect of creating or of canceling a contract, or of changing the terms thereof, or of releasing the original parties from liability.

SEC. 9. No party to a contract shall be compelled to accept a substitute principal, unless the name proposed to be substituted shall be declared in making the offer and as a part thereof.

Orders for the receipt or delivery of securities, issued by the Clearing-House, shall, however, be binding and enforceable upon members or firms using the facilities of the Clearing-House.

SEC. 10. When written contracts shall have been exchanged the signers thereof only are liable.

ARTICLE XXV.

Payment and Delivery.

SEC. 1. In all deliveries of securities, the party delivering shall have the right to require the purchase money to be paid upon delivery; if delivery is made by transfer, payment may be required at time and place of transfer.

SEC. 2. The Receiver of shares of stock shall have the option of requiring the delivery to be made either in certificates therefor or by transfer thereof; except that in cases where personal liability attaches to ownership, the Seller shall have the right to make delivery by transfer.

The right to require receipt or delivery by transfer shall not obtain while the transfer books are closed.

SEC. 3. Deliveries of securities on contracts subject to the rules of the Exchange shall in all cases conform to the requirements for regularity which may be made, from time to time, by the Committee on Securities.

SEC. 4. The Buyer must, not later than two-fifteen o'clock P. M., accept and pay for all, or any portion of a lot of stock contracted for, which may be tendered in lots of one hundred shares or multiples thereof; and he may buy in "under the rule" the undelivered portion, in accordance with the provisions of Article XXVIII.

This rule shall also apply to contracts for bonds when tender is made in lots of ten thousand dollars or multiples thereof.

ARTICLE XXVI.

Settlement of Contracts.

SEC. 1. All deliveries of securities must be made before quarter after two o'clock P. M., and when deliveries are not made by that time the contract may be closed "under the rule" in the manner provided in Article XXVIII of these Rules. In the absence of any notice or agreement the contract shall continue without interest until the following business day; but in every case of non-delivery of securities the party in default shall be liable for any damages which may accrue thereby; and all claims for such damages must be made before three o'clock P. M., on the business day following the default.

SEC. 2. The neglect or failure of a member or firm to exchange Clearing-House tickets on a contract, in conformity with the "Rules for Clearing," shall constitute a default; and such defaulted contract may be closed as provided in Article XXVIII; except that the limit of time for delivery of notice of intention to close such contract shall be ten-thirty o'clock A. M. of the following business day, and the time for closing shall not be before eleven o'clock A. M.

SEC. 3. Parties receiving securities shall not deduct, from the purchase price, any damages claimed for non-delivery, except by the consent of the party delivering the same.

SEC. 4. Notice for the return of loans of money, or of securities not admitted to the Clearing-House, must be given before one o'clock P. M. Notice for the return of loans of securities admitted to the Clearing-House must be given before three-thirty o'clock P. M., except on half-holidays observed by the Exchange, when such notice must be given before twelve-thirty o'clock P. M. All such notices shall be considered as in full force until delivery is made.

SEC. 5. On half-holidays observed by the Exchange, securities sold specifically for "Cash" must be delivered and received at or before eleven-thirty o'clock A. M. In case of default the contract may be closed after eleven-forty o'clock A. M. "under the rule," in manner provided in Article XXVIII.

ARTICLE XXVII.

Clearing-House.

SEC. 1. There shall be a Clearing-House for the purpose of acting as the common agent of the members of the Exchange in receiving and delivering such securities as may from time to time be designated by the Clearing-House Committee.

SEC. 2. Nothing in the conduct of the business of clearing shall attach any liability to the Exchange, or to any member of the Clearing-House Committee, and delays on the part of the Clearing-House shall not attach any liability to members who are clearing.

SEC. 3. The Clearing-House Committee shall designate from time to time the securities which shall be cleared, and, in all transactions in such securities, the deliveries shall be made through the Clearing-House, unless otherwise specially stipulated in the bid or offer or otherwise agreed upon.

SEC. 4. The "Rules for Clearing" and the "Rules for Dealing" adopted by the Governing Committee, and all amendments thereto, shall be binding upon the members of the Exchange equally with the laws included in the Constitution.

Amendments to "Rules for Clearing" or to "Rules for Dealing" may be adopted by a vote of two-thirds of all the existing members of the Governing Committee and need not be submitted to the members of the Exchange for approval.

ARTICLE XXVIII.

Closing Contracts "Under the Rule.'

SEC. 1. When the insolvency of a member or firm is announced to the Exchange, members having contracts subject to the rules of the Exchange with the member or firm, shall without unnecessary delay proceed to close the same. If the contracts involve securities admitted to quotation upon the Exchange the closing must be in the Exchange, either officially by the Chairman, or by personal purchase or sale. If the contracts involve securities not dealt in on the Exchange, the purchase or sale of such securities must be promptly made in the best available market. Should a contract not be closed, as above provided, the price of settlement shall be fixed by the price current at the time when such contract should have been closed under this rule.

SEC. 2. A contract which has not been fulfilled according to the terms thereof may be officially closed "under the rule" by the Chairman, as herein provided.

Notice of intention to make such closing of a contract must be delivered, at or before two-thirty o'clock P. M., at the registered office address of the member or firm in default. And the Chairman shall not close such contract before two thirty-five o'clock P. M.

SEC. 3. Every notice of intention to close a contract "under the rule," because of non-delivery, shall be in writing; and shall state the name of the member or firm by whom the order is given, also for whose account

— all of which shall be announced by the Chairman before closing the contract.

The closing of a contract "under the rule," made in conformity with such notice, shall be also for the account and liability of each succeeding party in interest.

SEC. 4. Notice of intention to close a contract "under the rule" may be given upon the entire amount in default or upon any portion thereof, but in this latter case for not less than one hundred shares of stock or ten thousand dollars of bonds.

SEC. 5. When notice that a contract will be closed "under the rule" is received too late for transmission to other members or firms interested in such contract, within the times stated therefor, the notified member or firm who is unable to so transmit said notice may, immediately after the official closing "under the rule," reëstablish such contract by a new purchase or sale in the "regular way"; and any loss arising therefrom shall be a valid claim against the successive party or parties in interest.

SEC. 6. When a member has issued a notice of intention to close a contract "under the rule," for default in delivery, he must receive and pay for securities due upon such contract if tendered at his office within five minutes of the official time for closing; or thereafter, if tendered at the rostrum of the Exchange, before the Chairman has closed the contract.

SEC. 7. When a contract has been closed "under the rule," the member or firm who gave the order must give prompt notice of such closing to the member or firm in default.

Notification to successive parties in interest must be transmitted without delay, and claims for damages, arising therefrom, must be made prior to three o'clock P. M. of the business day following the closing of the contract.

SEC. 8. When a contract has been closed "under the rule" the Chairman shall endorse upon the order therefor the name of the purchaser or seller, the price and the hour at which such contract is closed, and deliver the order to the Secretary of the Exchange, who shall ascertain whether the money difference, if any, has been paid. If such difference shall not be paid within twenty-four hours after the closing of the contract, the Secretary shall report such default to the President.

SEC. 9. When a contract is closed "under the rule," any member or firm accepting the bid or offer, as made by the Chairman, and not complying promptly therewith, shall be liable for any damages resulting therefrom.

The member or firm, for whose account a contract is being closed "under the rule," shall not be permitted to accept the bid or offer made by the Chairman.

SEC. 10. When a loan of money is not paid at or before two-fifteen o'clock P. M. of the day upon which it becomes due, the borrower shall be considered as in default, and the lender may sell "under the rule" the securities pledged therefor, or so much thereof as may be necessary to liquidate the loan, in the manner prescribed in the foregoing Sections of this Article.

ARTICLE XXIX.

Irregularity in Securities.

Reclamation for irregularity in a security, when such irregularity affects only its currency in the market, must be made within ten days from day of delivery of the security.

ARTICLE XXX.

Disagreement on Terms of Contract.

When a disagreement arising from a transaction in securities shall be discovered, the money difference shall forthwith be established by purchase or sale by the Chairman, or by mutual agreement.

ARTICLE XXXI.

Deposits on Contracts.

SEC. 1. Mutual cash deposits of not exceeding ten per cent. may be required at any time by either party to a contract. Whenever the margin of either party becomes reduced to five per cent. by reason of changes in the market value of the securities, further deposits may be called, from time to time, sufficient to restore the impaired margin.

SEC. 2. The holder of a due-bill issued for the dividend on stock contracted for, may require the maker of the due-bill to deposit the full amount due thereon, in a Trust Company, payable to the joint order of both parties.

SEC. 3. When deposits are called before two o'clock P. M., they must be made at or before two-thirty o'clock of the same day; if called after two o'clock P. M. they must be made at or before ten-thirty o'clock A. M. of the following business day.

On half-holidays observed by the Exchange, deposits called before eleven o'clock A. M. must be made at or before eleven-thirty o'clock A. M.; if called after eleven o'clock A. M. they must be made at or before ten-thirty o'clock A. M. of the next business day.

SEC. 4. Failure of either party to a contract to comply with a demand for a deposit shall constitute a default; and the other party to the contract may report such default to the Chairman, and instruct him to reestablish the contract forthwith, by a new purchase or sale "under the rule," and any difference arising therefrom shall be paid to the party entitled thereto.

Written notice of intention to reëstablish the contract shall be sent to the office of the party in default.

SEC. 5. Unless otherwise mutually agreed, deposits on contracts shall be made in the New York Life Insurance and Trust Company.

ARTICLE XXXII.

Dividends — Interest — Premium.

SEC. 1. On the day of closing of the transfer books of a corporation for a dividend upon its shares all transactions therein for "Cash" shall be "dividend on" up to the time officially designated for the closing of transfers; all transactions on that day other than for "Cash" shall be "ex-dividend."

Should the closing of transfers occur upon a holiday or half-holiday, observed by the Exchange, transactions on the preceding business day, other than for "Cash," shall be "ex-dividend."

Sec. 2. The buyer shall be entitled to receive all interest, dividends, rights and privileges, except voting power, which may pertain to the securities contracted for, and for which the transfer books shall close during the pendency of the contract.

When such contract shall mature before the official date for payment of interest or dividend, the seller shall deliver a due-bill therefor signed or endorsed by him.

When a security is sold before the day of closing books for "Rights" (and is quoted "ex-Rights" on that day), and is delivered thereafter, the buyer shall on its delivery pay only the market price of the security "ex-Rights." He shall pay the balance due on the contract, when the seller delivers the "Rights," at any time on or before the day set by the Committee on Securities for settlement of contracts in "Rights."

When a security is loaned before the day of closing books for "Rights" (and is quoted "ex-Rights" on that day), and is returned thereafter, the lender shall on its return pay only the market price of the security "ex-Rights." He shall pay the balance due on the contract, when the borrower delivers the "Rights," at any time on or before the day set by the Committee on Securities for settlement of contracts in "Rights."

SEC. 3. A charge of one per cent. may be made for collecting dividends. For scrip or stock dividends the charge shall be computed upon the market value of such scrip or stock.

No charge shall be made for collecting dividends accruing on securities deliverable on a contract.

SEC. 4. Offers to buy or sell dividends shall not be made publicly on the Exchange. The Chairman shall impose a fine of twenty-five dollars for each violation of this rule.

SEC. 5. When securities are borrowed or loaned the sum agreed upon, either as interest for carrying or as premium for use, shall be paid whether such securities are delivered or not.

SEC. 6. When money or securities are loaned at a premium said premium shall apply to the day for which the loan is made.

ARTICLE XXXIII.

Transfer and Registry.

SEC. 1. Corporations whose shares are admitted to dealings upon the Exchange will be required to maintain a Transfer Agency and a Registry office in the City of New York, Borough of Manhattan. Both the Transfer Agency and the Registrar must be acceptable to the Committee on Stock List, and the Registrar must file with the Secretary of the Exchange an agreement to comply with the requirements of the Exchange in regard to registration.

SEC. 2. When a corporation purposes to increase its

authorized capital stock, thirty days' notice of such proposed increase must be officially given to the Exchange, before such increase may be admitted to dealings.

SEC. 3. When the capital stock of a corporation is increased through conversion of convertible bonds, already listed, the issuing corporation shall give immediate notice to the Exchange and the Committee on Stock List may, thereupon, authorize the registration of such shares and add them to the list.

SEC. 4. The Governing Committee may suspend dealings in the securities of any corporation previously admitted to quotation upon the Exchange, or it may summarily remove any securities from the list.

SEC. 5. After the admission of a security to dealings upon the Exchange no change in the form of certificate, or of the Transfer Agency or the Registrar of Shares, or of the Trustee of Bonds shall be made without the approval of the Committee on Stock List.

ARTICLE XXXIV.

Commissions.

SEC. 1. Commissions shall be charged and paid, under all circumstances, upon all purchases or sales of securities dealt in upon the Exchange; and shall be absolutely net, and free from all or any rebatement, return, discount or allowance in any shape or manner whatsoever, or by any method or arrangement, direct or indirect; and no bonus, nor any percentage or portion of the commission, shall be given, paid or allowed, directly or indirectly, or as a salary, or portion of a salary, to any clerk or person, for business sought or procured for any member of the Exchange.

SEC. 2. All commissions shall be calculated upon the par value of securities and the rates shall be as follows:

(*a*) On business for parties not members of the Exchange, including joint-account transactions in which a non-member is interested, transactions for partners not members of the Exchange, and for firms of which the Exchange member or members are special partners only, the commission shall be not less than one-eighth of one per cent.

(*b*) On business for members of the Exchange, the commission shall be not less than one-thirty-second of one per cent., except when a principal is given up, in which case the commission shall be not less than one-fiftieth of one per cent.

(*c*) On Mining Shares, Subscription Rights, and Notes of Corporations, such rates, to members and non-members, as may be determined, from time to time, by the Committee on Commissions, with the approval of the Governing Committee.

(*d*) Government and Municipal Securities are exempted from the provisions of this Article.

SEC. 3. A firm having as a general partner a member of the Exchange, shall be entitled to have its business transacted at the rates of commission hereinbefore prescribed for members. A member of the Exchange cannot confer this privilege upon more than one firm at any one time.

The privileges provided for under this Section can only be conferred upon a *Branch House in this country* when established under the same name as the parent firm and in which the partners and their respective interests are identical with those of the parent firm.

SEC. 4. A proposition for the transaction of business, at less than the minimum rates of commission herein provided, shall constitute a violation of this article.

SEC. 5. A member suspended by the Governing Committee shall not, during the time of his suspension, be entitled to have his business transacted at member's rates of commission.

A member who is in suspension by reason of insolvency may have his business transacted at member's rates.

SEC. 6. If the Governing Committee shall, by a majority vote of all its existing members, determine that a member of the Exchange has violated the provisions of this Article, it shall suspend such member, for the first offense, for such period not less than one year nor more than five years, as a majority of the members of said Committee present may determine. A member adjudged guilty of a second offense, by a majority vote of all the existing members of the Governing Committee, shall be expelled by a like vote.

ARTICLE XXXV.

Office Address — Partnerships — Branch Offices.

SEC. 1. Every member shall register with the Secretary an address, and subsequent changes thereof, where notices may be served. The registered address of every member transacting business upon the Exchange must be in its vicinity.

SEC. 2. When a member shall form a partnership he shall immediately register the same with the Secretary; official announcement thereof shall be made to the Exchange and notice posted upon the bulletin for ten days. Notice of dissolution of partnership must be given in like manner.

SEC. 3. No person shall be eligible to either general or special partnership in more than one registered firm at the same time.

This law shall not obtain, however, when a member of a registered firm forms a partnership in a foreign country under the same or different name from that of his firm in this country; provided, however, that the firm in said foreign country shall not derive any benefit from the privileges which attach to members of firms registered at the Stock Exchange.

Sec. 4. A member shall not form a partnership with a suspended member of the Exchange, nor with any person who has been expelled therefrom; nor with any insolvent person, or with any person who may have previously been a member of the Exchange, and against whom any member holds a claim, arising out of transactions made during the time of such membership, and which has not been released, or settled in accordance with the laws of the Exchange.

A member, who is a special partner in a firm, does not thereby confer any of the privileges of the Exchange on such firm.

SEC. 5. A member of the Exchange who is a general partner in a firm represented thereon is liable to the same discipline and penalties for any act or omission of said firm as if the same were committed by him personally; but the Governing Committee may in its discretion by a vote of not less than thirty members relieve him from the penalty therefor.

SEC. 6. Members may, by the consent and approval of the Committee on Commissions, establish Branch Offices. Such offices must be in charge of either a partner, or of a manager or clerk acceptable to said Committee.

The member or firm establishing a Branch Office shall register it with the Secretary of the Exchange, and shall be directly responsible for the conduct of its business.

The managing clerk and all other employees must be paid fixed salaries, not varying with the business.

No agents for the solicitation of business, shall be employed on any other than the foregoing basis.

SEC. 7. Whenever it shall appear to the Governing Committee that a member has formed a partnership, or established a branch office, or is individually or through any member of his firm, interested in a partnership in a foreign country, whereby the interest or good repute of the Exchange may suffer, the Committee may require the dissolution of such partnership, the discontinuance of the interest in said foreign partnership, or of such branch office, as the case may be.

SEC. 8. Any member failing to comply with any requirement of this Article, or with any requirement of the Governing Committee in regard thereto, shall be liable to suspension for a period not exceeding one year.

ARTICLE XXXVI.

Disorderly Conduct.

SEC. 1. Indecorous language, or an act subversive of good order and decorum, or serious interference with the personal comfort or safety of another person is forbidden. Any member who shall violate this rule, within the limits of any department of the Exchange, may be fined by the Chairman, or by the Committee of Arrangements, in a sum not exceeding fifty dollars; or upon complaint made may be summoned before the Governing Committee and suspended for a period not exceeding sixty days.

SEC. 2. The Committee of Arrangements may make rules to govern the conduct of members upon the Exchange; it may impose a fine, not exceeding fifty dollars, for each violation thereof, or may report the delinquent to the Governing Committee, who may suspend him for a period not exceeding sixty days.

SEC. 3. Betting or offering to bet, upon the floor of the Exchange, is forbidden. A member violating this rule shall be subject to the penalties prescribed in the preceding Section of this Article.

ARTICLE XXXVII.

Minutes — Visitors — Communications.

SEC. 1. Members shall have access to the minutes of the Exchange.

SEC. 2. Visitors shall not be admitted to the floor of the Exchange except by permission of the President or the Committee of Arrangements.

SEC. 3. Communications shall not be read to the Exchange without the consent of the President or the Committee of Arrangements.

ARTICLE XXXVIII.

Alterations of the Constitution.

The Governing Committee may make additions, alterations or amendments to the Constitution by a majority vote of all its existing members. Every proposed addition, alteration or amendment must be presented, in writing, at a regular meeting of the Governing Committee, and referred to the Committee on Constitution, which shall report thereon at the next regular meeting of the Governing Committee, or at a special meeting called for the sole purpose of considering it. Action thereon may be postponed to a fixed date by a vote of two-thirds of the members of the Governing Committee present. Such alterations when adopted by the Governing Committee shall be submitted to the Exchange and shall stand as the law of the Exchange, if not disapproved within one week by a majority vote of the entire membership.

No alteration of Article XVIII shall ever be made which will impair, in any essential particular, the obligation of each member to contribute, as therein provided, to the provision for the families of deceased members.

Resolutions Adopted by the Governing Committee.

Advertising.

FEBRUARY 9, 1898.

"That in future the publication of an advertisement of other than a strictly legitimate business character, by a member of the Exchange, shall be deemed an act detrimental to the interest and welfare of the Exchange."

Arbitrage Dealings.

JANUARY 26, 1898.

"Whereas, The so-called Arbitrage business or trading between this Exchange and that of any other city in the United States, based upon quotations from the floor of this Exchange, has resulted in practically ignoring the commission law; therefore

"Resolved, That in the judgment of this Committee the sending of continuous quotations or quotations at frequent intervals by members of this Exchange, from the floor of the Exchange, is detrimental to the interest and welfare of the Exchange, and that any member engaging in such business or trading shall be proceeded against under Section 8 of Article XVII of the Constitution;

"Resolved, That the Committee of Arrangements be and they hereby are authorized and instructed to prevent the transaction of any such business or trading by any member of this Exchange, and to prefer charges against any member engaging therein."

Foreign Arbitrage — Joint Accounts.

APRIL 20, 1911.

(To take effect July 1, 1911.)

"Whereas, The so-called Arbitrage business by means of joint account trading between this Exchange and foreign cities, where each party interested charges a commission or allowance, has resulted in practically nullifying the Commission Law; therefore

"Resolved, That any business, domestic or foreign, for the joint account of a member of the Exchange and a non-member, where each party in interest charges a commission or allowance, is hereby prohibited;

"Resolved, That any business, domestic or foreign, conducted under an arrangement of accounts, not joint account in name, but designed to produce results similar to those of the above described joint account, is hereby prohibited."

Bids and Offers.

DECEMBER 14, 1898.

"That where parties have orders to buy and orders to sell the same security, said parties must offer said security, whether it be stock or bonds, at one-eighth per cent. higher than their bid before making transactions with themselves."

Rules Covering Bids and Offers.

MARCH 30, 1910.

(Amended May 12, 1911.)

1. That the recognized quotation on stocks shall be public bids and offers on lots of 100 shares.

2. All bids and offers on larger lots shall be considered to be for any part thereof in lots of 100 shares or of multiples thereof, whether so stated in the bid or offer or not.

3. If a bid is made for a larger lot of stock above the price at which smaller lots are offered, or if a transaction is made in a larger lot above the price at which smaller lots are offered, such bidder or buyer shall be compelled to buy any or all of the smaller lots which were publicly offered at the time, at the lower price, up to the amount of the bid for the larger lot. If the bid for the larger lot is accepted, and the buyer is unwilling to buy more, the seller must give up to the members who were publicly offering to sell at the lower price, such amounts as they were publicly offering to sell at the lower price, if such claim is made immediately.

4. If an offer is made to sell a larger lot of stock below the price which is bid for smaller lots, or if a transaction is made in a larger lot below the price which is bid for smaller lots, such member offering to sell, or the seller, shall be compelled to sell any or all of the smaller lots which were publicly bid for at the time, at the higher price, up to the amount of the offer of the larger lot. If the offer of the larger lot is accepted, and the seller is unwilling to sell more, the buyer must give up to the members who were publicly bidding the higher price, such amounts as they were publicly bidding for, at the higher price, if such claim is made immediately.

5. A member may sell on offer the largest amount bid for without regard to priority of bids. Should the

offer be of an amount larger than the largest bid, the balance shall go to the next largest bidder in sequence; bids for equal amounts being on a par.

A member may buy on bids under the same rule.

6. Attention is directed to the resolution of the Governing Committee adopted October 26, 1892, which reads as follows:

"When a purchase or sale is claimed by a party who states that he had on the floor a prior or better bid or offer such claim shall not be sustained if the bid or offer was not made with the publicity and frequency necessary to make the existence of such bid or offer generally known at the time of the transaction."

7. Disputes arising from a question as to priority of bid or offer, if not settled by agreement between the members interested, shall be settled by vote of the members knowing of the transaction in question.

Disputes as to the application of rules relating to the transaction in question, if not settled by agreement between the members interested, shall be settled by any member of the Committee of Arrangements.

8. The above rules shall not apply to lots of less than 100 shares, nor to active openings when bids and offers are simultaneous.

Members Dealing with Themselves — Specialists.

MARCH 30, 1910.

(To take effect April 4, 1910.)

"Resolved, That any member of the Exchange who, while acting as a broker, either as a 'Specialist' or otherwise, shall buy or sell directly or indirectly for his own account, for account of a partner, or for any account in which he has an interest, the securities, the order for the purchase or sale of which has been accepted by him for execution, shall be deemed guilty of conduct or proceeding inconsistent with just and equitable principles of trade, and shall be subject to the penalties provided in Article XVII, Section 6, of the Constitution.

"The foregoing rule shall not apply to the act of a member who by reason of his neglect to execute an order is compelled to take or to supply on his own account the securities named in the order; in such case the member is not acting as a broker and shall not charge a commission.

"A member, acting as a broker, is permitted to report to his principal a transaction as made with himself, only when he has orders both to buy and to sell and not to give up, and then he must add to his name on the report, 'on order,' or words to that effect."

Bucket-shops.

MAY 19, 1909.

"That any member of this Exchange who is interested in, or associated in business with, or whose office is connected, directly or indirectly, by public or private wire or other method or contrivance with, or who transacts any business directly or indirectly with or for, any organization, firm or individual engaged in the business of dealing in differences or quotations (commonly called a bucket-shop) shall, on conviction thereof, be deemed to have committed an act or acts detrimental to the interest and welfare of this Exchange."

Clearing Charges.

NOVEMBER 23, 1881.

"That in transactions where orders are received from a non-member, wherein the broker filling the order is directed to give up another broker or clearing-house, the responsibility of collecting the full commission of one-eighth per cent. shall rest with the broker or clearing-house settling the transaction."

OCTOBER 24, 1894.

"That in transactions where orders are received from a member, on which a clearing firm is given up by said member or by his order, the responsibility of collecting the full commission of one-thirty-second of one per cent. shall rest with said clearing firm; and it shall be the duty of the broker who executes such orders to report the transactions to the clearing firm and render to them and collect his bill therefor at the rate of one-fiftieth of one per cent.; and also that where a broker executes an order for a member and clears the security himself, he must charge one-thirty-second of one per cent."

DECEMBER 28, 1911.

"That hereafter when a member of the Exchange receives and delivers securities for another member, the clearing charge for said service may be a matter of mutual agreement."

JANUARY 24, 1912.

"That the Governing Committee rules that in the matter of clearing charges between members of the Exchange, said charges shall be based upon a stipulated sum of money for each one hundred shares of stock or ten thousand dollars of bonds, or portions thereof.

"The payment of a certain sum of money for any period of time for said service, irrespective of the number of shares or amount of bonds cleared, is forbidden."

Clerks in Nominal Positions.

JANUARY 23, 1901.

"That the employment of a clerk or clerks in a nominal position because of the business obtained by such clerk or clerks for their employer, is a violation of the rules." Articles XXXIV and XXXV of the Constitution.

Clerks, Speculative Transactions for.

MARCH 30, 1910.

(To take effect April 4, 1910.)

"That the taking or carrying of a speculative account, or the making of a speculative transaction, in which a clerk of the Exchange, or of a member of the Exchange, or of a bank, trust company, banker or insurance company, is directly or indirectly interested, unless the written consent of the employer has been first obtained, shall be deemed an act detrimental to the interest and welfare of the Exchange.

Responsibility for Accounts — Fictitious Names, etc.

"That every member of the Exchange be required to use due diligence to learn the essential facts relating to every account accepted by himself or by his clerks or representatives, and also relating to the possible use of a name for the account other than that of the party interested."

Commissions.

Reciprocal Business.

APRIL 14, 1897.

"That transacting or offering to transact business in grain, produce, cotton or other commodities, without commission, or for a nominal commission, by any member of this Exchange or firm represented therein, for a customer dealing in securities dealt in at the Exchange, is a method or arrangement for rebatement of commissions, and is a violation of the commission law.

"That giving or offering to give reciprocal business in grain, produce, cotton or other commodities dependent upon the amount of Stock Exchange business received is a method or arrangement for rebatement of commissions and is a violation of the commission law."

Commission on Mining Shares.

APRIL 13, 1910.

"That the rates of commission on mining shares shall be based upon selling price, regardless of par value, and shall not be less than the following, for each one hundred shares:

Selling at	For Non-Members.	For Members, if cleared,	For Members, if given up.
$10 and above,	$12.50	$3.12½	$2.00
Below $10,	6.25	1.56¼	1.00

Taking Over or Accepting Transactions.

APRIL 12, 1911.

"Whenever a non-member of this Exchange shall cause to be executed in any market outside of the United States any order or orders for the purchase or sale of securities listed on this Exchange, other than Government, State or Municipal securities, and said purchase or sale shall be accepted by a member or a firm who are members of this Exchange, for the account of said non-member, one-eighth of one per cent. commission shall be charged said non-member in addition to any commission charged by the party or parties making the transaction."

Commissions.

(*Bunched Orders.*)

JUNE 12, 1912.

The Committee on Commissions reported to the Governing Committee that complaint had been made that a custom prevails upon the Floor of what is called "bunched" orders — that is, when one member has 300 shares of stock to sell, another 200 and another 500, they "bunch" the lots, one of said members offering the entire lot of 1,000 shares; if he succeeds in disposing of said lot, it is not the custom for him to charge his associates in the sale any commission.

The Committee on Commissions expressed the opinion that such an arrangement or custom is contrary to the commission law and should not be permitted, and asked the confirmation of said opinion by the Governing Committee.

On motion, said opinion was confirmed.

Commission on Government Securities.

JUNE 12, 1907.

"That the Commission Law, in Subdivision *d*, Section 2, Article XXXIV, of the Constitution, which reads as follows:

"'Government and Municipal Securities are exempted from the provisions of this article,' refers only to securities of the United States, Porto Rico, or the Philippine Islands, and of States and Municipalities therein."

Comparisons.

NOVEMBER 9, 1904

"That when a mistake in comparison is made, either by a member in person or by his clerks, thereby causing a loss to another member, or when a failure to promptly fulfill the duties imposed by the comparison law causes a loss to another member, the member sustaining the loss may bring a suit before the Arbitration Committee, joining as defendants, if he so elects, any or all of the parties concerned, and the Arbitration Committee may render such verdict against any or all of the defendants as the facts in the case may warrant."

Interest.

MARCH 26, 1902.

"That any agreement or arrangement entered into between a member or his firm, and his or their customer, whereby special and unusual rates of interest are stipulated for, or money-advances upon unusual terms are made a condition, in connection with the conducting of an account, with intent thereby to give special or unusual advantages to such customer, for the purpose of securing his business, shall be deemed to be a violation of Article XXXIV of the Constitution, commonly known as the Commission Law."

Money Loans — Interest.

OCTOBER 25, 1899.

"When a member has contracted to borrow money on collateral, the simple payment of the interest by the borrower to the lender, after three o'clock P. M., without actually effecting or properly endeavoring to effect a loan, shall be held to be an evasion of the contract and an act detrimental to the interest and welfare of the Exchange, and the offending member may be proceeded against under Section 8, Article XVII, of the Constitution."

Stamp Tax.

MAY 24, 1905.

"That in the judgment of the Governing Committee any member of the Exchange who, by agreement or otherwise, directly or indirectly, assumes or bears for his own account, or relieves his principal from any part of the Stamp Tax imposed by the Act of the Legislature of the State of New York, approved April 19, 1905, is guilty of a violation of Article XXXIV of the Constitution relating to commissions.

Failure to Affix Stamps.

NOVEMBER 9, 1910.

"The Governing Committee calls the attention of members to the following resolution adopted on May 26, 1905:

" 'In order to constitute a good delivery after June 1, 1905, all deliveries on sales of stock, whether by Clearing-House delivery ticket or by certificate of stock, must be accompanied by a sales ticket stamped in accordance with the Act of the Legislature of the State of New York, adopted April 19, 1905, providing for a Tax on Transfers of Stock.'

"Any wilful failure on the part of a member to affix the stamps required by Article XII of the Tax Law relating to the Tax on Transfers or *Sales* of Stock, will be deemed by the Governing Committee an act detrimental to the interest and welfare of the Exchange.'

Stock List.

MARCH 27, 1895.

"Whenever it shall appear to the Committee on Stock List that the outstanding amount of any security listed upon the Stock Exchange has become so reduced as to make inadvisable further dealings therein upon the Exchange, the said Committee may direct that such security shall be taken from the list and further dealings therein prohibited."

Telephones.

NOVEMBER 8, 1911.

"That the resolution adopted by the Governing Committee on March 28, 1900, be amended by striking out the words 'Sec. 8,' and inserting in lieu thereof the words 'Sec. 10,' so that said resolution as amended shall read as follows, viz.:

"Resolved, That the privilege of telephonic communication between the offices of members and the building of the New York Stock Exchange shall not be enjoyed as of right but shall rest in the discretion of the Committee of Arrangements or the Governing Committee, and that the Committee of Arrangements shall have power in their discretion, at any time, and from time to time, to withhold such privilege from any member, and to disconnect, or cause to be disconnected, any private telephone in the Stock Exchange building. Said Committee shall also have power in their discretion, at any time, and from time to time, to deprive any member of the privilege of using any public telephone in the Stock Exchange building; said Committee shall not be obliged to assign any reason or cause for any action taken by them under this resolution.

"Any member aggrieved by any decision of the Committee of Arrangements under this resolution shall have the right to appeal therefrom to the Governing Committee, and to appear in person before the Governing Committee to be heard upon such appeal.

"No such appeal shall suspend the operation of the decision appealed from.

"Every decision of the Committee of Arrangements by which the privilege of telephonic communication with the Stock Exchange building shall be withheld from any member, pursuant to this resolution, shall be immediately posted upon the bulletin board in the Exchange, and every member of the Exchange shall be deemed to have notice thereof. If after any such notice shall have been posted, any member of the Stock Exchange shall furnish to the member named therein, or to his partner or firm or office any facilities for communication between the office of such member and the Stock Exchange building, or between the office of the member named in such notice and the office of any other member of the Exchange by means of private wire, telephone or any electric or other device, contrivance or apparatus, he may be suspended by the Governing Committee for a period not exceeding two months, pursuant to the provisions of Sec. 10 Article XVII of the Constitution of the Exchange."

Telephone or Telegraph Connections.

MAY 9, 1900.

(To take effect on June 1, 1900.)

"*First.* — That hereafter no member of the Stock Exchange and no firm of which such member is a partner, shall establish telephonic or telegraphic wire connection between the office of such member or firm and the office of any firm or individual not a member of the Stock Exchange transacting a banking or brokerage business, unless application therefor shall first be made to the Committee of Arrangements, and shall have been approved by them.

"*Second.* — Every such telephonic or telegraphic wire connection which shall be so authorized by the Committee of Arrangements, as well as all existing telephonic or telegraphic wire connections of the same character, shall be registered with the Committee of Arrangements, who shall make such regulations governing the matter as they shall deem necessary.

"*Third.* — That the Committee of Arrangements shall have power, at any time, in their discretion, to order any connection of the character described in these resolutions to be discontinued.

"*Fourth.* — While members of the Stock Exchange may connect their offices by wire with the offices of non-members, in accordance with the provisions of these resolutions, and pay for such wire connection, nevertheless no such member shall directly or indirectly, by himself or through his firm, pay the cost of telegraph operators or any other expense pertaining to non-members' offices.

"*Fifth.* — No office in the City of New York of any member of the Stock Exchange, or of any firm of which such member is a partner, shall be connected by telegraphic or telephonic wire with any point outside of the City of New York unless such wire shall be furnished by a telegraph or telephone company approved by the Committee of Arrangements. Said Committee shall from time to time formulate a list of such approved companies.

"*Sixth.* — Any member violating any provision of these resolutions, or any regulation made by the Committee of Arrangements in pursuance thereof, shall be deemed to be guilty of an act detrimental to the interest and welfare of the Exchange."

Privileges.

FEBRUARY 14, 1912.

"When securities are received or delivered on a privilege for a non-member, one-eighth of one per cent. commission must be charged whether said securities are received or delivered upon the day of expiration of said privilege or prior thereto."

Margins — Improper Use of Customers' Securities — Reckless and Unbusinesslike Dealing.

FEBRUARY 13, 1913.

"That the acceptance and carrying of an account for a customer, either a member or a non-member, without proper and adequate margin may constitute an act detrimental to the interest and welfare of the Exchange, and the offending member may be proceeded against under Section 8 of Article XVII of the Constitution.

"That the improper use of a customer's securities by a member or his firm, is an act not in accordance with just and equitable principles of trade, and the offending member shall be subject to the penalties provided in Section 6 of Article XVII of the Constitution.

"That reckless or unbusinesslike dealing is contrary to just and equitable principles of trade, and the offending member shall be subject to the penalties provided in Section 6 of Article XVII of the Constitution, in every case in which the offense does not come within the provisions of Section 5 of Article XVI thereof."

Sales With no Change of Ownership.

FEBRUARY 5, 1913.

Resolved, That no Stock Exchange Member, or member of a stock Exchange firm shall give, or with knowledge execute, orders for the purchase or sale of securities which would involve no change of ownership.

The punishment for this offense shall be as prescribed in Section 8 of Article XXIII of the Constitution regarding fictitious transactions.

PART V

LAWS OF THE STATE OF NEW YORK RELATING TO STOCKBROKERS

PART V

LAWS OF THE STATE OF NEW YORK RELATING TO STOCKBROKERS

Penal Law

(L. 1909. chap. 88. Consol. Laws, chap. 40.)

SEC. 295. *Receiving deposits in insolvent bank.*—An officer, agent, teller or clerk of any bank, banking association or savings bank, and every individual banker or agent, and every private banker or agent and any teller or clerk of an individual banker, or of a private banker who receives any deposit, knowing that such bank or association or banker is insolvent, is guilty of a misdemeanor, if the amount or value of such deposit be less than twenty-five dollars; if the amount or value of such deposit be twenty-five dollars or over, such person shall be guilty of a felony, punishable by imprisonment for not less than one nor more than five years or by a fine of not less than five hundred nor more than three thousand dollars, or by both.

Source.—Penal Code, Sec. 601, as amended by L. 1902, ch. 148.

Application of section. — Cragie v. Hadley, 99 N. Y. 131 (1885); Atkinson v. Rochester Printing Co. 114 N. Y. 175 (1889); Hall v. Baker, 66 App. Div. 131, 135, 72 N. Y Supp. 965 (1901).

Guilty knowledge must be shown on the part of the officers. Stapelton v. O'Dell, 21 Misc. 94, 47 N. Y. Supp. 13 (1897). The fact that the state superintendent of banks had closed the bank does not tend to prove such guilty knowledge. The condition of the bank, whether solvent or not, is yet undetermined. People v. St. Nicholas Bank, 77 Hun, 159, 166, 28 N. Y. Supp. 407 (1894).

Admission of unproved paper on the trial of an indictment under this section may be reversible error. People v. Severance, 67 Hun, 182, 22 N. Y. Supp. 91 (1893).

(L. 1909, chap. 88. Consol. Laws 1909, chap. 40.)

SEC. 298. *Misconduct by banks and bankers.* — Any moneyed corporation or individual banker authorized to carry on the business of banking under the laws of this state, who:

1. Receives, pays out, gives or offers in payment as money to circulate, or who attempts to circulate as money, any bill, note or other evidence of debt issued or purporting to have been issued by any corporation or individual, situated or residing without this state, and which bill, note or other evidence of debt shall, upon any part thereof, purport to be payable or redeemable at any place or by any corporation or individual within this state; or,

2. Issues, utters, or circulates, as money, or in any way, directly or indirectly, aids or assists in the issuing, uttering or circulating as money within this state, of any bank bill, note or other evidence of debt in the similitude of a bank note issued or purporting to have been issued

by any corporation or individual situated or residing without this state; or procures or receives, in any manner whatever, any such bank bill, note or other evidence of debt with intent to issue, utter or circulate, or with intent to aid in issuing, uttering or circulating the same as money within this state; or,

3. Directly or indirectly lends or pays out for paper discounted or purchased any bank bill, note or other evidence of debt, which is not received at par by such corporation or banker for debts due such corporation or banker; or,

4. Issues or puts in circulation any bank bill or note of any such corporation or banker, unless the same shall be made payable on demand and without interest, except bills of exchange on foreign countries or places beyond the limits or jurisdiction of the United States,

Is guilty of a misdemeanor.

Nothing in this section contained shall be construed to prohibit any such corporation or banker from receiving and paying out such foreign bank bills as they shall receive at par in the ordinary course of their business, or to prohibit such corporation or banker from receiving foreign notes from their dealers and customers in the regular and usual course of their business, at a rate of discount not exceeding that which is or shall be at the time fixed by law, for the redemption of the bills of the banks of this state at their agencies, or from obtaining from the corporations, associations or individuals by which such foreign notes are made, the payment or redemption thereof.

Source.—Penal Code, sec. 604, as amended by L. 1892, ch. 692, Sec. 1.

SEC. 299. *Unlawful discount of bills of foreign banks.*— Any person, association or corporation within the state who, directly or indirectly, on any pretense whatever, procures or receives or offers to receive from any corporation or person any bank bill or note or other evidence of debt in the similitude of a bank note, issued or purporting to have been issued by any corporation or individual, situated or residing without this state, at a greater rate of discount than is or shall be at the time fixed by law, for the redemption of the bills of the banks of this state at their agencies, is guilty of a misdemeanor.

Source.— Penal Code, sec. 605, as amended by L. 1892, ch. 692, sec. 1.

SEC. 302. *Unauthorized use of the term "bank."* Any person engaged in banking in this state, not subject to the supervision of the superintendent of banks, and not required by law to report to such superintendent, who was not engaged in such banking before May twenty-third, eighteen hundred and eighty-five, who:

1. Uses an office sign at the place where such business is transacted, having thereon any artificial or corporate name, or other words indicating that such place or office is the place or office of a bank; or,

2. Uses or circulates any letter-heads, bill-heads, blank notes, blank receipts, certificates, circulars or any written

or printed paper whatever, having thereon any artificial or corporate name, or other word or words indicating that such business is the business of a bank,

Is guilty of a misdemeanor.

Source. — Penal Code, Sec. 609, as amended by L. 1892, ch. 692, Sec. 1.

Application of section. — Hall v. Baker, 66 App. Div. 131, 72 N. Y., Supp. 965 (1901).

"Bucket-Shop" Act.

SEC. 390 *Acts prohibited; penalty for violation.* Any person, copartnership, firm, association or corporation whether acting in his, their or its own right, or as the officer, agent, servant, correspondent or representative of another, who shall,

1. Make or offer to make, or assist in making or offering to make any contract respecting the purchase or sale, either upon credit or margin, of any securities or commodities, including all evidences of debt or property and options for the purchase thereof, shares in any corporation or association, bonds, coupons, scrip, rights, choses in action and other evidences of debt or property, and options for the purchase thereof or anything movable that is bought and sold, intending that such contract shall be terminated, closed or settled according to, or upon, the basis of the public market quotations of prices made on any board of trade or Exchange upon which such commodities or securities are dealt in, and without intending a bona fide purchase or sale of the same; or,

2. Makes or offers to make or assists in making or offer-

ing to make any contract respecting the purchase or sale, either upon credit or margin, of any such securities or commodities wherein both parties intend that such contract shall be deemed, terminated, closed and settled when such market quotations of prices for such securities or commodities named in such contract shall reach a certain figure, without intending a bona fide purchase or sale of the same; or,

3. Makes or offers to make, or assists in making or offering to make any contract respecting the purchase or sale, either upon credit or margin, of any such securities or commodities, not intending the actual bona fide receipt or delivery of such securities or commodities, but intending a settlement of such contract based upon the difference in such public market quotations of prices at which said securities or commodities are, or are asserted to be, bought or sold; or,

4. Shall, as owner, keeper, proprietor or person in charge of, or as officer, director, stockholder, agent, servant, correspondent or representative of such owner, keeper, proprietor or person in charge, or of any other person, keep, conduct or operate any bucket-shop, as hereinafter defined; or knowingly permit or allow or induce any person, co-partnership, firm, association or corporation whether acting in his, their or its own right, or as the officer, agent, servant, correspondent or representative of another to make or offer to make therein, or in offering to make therein, any of the contracts specified in any of the three preceding subdivisions of this section.

Shall be guilty of a felony and on conviction thereof shall, if a corporation, be punished by a fine of not more than five thousand dollars for each offense, and all other persons so convicted shall be punished by a fine of not more than one thousand dollars or by imprisonment for not more than five years, or by both such fine and imprisonment. The prosecution, conviction and punishment of a corporation hereunder shall not be deemed to be a prosecution, conviction or punishment of any of its officers, directors or stockholders.

(Amended by Laws 1913, ch. 236. In effect April 9, 1913.)

SEC. 391. *Exhibiting quotations; penalty for violation.* Any person, firm, copartnership, association or corporation receiving, communicating, exhibiting or displaying in any manner any statement of quotations of prices of any such securities or commodities with an intent to make or offer to make or to assist in making or offering to make any contract prohibited in this article shall be guilty of a felony and on conviction thereof shall be punished as provided in section three hundred and ninety of this chapter.

Source. — Penal Code, sec. 355-b, as added by L. 1908, ch. 458.

SEC. 392. *Written statement to be furnished; presumption.* Every person, firm, association, copartnership or corporation shall furnish upon written demand to any customer, or principal for whom such person has executed an order for the actual purchase or sale of any such securities or commodities, either for immediate or future delivery, a written statement containing the names of the persons from whom such property was bought, or to whom it has been sold, as the case may be, the time when, place where, the amount of and the price at which the same was either bought or sold; and if such person, firm, association, copartnership or corporation shall refuse or neglect to furnish such statement within forty-eight hours after such demand, such refusal shall be prima facie evidence that such purchase or sale was made in violation of this article.

Source. — Penal Code, sec. 355-c, as added by L. 1908, ch. 458.

SEC. 393. *Corporations; additional penalty for second offense.* If a domestic corporation shall be convicted of a second offense hereunder the supreme court shall have jurisdiction upon an action brought by the attorney-general, in the name of the people, for that purpose, to dissolve such corporation; and if a foreign corporation shall be convicted of a second offense, such court shall have jurisdiction in an action brought in like manner to restrain such corporation from doing business in this state.

Source.— Penal Code, sec. 355-d, as added by L. 1908, ch. 458.

SEC. 394. *Definitions.* "Bucket-shop" shall mean any building, or any room, apartment, booth, office or store therein or any other place where any contract prohibited by this article is made or offered to be made.

Source — Penal Code, sec. 355-e, as added by L. 1908, ch. 458.

SEC. 444. *Discriminations by Exchanges or Members.* No exchange, voluntary association, or corporation, heretofore or hereafter formed or organized, for the purpose of affording to its members, or to others, facilities for dealing or trading in stocks, bonds, or other securities, or in commodities, shall make or enforce any by-law, rule, regulation, resolution or agreement the purpose or result of which shall be to forbid or prevent the members of such exchange, voluntary association, or corporation, from dealing, at the regular rates of commission with or for the members of any other exchange, voluntary association, or corporation formed or organized for like purposes, nor shall any such exchange, voluntary association, or corporation, penalize or discipline or attempt to penalize or discipline its members or any of them, for an infraction of any such by-law, rule, regulation, resolution or agreement. Any corporation violating any of the foregoing provisions, and any person participating in the acts herein forbidden to be done by any exchange, voluntary association, or corporation, and any member of any such exchange, voluntary association, or corporation refusing to deal with or for any customer as above provided, on the ground that said customer is a member of some other Exchange, voluntary association, or corporation of like character, is guilty of a misdemeanor.

(Added by Laws 1913, ch. 477. In effect Sept. 1, 1913.)

(L. 1909, chap. 88. Consol. Laws 1909, chap. 40.)

SEC. 660. *Frauds in the organization of corporations.*—A person who:

1. Without authority subscribes the names of another to or inserts the name of another in any prospectus. circular or other advertisement or announcement of any corporation or joint-stock association existing or intended to be formed, with intent to permit the same to be published, and thereby to lead persons to believe that the person whose name is so subscribed is an officer, agent, member or promoter of such corporation or association; or,

2. Signs the name of a fictitious person to any subscription for or agreement to take stock in any corporation, existing or proposed; or,

3. Signs to any such subscription or agreement the name of any person, knowing that such person does not intend in good faith to comply with the terms thereof, or under any understanding or agreement, that the terms of such subscription or agreement are not to be complied with or enforced,

Is guilty of a misdemeanor.

Source.—Penal Code, sec. 590, as amended by L. 1892, sec. 1.

SEC. 662. *Fraudulent issue of stocks and bonds.*—An officer, agent, or other person in the service of any joint-stock company or corporation formed or existing under the laws of this state, or of the United States or of any state or territory thereof, or of any foreign government or country, who wilfully and knowingly with intent to defraud;

1. Sells, pledges or issues, or causes to be sold, pledged or issued, or signs or executes, or causes to be signed or executed with intent to sell, pledge or issue, or cause to be sold, pledged or issued, any certificate or instrument purporting to be a certificate or evidence of the ownership of any share or shares of such company or corporation or any bond or evidence of debt, or writing purporting to be a bond or evidence of debt of such company or corporation, without being first thereto duly authorized by such company or corporation, or contrary to the charter or laws under which such corporation or company, exists, or in excess of the power of such company or corporation or of the limit imposed by law or otherwise upon its power to create or issue stock or evidences of debt; or,

2. Reissues, sells, pledges or disposes of, or causes to be reissued, sold, pledged or disposed of, any surrendered or canceled certificates, or other evidence of the transfer or ownership of any such share or shares,

Is punishable by imprisonment for a term not exceeding seven years, or by a fine not exceeding three thousand dollars, or by both.

Source. — Penal Code, sec. 591, as amended by L. 1892, ch. 662, sec. 19.

(L. 1909, chap. 88. Consol. Laws 1909, chap. 40.)

SEC. 663. *Acting for foreign corporations not auth-*

orized to do business in this state.—Any person, or corporation, who:

1. Acts as agent or representative of any mortgage, loan or investment corporation or building and mutual loan corporation or association or coöperative savings and loan association organized outside of this state, while such mortgage, loan or investment corporation or building and mutual loan corporation or association or coöperative savings and loan association shall not be authorized under a license of the superintendent of banks to do business in this state; or,

2. Acts as agent or representative in this state of a foreign corporation, other than a moneyed corporation, with the words "trust," "bank," "banking," "insurance," "assurance," "indemnity," "guarantee," "guaranty," "savings," "investment," "loan," "benefit," or any other words or terms indicating, representing or holding out such company to be a moneyed corporation as a part of its name or corporate title, or who, in connection with such corporation or otherwise, shall put forth any sign containing said name, or who shall advertise or publish the said company as doing business in this state, directly or indirectly, through agents or otherwise, while such company shall not be authorized under a certificate procured from the secretary of state pursuant to section fifteen of the general corporation law to do business, in this state,

Is guilty of a misdemeanor.

Source. — Penal Code, sec. 593, as amended by L. 1892, ch. 692, sec. 1; L. 1904, ch. 489, sec. 1; L. 1908, ch. 118.

SEC. 926. *False rumors as to stocks, bonds or public funds.*—A person who, with intent to affect the market price of the public funds of this state or of the United States, or of any state or territory thereof or of a foreign country or government, or of the stocks, bonds, or other evidences of debt of a corporation or association, or the market price of gold or silver coin or bullion, or any merchandise or commodity whatever;

1. Without lawful authority, falsely signs the name of an officer of a corporation, or of any other person to a letter, message, or other paper: or,

2. Utters or circulates such a letter, message, or paper, knowing that the same has been so falsely signed; or,

3. Knowingly circulates any false statement, rumor, or intelligence,

Is punishable by a fine of not more than five thousand dollars, or by imprisonment for not more than three years, or both.

Source.— Penal Code, sec. 435.

Circulating a false report that a stock corporation is going into a receiver's hands is a violation of this action. People v. Goslin, 67 App. Div., 16; 73 N. Y., Supp. 520 (1901); aff'd 171 N. Y. 627.

SEC. 951. *Reporting or publishing fictitious transactions in securities.*—A person who with intent to deceive, reports or publishes, or causes to be reported or published as a purchase or sale of the stocks, bonds or other evidences of debt of a corporation, company or association, any transaction therein, whereby no actual change of ownership or interest is effected, is guilty of a felony, punishable by a fine of not more than five thousand dollars, or by imprisonment for not more than two years, or by both.

(Added by Laws 1913, ch. 476. In effect May 9, 1913.)

SEC. 952. *False statement or advertisement as to securities.* — Any person who, with intent to deceive, makes, issues or publishes, or causes to be made, issued or published, any statement or advertisement as to the value or as to facts affecting the value of the stocks, bonds or other evidences of debt of a corporation, company or association, or to facts affecting the financial condition of any corporation, company or association which has issued, is issuing or is about to issue stocks, bonds or other evidences of debt, and who knows, or has reasonable ground to believe that any material representation, prediction or promise made in such statement or advertisement is false, is guilty of a felony, punishable by a fine of not more than five thousand dollars, or by imprisonment for not more than three years, or by both.

(Added by Laws 1913, ch. 475. In effect May 9, 1913.)

SEC. 953. *Manipulation of prices of securities.*—Any person who inflates, depresses, or causes fluctuations in, or attempts to inflate, depress or cause fluctuations in, or combines or conspires with any other person or persons to inflate, depress or cause fluctuations in, the market prices of the stocks, bonds or other evidences of debt of a corporation, company or association, or of an issue or any part of an issue of the stock, bonds or evidences of debt of a corporation, company or association, by means of pretended purchases and sales thereof, or by any other fictitious transactions of devices for or on account of such person or of any other person, or for or on account of the persons so combining or conspiring, whereby either in whole or in part a simultaneous change of ownership of or interest in such stocks, bonds or evidences of debt, or of such issue or part of an issue thereof, is not effected, is guilty of a felony, punishable by a fine of not more than five thousand dollars or by imprisonment for not more than two years, or by both.

A pretended purchase or sale of any such stocks, bonds or other evidences of debt whereby, in whole or in part, no simultaneous change of ownership or interest therein is effected, shall be prima facie evidence of the violation of this section by the person or persons taking part in the transactions of such pretended purchase or sale.

(Added by Laws 1913, ch. 253. In effect April 10, 1913.)

SEC. 954. *Trading by brokers against customers' orders.* —A broker who, being employed by a customer to buy and carry upon margin the stocks, bonds or other evidences of debt of a corporation, company or association, while acting as broker for such customer in respect of such stocks, bonds or other evidences of debt, sells for his own account the same kind or issue of stocks, bonds or other evidences of debt of such corporation, company or association, with intent to trade against the customer's order, or, who, being employed by a customer to sell the stocks, bonds or other evidences of debt of a corporation, company or association, while acting as broker for such customer in respect to the sale of such stocks, bonds or other evidences of debt, purchases for his own account the same kind or issue of stocks, bonds or other evidences of debt of such corporation, company or association, with intent to trade against the customer's order, is guilty of a felony, punishable by a fine of not more than five thousand dollars, or by imprisonment for not more than one year, or by both. Every member of a firm of brokers, who either does, or consents or assents to the doing of any act which by the provisions of this section is made a felony, shall be guilty of a violation thereof.

(Added by Laws 1913, ch. 592. In effect May 17, 1913.)

SEC. 955. *Transactions by brokers after insolvency.*— A person engaged in the business of purchasing and selling as broker, stocks, bonds or other evidences of debt of corporations, companies or associations who, knowing that he is insolvent, accepts or receives from a customer ignorant of such broker's insolvency, money, stocks, bonds or other evidences of debt belonging to the customer otherwise than in liquidation of, or as security for, an existing indebtedness, and who thereby causes the customer to lose in whole or in part such money, stocks, bonds or other evidences of debt, is guilty of a felony punishable by fine of not more than five thousand dollars or by imprisonment for not more than two years, or by both. A person shall be deemed insolvent within the meaning of this section whenever the aggregate of his property shall not, at a fair valuation, be sufficient in amount to pay his debts.

(Added by Laws 1913, ch. 500. In effect May 8, 1913.)

(L. 1909, ch. 88. Consol. Laws 1909, ch. 40.)

SEC. 956. *Hypothecation of customer's securities.*—A person engaged in the business of purchasing and selling as a broker stocks, bonds or other evidences of debt of corporations, companies or associations, who,

1. Having in his possession, for safe keeping or otherwise, stocks, bonds or other evidences of debt of a corporation, company or association belonging to a customer without having any lien thereon or any special property therein, pledges or disposes thereof without such customer's consent or,

2. Having in his possession stocks, bonds or other evidences of debt of a corporation, company or association belonging to a customer on which he has a lien for indebtedness due to him by the customer,

Pledges the same for more than the amount due to him thereon, or otherwise disposes thereof for his own benefit, without the customer's consent, and without having in his possession or subject to his control, stocks, bonds or other evidences of debt of the kind and amount to which the customer is then entitled, for delivery to him upon his demand therefor and tender of the amount due thereon, and thereby causes the customer to lose, in whole or in part, such stocks, bonds or other evidences of debt, or the value thereof, is guilty of a felony, punishable by a fine of not more than five thousand dollars or by imprisonment for not more than two years, or by both.

Every member of a firm of brokers, who either does, or consents or assents to the doing of any act which by the provisions of this or the last preceding section is made a felony, shall be guilty thereof.

(Added by Laws 1913, ch. 500. In effect May 8, 1913.)

SEC. 957. *Delivery to customers of memoranda of transactions by brokers.* A person engaged in the business of purchasing or selling as broker, stocks, bonds and other evidences of debt of corporations, companies or associations shall deliver to each customer on whose behalf a purchase or sale of such securities is made by him a statement or memorandum of such purchase or sale, a description of the securities purchased or sold, the name of the person, firm or corporation from whom such securities were purchased, or to which the same were sold, and the day, and the hours between which the transactions took place. A broker who refuses to deliver such statement or memorandum to a customer within twenty-four hours after a written demand therefor, or who delivers a statement or memorandum which is false in any material respect, is guilty of a misdemeanor, punishable by a fine of not more than five hundred dollars, or imprisonment for not more than one year, or both.

(Added by Laws, 1913, ch. 593. In effect Sept. 1, 1913.)

Personal Property Law

(L. 1909, chap 45. Consol. Laws 1909, chap 41.)

SEC. 33. *Validity of certain agreements made without consideration.* An agreement for the purchase, sale, transfer or delivery of a certificate or other evidence of debt, issued by the United States or by any state, or a municipal or other corporation, or of any share or interest in the stock of any bank corporation or joint stock association, incorporated or organized under the laws of the United States or of any state, is not void or voidable, for want of consideration, or because of the non-payment of consideration, or because the vendor, at the time of making such contract, is not the owner or possessor of the certificate or certificates or other evidence of debt, share or interest.

Source. Former Pers. Prop. L. (L. 1897, ch. 417.) Sec. 22; originally revised from L. 1858, ch. 134.

For rule and practice prior to act of 1858, and under the Revised Statutes, see Staples v. Gould, 9 N. Y. 520 (1854); Washburn v. Franklin, 28 Barb. 27 (1858).

ARTICLE VI.

(Laws 1909, ch. 45 Consol. Laws 1909, ch. 41.)

Transfers of Certificates and Shares of Stock.

This new article is added by Laws 1913, ch. 660.

As originally enacted the Personal Property Law contained five articles. By Laws 1911, ch. 571, a new article 5 was added, and the original article 5, renumbered article 6, which, with the new article added by said

Laws 1913, ch. 600, leaves the law with two articles numbered 6.

SEC. 162. *How title to certificates and shares may be transferred.* Title to a certificate and to the shares represented thereby can be transferred only,

(*a*) By delivery of the certificate endorsed either in blank or to a specified person by the person appearing by the certificate to be the owner of the shares represented thereby, or

(*b*) By delivery of the certificate and a separate document containing a written assignment of the certificate or a power of attorney to sell, assign or transfer the same or the shares represented thereby, signed by the person appearing by the certificate to be the owner of the shares represented thereby. Such assignment or power of attorney may be either in blank or to a specified person.

The provisions of this section shall be applicable although the charter or articles of incorporation or code of regulations or by-laws of the corporation issuing the certificate and the certificate itself provide that the shares represented thereby shall be transferable only on the books of the corporation or shall be registered by a registrar or transferred by a transfer agent.

(Added by Laws 1913, ch. 600. In effect Sept. 1, 1913.)

SEC. 163. *Powers of those lacking full legal capacity and of fiduciaries not enlarged.* Nothing in this article shall be construed as enlarging the powers of an infant or other person lacking full legal capacity, or of a trustee, executor or administrator, or other fiduciary, to make a valid endorsement, assignment or power of attorney.

(Added by Laws 1913, ch. 600. In effect Sept. 1, 1913.)

SEC. 164. *Corporations not forbidden to treat registered holder as owner.* Nothing in this article shall be construed as forbidding a corporation,

(*a*) To recognize the exclusive right of a person registered on its books as the owner of shares to receive dividends and to vote as such owner, or

(*b*) To hold liable for calls and assessments a person registered on its books as the owner of shares.

(Added by Laws 1913, ch. 600. In effect Sept 1, 1913.)

SEC. 165. *Title derived from certificate extinguishes title derived from a separate document.* The title of a transferee of a certificate under a power of attorney or assignment not written upon the certificate, and the title of any person claiming under such transferee, shall cease and determine if, at any time prior to the surrender of the certificate to the corporation issuing it, another person, for value in good faith, and without notice of the prior transfer, shall purchase and obtain delivery of such certificate with the indorsement of the person appearing by the certificate to be the owner thereof, or shall purchase and obtain delivery of such certificate and the written assignment or power of attorney of such person though contained in a separate document.

(Added by Laws 1913, ch. 600. In effect Sept. 1 1913.)

Sec. 166. *Who may deliver a certificate.*—The delivery of a certificate to transfer title in accordance with the provisions of section one hundred and sixty-two is effectual, except as provided in section one hundred and sixty-eight, though made by one having no right of possession and having no authority from the owner of the certificate or from the person purporting to transfer the title.

(Added by Laws 1913, ch. 600. In effect Sept. 1, 1913.)

Sec. 167. *Endorsement effectual in spite of fraud, duress, mistake, revocation, death, incapacity or lack of consideration or authority.*—The endorsement of a certificate by the person appearing by the certificate to be the owner of the shares represented thereby is effectual, except as provided in section one hundred and sixty-eight, though the endorser or transferor,

(*a*) was induced by fraud, duress or mistake to make the endorsement or delivery, or

(*b*) has revoked the delivery of the certificate, or the authority given by the endorsement or delivery of the certificate, or

(*c*) has died or become legally incapacitated after the endorsement, whether before or after the delivery of the certificate, or (*d*) has received no consideration.

(Added by Laws 1913, ch. 600. In effect Sept. 1, 1913.)

SEC. 168. *Rescission of transfer.*—If the endorsement or delivery of a certificate,

(*a*) was procured by fraud or duress, or

(*b*) was made under such mistake as to make the endorsement or delivery inequitable; or

If the delivery of a certificate was made

(*c*) without authority from the owner, or

(*d*) after the owner's death or legal incapacity,

The possession of the certificate may be reclaimed and the transfer thereof rescinded, unless:

1. The certificate has been transferred to a purchaser for value in good faith without notice of any facts making the transfer wrongful, or

2. The injured person has elected to waive the injury, or has been guilty of laches in endeavoring to enforce his rights.

Any court of appropriate jurisdiction may enforce specifically such right to reclaim the possession of the certificate or to rescind the transfer thereof and, pending litigation, may enjoin the further transfer of the certificate or impound it.

(Added by Laws 1913, ch. 600. In effect Sept. 1, 1913.)

SEC. 169. *Rescission of transfer of certificate does not invalidate subsequent transfer by transferee in possession.*—Although the transfer of a certificate or of shares represented thereby has been rescinded or set aside, nevertheless, if the transferee has possession of the certificate or of a new certificate representing part or the whole of the same shares of stock, a subsequent transfer of such certificate by the transferee, mediately or immediately, to a purchaser for value in good faith, without notice of any facts making the transfer wrongful, shall give such purchaser an indefeasible right to the certificate and the shares represented thereby.

(Added by Laws 1913, ch. 600. In effect Sept. 1, 1913.)

SEC. 170. *Delivery of unendorsed certificate imposes obligation to endorse.*—The delivery of a certificate by the person appearing by the certificate to be the owner thereof without the endorsement requisite for the transfer of the certificate and the shares represented thereby, but with intent to transfer such certificate or shares, shall impose an obligation, in the absence of an agreement to the contrary, upon the person so delivering, to complete the transfer by making the necessary endorsement. The transfer shall take effect as of the time when the endorsement is actually made. This obligation may be specifically enforced.

(Added by Laws 1913, ch. 600. In effect Sept. 1, 1913.)

SEC. 171. *Ineffectual attempt to transfer amounts to a promise to transfer.*—An attempted transfer of title to a certificate or to the shares represented thereby without delivery of the certificate shall have the effect of a promise to transfer and the obligation, if any, imposed by such promise shall be determined by the law governing the formation and performance of contracts.

(Added by Laws 1913, ch. 600. In effect Sept. 1, 1913.)

SEC. 172. *Warranties on sale of certificate.*—A person who for value transfers a certificate, including one who assigns for value a claim secured by a certificate, unless a contrary intention appears, warrants —

(*a*) that the certificate is genuine,

(*b*) that he has a legal right to transfer it, and

(*c*) that he has no knowledge of any fact which would impair the validity of the certificate.

In the case of an assignment of a claim secured by a certificate, the liability of the assignor upon such warranty shall not exceed the amount of the claim.

(Added by Laws 1913, ch. 600. In effect Sept. 1, 1913.)

SEC. 173. *No warranty implied from accepting payment of a debt.*—A mortgagee, pledgee or other holder for security of a certificate who in good faith demands or receives payment of the debt for which such certificate is security, whether from a party to a draft drawn for such debt, or from any other person, shall not by so doing be deemed to represent or to warrant the genuineness of such certificate, or the value of the shares represented thereby.

(Added by Laws 1913, ch. 600. In effect Sept. 1, 1913.)

SEC. 174. *No attachment or levy upon shares unless certificate surrendered or transfer enjoined.*—No attachment or levy upon shares of stock for which a certificate is outstanding shall be valid until such certificate be actually seized by the officer making the attachment or levy, or be surrendered to the corporation which issued it, or its transfer by the holder be enjoined. Except where a certificate is lost or destroyed, such corporation shall not be compelled to issue a new certificate for the stock until the old certificate is surrendered to it.

(Added by Laws 1913, ch. 600. In effect Sept. 1, 1913.)

SEC. 175. *Creditor's remedies to reach certificate.*—A creditor whose debtor is the owner of a certificate shall be entitled to such aid from courts of appropriate jurisdiction, by injunction and otherwise, in attaching such certificate or in satisfying the claim by means thereof as is allowed at law or in equity, in regard to property which cannot readily be attached or levied upon by ordinary legal process.

(Added by Laws 1913, ch. 600. In effect Sept. 1, 1913.)

SEC. 176. *There shall be no lien or restriction unless indicated on certificate.*—There shall be no lien in favor of a corporation upon the shares represented by a certificate issued by such corporation and there shall be no restriction upon the transfer of shares so represented by virtue of any by-law of such corporation or otherwise, unless the right of the corporation to such lien or the restriction is stated upon the certificate.

(Added by Laws 1913, ch. 600. In effect Sept. 1, 1913.)

SEC. 177. *Alteration of certificate does not divest title to shares.*—The alteration of a certificate, whether fraudulent or not and by whomsoever made, shall not deprive the owner of his title to the certificate and the shares originally represented thereby, and the transfer of such a certificate shall convey to the transferee a good title to such certificate and to the shares originally represented thereby.

(Added by Laws 1913, ch. 600. In effect Sept. 1, 1913.)

SEC. 178. *Lost or destroyed certificate.*—Where a certificate has been lost or destroyed, a court of competent jurisdiction may order the issue of a new certificate therefor on service of process upon the corporation and on reasonable notice by publication, and in any other way which the court may direct, to all persons interested and upon satisfactory proof of such loss or destruction and upon the giving of a bond with sufficient surety to be approved by the court to protect the corporation or any person injured by the issue of a new certificate from any liability or expense, which it or they may incur by reason of the original certificate remaining outstanding. The court may also in its discretion order the payment of the corporation's reasonable costs and counsel fees. The issue of a new certificate under an order of the court as provided in this section shall not relieve the corporation from liability in damages to a person to whom the original certificate has been or shall be transferred for value without notice of the proceedings or of the issuance of the new certificates.

(Added by Laws 1913, ch. 600. In effect Sept. 1, 1913.)

SEC. 179. *Rule for cases not provided for by this act.*—In any case not provided for by this act, the rules of law and equity, including the law merchant, and in particular the rules relating to the law of principal and agent, executors, administrators and trustees and to the effect of fraud, misrepresentation, duress or coercion, mistake, bankruptcy or other invalidating cause, shall govern.

(Added by Laws 1913, ch. 600. In effect Sept. 1, 1913.)

SEC. 180. *Interpretation shall give effect to purpose of uniformity.*—This act shall be so interpreted and construed as to effectuate its general purpose to make uniform the law of those states which enact it.

(Added by Laws 1913, ch. 600. In effect Sept. 1, 1913.)

SEC. 181. *Definition of endorsement.*—A certificate is endorsed when an assignment or a power of attorney to sell, assign or transfer the certificate or the shares represented thereby is written on the certificate and signed by the person appearing by the certificate to be the owner of the shares represented thereby, or when the signature of such person is written without more upon the back of the certificate. In any of such cases a certificate is endorsed though it has not been delivered.

(Added by Laws 1913, ch. 600. In effect Sept. 1, 1913.)

SEC. 182. *Definition of person appearing to be the owner of certificate.*—The person to whom a certificate was originally issued is the person appearing by the certificate to be the owner thereof, and of the shares represented thereby, until and unless he endorses the certificate to another specified person, and thereupon such other specified person is the person appearing by the certificate to be the owner thereof until and unless he also endorses the certificate to another specified person. Subsequent special endorsements may be made with like effect.

(Added by Laws 1913, ch. 600. In effect Sept. 1, 1913.)

SEC. 183. *Other definitions.*—1. In this article, unless the context or subject-matter otherwise requires —

"Certificate" means a certificate of stock in a corporation organized under the laws of this state or of another state whose laws are consistent with this act.

"Delivery" means voluntary transfer of possession from one person to another.

"Person" includes a corporation or partnership or two or more persons having a joint or common interest.

To "purchase" includes to take as mortgagee or as pledgee.

"Purchaser" includes mortgagee and pledgee.

"Shares" means a share or shares of stock in a corporation organized under the laws of this state or of another state whose laws are consistent with this act.

"State" includes state, territory, district and insular possession of the United States.

"Transfer" means transfer of legal title.

"Title" means legal title and does not include a merely equitable or beneficial ownership or interest.

"Value" is any consideration sufficient to support a simple contract. An antecedent or preëxisting obligation, whether for money or not, constitutes value where a certificate is taken either in satisfaction thereof or a security therefor.

2. A thing is done "in good faith" within the meaning of this act, when it is in fact done honestly, whether it be done negligently or not.

(Added by Laws 1913, ch. 600. In effect Sept. 1, 1913.)

SEC. 184. *Article does not apply to existing certificates.* The provisions of this article apply only to certificates issued after the taking effect of this article.

(Added by Laws 1913, ch. 600. In effect Sept. 1, 1913.)

SEC. 185. *Inconsistent legislation repealed.* All acts or parts of acts inconsistent with this article are hereby repealed.

(Added by Laws 1913, ch. 600. In effect Sept. 1, 1913.)

The enacting clause of this law (Laws, 1913, ch. 600) provided that the article should consist of 25 sections, to be numbered 162-186, inclusive, but the body of the law contains only 24 sections, one short of the number designated in the enacting clause.

General Business Law

(L. 1909, chap. 25. Laws 1909, chap. 20.)

Banking Licenses.

SEC. 25. *Licenses, bonds and deposits.* — Except as provided in section twenty-nine-d, no individual or partnership shall hereafter engage directly or indirectly in the business of receiving deposits of money for safe-keeping or for the purpose of transmission to another or for any other purpose in cities of the first class without having first obtained from the comptroller a license to engage in such business. Before receiving such license, the applicant therefor shall file with the comptroller a written statement in the form to be prescribed by the comptroller and verified by the individual or members of the firm making the application, showing the amount of the assets and liabilities of the applicant, designating the place where the applicant proposes to engage in business, that the applicant has been, or if the applicant shall constitute a partnership, that a majority of the members thereof having a controlling interest in the business of such partnership have been continuously for a period of five years immediately preceding the date of such appiication resident in the United States. Such applicant shall at the same time deposit with the comptroller ten thousand dollars in money or in securities which shall consist of bonds of the United States, of this state or of any municipality thereof, or other bonds approved by the comptroller, and if a deposit of securities shall be so made in lieu of ten thousand dollars in money, the comptroller shall thereafter require the applicant to maintain such deposit at all times at a value which shall equal the sum of ten thousand dollars. In addition thereto there shall be presented to the comptroller a bond to the people of the state of New York executed by the applicant and by a surety company approved by the comptroller, conditioned upon the faithful holding of all moneys that may be deposited with the applicant, in accordance with the terms of the deposit and the repayment of such moneys so deposited and upon the faithful transmission of any money which shall be delivered to such applicant for transmission to another, and in the event of the insolvency or bankruptcy of the applicant, upon the payment of the full amount of such bond to the assignee, receiver or trustee of the applicant, as the case may require, for the benefit of the persons making such deposits and of such persons as shall deliver money to the applicant for transmission to another. The penalty of the bond shall be a sum fixed by the comptroller, which shall not be more than fifty thousand dollars nor less than ten thousand dollars. In lieu of the aforesaid bond the applicant may deposit and the comptroller shall accept, money and securities of the character above described. The money and securities so deposited shall be held on the conditions specified in the aforesaid bond. If securities be deposited in lieu of the aforesaid bond, and be accepted as hereinafter provided, the comptroller shall require the applicant to maintain such deposit at a value equal to the amount fixed as the penalty of the bond in lieu of which such money and securities shall be so deposited. Upon the receipt of such application the comptroller shall cause to be posted upon a bulletin to be maintained by him in his office in a place accessible to the general public, at noon of the succeeding Friday the name of the applicant and whether individual or partnership, and the proposed business address designated in the application. After notice of the application shall have been so posted for a period of two weeks, he may in his discretion approve or disapprove the application. In the event of his approval he shall accept the money, securities and bond, if there be one, and hold them for the purposes herein set forth, and shall issue a license authorizing the applicant to carry on the aforesaid business at the place designated in the application and to be specified in the license certificate. For such license the licensee shall pay a fee of fifty dollars. Such license shall not be transferred or assigned. It shall not authorize the transaction of business at any place other than that described in the license certificate, except with the written approval of the comptroller. Immediately upon the receipt of the license certificate issued by the comptroller pursuant to this article the licensee named therein shall cause such license certificate to be posted and at all times conspicuously displayed in the place of business for which it is issued, so that all persons visiting such place may readily see the same. It shall be unlawful for any person or partnership holding such license certificate to post such certificate or to permit such certificate to be posted upon premises other than those designated therein or to which it has been transferred pursuant to the provisions of this article, or knowingly to deface or destroy any such license certificate. If it shall be established to the satisfaction of the comptroller in accordance with the rules and regulations by him prescribed, that an unexpired license certificate issued in accordance with the provisions of this article has been lost or destroyed without fault on the part of the holder, the comptroller shall issue a duplicate license therefor. The money and securities deposited with the comptroller as herein provided and the money which in case of default shall be paid on the aforesaid bond by any applicant or the surety thereof, shall constitute a trust fund for the benefit of the depositors of the licensee and of such persons as shall deliver money to such licensee for transmission to another, and such beneficiaries shall be entitled to an absolute preference as to such money or securities, over all general creditors of the licensee. Such money and securities shall in the event of the insolvency or bankruptcy of the licensee be delivered by the comptroller on the order or judgment of a court of competent jurisdiction to the assignee, receiver or trustee of the licensee designated in such order or judgment. The comptroller shall keep a book or books in which the licenses granted and the bonds filed shall be entered in alphabetical order, together with a statement of the date of the issuance of the license, the name or names of the principals, the place where the business licensed is to be transacted and the name of the surety company upon the bond filed, and the amount of all moneys and a description of all securities deposited, which record shall be open to public inspection. The comptroller shall cause to be printed annually on the first day of January and distributed upon application, a list of all licenses granted and remaining unrevoked. The comptroller shall from time to time pay over to each such licensee all moneys received by him as interest upon any moneys or securities deposited in accordance with the provisions of this article.

(Added by L. 1910, ch. 348. In effect Sept. 1, 1910.)

Constitutionality; waiver of a constitutional privilege by an individual. — The regulations of the business of receiving deposits is plainly within the power possessed by the state to regulate the conduct of various pursuits when necessary for the protection of the public; and the action of the Legislature in subjecting to regulation the particular class of people designated by this statute is clearly constitutional. The conditions made known by the commission of immigration recently appointed by the Governor to inquire into the condition and welfare of aliens in this state as to the widespread frauds upon and losses by ignorant depositors of the class sought to be protected and the knowledge of the Legislature of these conditions justify the selection for regulations of the persons selected. An individual may waive even a constitutional provision for his benefit, when no question of public policy or public morals is involved; and when a bond is given in accordance with this section the person giving such bond thereby waives the right to question the constitutionality of this statute, and his surety is estopped from raising that question in an action, thereafter brought against it, by those who made deposits on the faith of the undertaking. Nor is the statute unconstitutional as infringing on the exclusive right of Congress to regulate foreign and interstate commerce. It is doubtless true that this statute may incidentally and indirectly affect the business of transmitting moneys abroad. But it is well settled that the law although in a limited degree affecting interstate commerce is not for that reason a needless intrusion upon Federal jurisdiction or strictly a regulation of interstate commerce, but is to be considered as an ordinary police regulation and therefore not invalid. Musco v. United Surety Co., 196 N. Y. 459 (1909), affg. 132 App. Div. 300, 117 N. Y. Supp. 21; Guffanti v. National Surety Co., 196 N. Y. 452 (1909), affg. 133 App. Div. 610, 118 N. Y. Supp. 207; Benvegna v. United Surety Co., 196 N. Y. 453, (1909), affg. 132 App. Div. 925, 117 N. Y. Supp. 26.

SEC. 26. *Books to be kept and records to be made; revocation of licenses.*— Each licensee shall keep books of account showing full and complete records of all business transacted and a full statement of all assets and iabilities, and shall four times in each year as of such lays as the comptroller shall designate by a notice to be posted on the bulletin in his office and by written notice delivered at the place of business of such licensee or deposited in the post-office in a postpaid wrapper directed to him at such place of business, filed in the comptroller's office within ten days after the date of such notice, a written statement under oath in such form as shall be prescribed by the comptroller, showing the amount of the assets and liabilities of the licensee, which report shall be accessible to the public at all reasonable times. The license issued shall be revocable at all times by the comptroller for cause shown, and in the event of such revocation or of a surrender of such license, no refund shall be made in respect of any license fee paid under the provisions of this article. Every license certificate shall be surrendered to the comptroller within twenty-four hours after notice in writing to the holder that such license has been revoked. In case of the revocation of such license the money and securities and the bond, if there be one, received from the licensee, shall continue to be held by the comptroller, until otherwise directed by the order or judgment of a court of competent jurisdiction.

(Added by L. 1910, ch. 348. In effect Sept. 1, 1910.)

SEC. 27. *Penalties for conducting business without license, et cetera.*—Any person or partnership carrying on the business specified in section twenty-five of this article without having obtained from the comptroller a license therefor, or who shall carry on such business after the revocation of a license to carry on such business, or who, without such license shall, on any sign, letter-head, advertisement or publication of any kind use the word "banking" or "banker" or any equivalent term, in any language, in connection with any business whatsoever, or who shall fail to display the license certificate as provided in section twenty-five hereof, or who shall fail to keep books of account or to make the reports as herein provided, or who shall advertise or publish in any manner whatsoever, either orally or in writing, any statement intended to convey or actually conveying the idea or impression that such licensee is in any way under the supervision of this state or of any officer thereof, or that this state or any officer thereof has passed in any way whatsoever upon the responsibility, solvency or qualifications of such licensee to engage in such business, or that this state or any officer thereof has examined any accounts of said licensee or has in any way certified that such licensee is in any way a fit person to carry on such business, shall be guilty of a misdemeanor.

(Added by L. 1910, ch. 348, in effect Sept. 1, 1910.)

SEC. 28. *Perjury.*—Any person who in any application for a license presented to the comptroller, or in any report made under this article, shall swear falsely as to the amount of the assets or liabilities of the applicant, or as to the amount of the assets or liabilities of a licensee, or in any other particular, or in any affidavit made under section twenty-nine-d of this article shall swear falsely as to any fact therein stated, is guilty of perjury.

(Added by L. 1910, ch. 348, in effect Sept. 1, 1910.)

SEC. 29. *Penalty for failure to make reports.*—Any person or partnership who shall fail to make any report required by this article within the time specified for the same, shall forfeit to the people of the state of New York the sum of one hundred dollars for every day that such report shall be delayed or withheld. The money forfeited under this section shall be recovered in an action brought in the name of the people of the state, and with all moneys received as fees for the issuance of the licenses provided for herein shall be paid into the state treasury to the credit of the general fund.

(Added by L. 1910, ch. 348, in effect Sept. 1, 1910.)

(L. 1909, chap. 25. Consol. Laws 1909, chap. 20.)

SEC. 379. *Interest permitted on advances on collateral security.*—In any case hereafter in which advances of money, repayable on demand, to an amount not less than five thousand dollars, are made upon warehouse receipts, bills of lading, certificates of stock, certificates of deposit, bills of exchange, bonds or other negotiable instruments pledged as collateral security for such repayment, it shall be lawful to receive or to contract to receive and collect, as compensation for making such advances, any sum to be agreed upon in writing, by the parties to such transaction.

Source.—L. 1882, ch. 237, sec. 1.

Reference.—See Banking L., sec. 75.

Written contract is not necessary. In re Wilde's Sons, 138 Fed. Rept. 562 (1904).

Effect.—Hawley v. Kountze, 6 App. Div. 217, 39 N. Y. Supp. 897 (1896).

(L. 1909, chap. 25. Consol. Laws 1909, chap. 22.)

SEC. 380. *Brokerage on loans.*—No person shall, directly or indirectly, take or receive more than fifty cents for a brokerage, soliciting, driving or procuring the loan or forbearance of one hundred dollars, and in that proportion for a greater or less sum, except loans on real estate security; nor more than thirty-eight cents for making or renewing any bond, bill, note or other security given for such loan or forbearance, or for any counter bond, bill, note or other security concerning the same.

Source.—R. S. pt. 1, ch. 20, tit. 19, sec. 1, as amended by L. 1895, ch. 467.

Effect of statute is not to render contract wholly void. Buchanan v. Tilden, 18 App. Div. 123; 45 N. Y. Supp. 417 (1897).

Length of time loan is to run does not affect commission. Corp. v. Brown, 2 Sandf. 293 (1848); Broad v. Hoffman, 6 Barb. 177 (1848); Cook v. Phillips, 56 N. Y. 310 (1874).

Computation is upon the value of the currency called for by contract. Brown v. Post, 6 Robt. 111 (1868).

Promise to pay illegal compensation does not affect broker's right to recover legal compensation. Vanderpoel v. Kearns, 2 E. D. Smith, 170 (1853)

SEC. 381. *Recovery of excess.*—Every person who shall pay, deliver or deposit any money, property or thing in action, over and above the rate aforesaid, and his personal representatives may, within one year after such payment, delivery or deposit, sue for and recover the same of the person so taking or receiving such money, property or thing in action, or of his personal representatives.

In case such suit shall not be brought within the time above prescribed in good faith, or in case it shall be discontinued, or wilfully delayed, then the overseers of the poor of the city or town where the offense was committed, may within one year after such neglect, discontinuance or delay, sue for and recover the money, property or thing in action, so received, delivered or deposited, from the person receiving the same, or his personal representatives, for the use of the poor of the county.

Source.—R. S. pt. 1, ch. 20, title 19, secs. 2, 3.

Action for recovery may be commenced before contract is fully performed. Woodward v. Stearns, 10 Abb. Pr. N. S. 395 (1871).

SEC. 382. *Restitution a bar to further penalties.*—Upon the repayment and return of the money, property or other thing so illegally received, with the payment of the costs of such suit, the person making such return shall be acquitted and discharged from any other punishment, forfeiture or penalty which he may have incurred by reason of having so illegally received such money, property or other thing so returned.

Source.—R. S. pt. 1, ch. 20, tit. 19, sec. 5.

Tax Law

(L. 1909, chap. 62. Consol. Laws 1909, chap. 60.)

SEC. 270. *Amount of tax.*—There is hereby imposed and shall immediately accrue and be collected a tax, as herein provided, on all sales, or agreements to sell, or memoranda of sales of stock, and upon any and all deliveries of transfers of shares, or certificates of stock, in any domestic or foreign association, company or corporation, made after the first day of June, nineteen hundred and five, whether made upon or shown by the books of the association, company or corporation, or by any assignment in blank, or by any delivery, or by any paper or agreement or memorandum or other evidence of sale or transfer, whether intermediate or final, and whether investing the holder with the beneficial interest in or legal title to said stock, or merely with the possession or use thereof for any purpose, or to secure the future payment of money, or the future transfer of any stock, on each hundred dollars of face value or fraction thereof, two cents. It shall be the duty of the person or persons making or effectuating the sale or transfer to procure and affix the stamps and pay the tax provided by this article. It is not intended by this act to impose a tax upon an agreement evidencing the deposit of stock certificates as collateral security for money loaned thereon which stock certificates are not actually sold, nor upon such stock certificates so deposited, nor upon mere loans of stock for the return thereof. The payment of such tax shall be denoted by an adhesive stamp or stamps affixed as follows: In the case of a sale or transfer, where the evidence of the transaction is shown only by the books of the association, company or corporation, the stamp shall be placed upon such books, and it shall be the duty of the person making or effectuating such sale or transfer to procure and furnish to the association, company or corporation the requisite stamps, and of such association, company or corporation to affix and cancel the same. Where the transaction is effected by the delivery or transfer of a certificate, the stamp shall be placed upon the surrendered certificate; and in cases of an agreement to sell, or where the sale is effected by delivery of the certificate assigned in blank, there shall be made and delivered by the seller to the buyer, a bill or memorandum of such sale to which the stamp provided for by this article shall be affixed. Every such bill or memorandum of sale or agreement to sell shall show the date of the transaction which it evidences, the name of the seller, the stock to which it relates, and the number of shares thereof; and no further tax is hereby imposed upon the delivery of the certificate of stock, or upon the actual issue of a new certificate when the original certificate of stock is accompanied by the duly stamped memorandum of sale as herein provided. (Amended by L. 1910, ch. 38; L. 1911, ch. 352, and L. 1912, ch. 292, in effect May 1, 1912.)

Application. — The statute relates to sales or transfers of shares or certificates of stock in "associations and companies" as well as in corporations. Rept. of Atty. Genl. (1911), Vol. 2, p. 692.

No tax is imposed on a deposit of stock as collateral

security to a loan when the title to the stock is not actually transferred on the books of the corporation. The rule is otherwise, however, if by reason of a default in the payment of the loan or otherwise the transfer ripens into a sale. Rept. of Atty. Genl. (1911), Vol. 2, p. 577.

Effect of amendment of 1911.— Prior to the adoption of this amendment it was frequently contended that the statute related only to sales or transfers of stock which operated to invest the transferee with the beneficial interest in or ownership of the stock, and the amendment in question providing in express terms for a tax, not only upon sales or transfers of stock but upon deliveries or transfers of shares or certificates of stock, "whether investing the holder with the beneficial interest in or legal title to stock or merely with the possession or use thereof for any purpose," was adopted to settle this dispute. Rept. of Atty. Genl. (1911), Vol. 2, p. 697.

Since the amendment of 1911 transfers which operate to effect a change in the legal title to stock are taxable though the intermediate holder of the stock be acting merely as a trustee for the transferee. Rept. of Atty. Genl. (1911), Vol. 2, p. 695. Transfers of stock to voting trustees or nominees are taxable. Rept. of Atty. Genl. (1911), Vol. 2, p. 616.

Taxable transfers. — Where stock is issued pursuant to an agreement whereby the subscriber is on certain conditions to return a portion thereof to the treasury of the company, and a return is made accordingly, the latter transfer is taxable. Rept. of Atty. Genl. (1911), Vol. 2, p. 554.

Surrenders of certificates of stock, held by the Standard Oil Company, to its various subsidiary corporations and the issuance of new certificates of those companies to the stockholder of the Standard Oil Company are taxable transfers. Rept. of Atty. Genl., Mch. 7, 1912.

Where a corporation, as a consideration for the sale to it of the assets of a second corporation, issues and delivers certificate of its capital stock to and in the name of the selling corporation, the subsequent distribution of said stock by the directors of the latter among its stockholders according to their respective holding in said corporation constitutes taxable transfers. Rept. of Atty. Genl. (1911), Vol. 2, p. 697.

Where foreign insurance company has, in compliance with the provisions of section 27 of the Insurance Law, by a deed of trust transferred to certain individual trustees corporate stock, the subsequent transfer of said stock to a corporation substituted as trustee in place of such individual trustee is taxable. Rept. of Atty. Genl. (1911), Vol. 2, p. 575.

Transfers of stock to or from "nominee" are taxable under the law as amended by Chapter 352 of the Laws of 1911. Deliveries of certificates of stock, made against receipt, but without payment, by order and for account of a foreign client are taxable. Rept. of Atty. Genl. (1911), Vol. 2, p. 586.

Transfers of voting trust certificates constitute transfers of stock within the meaning of the Stock Transfer Tax Law and accordingly are taxable. Rept. of Atty. Genl. (1911), Vol. 2, p. 616.

A compromise of claims for stock transfer taxes cannot be made by the Comptroller. Rept. of Atty. Genl. (1911), Vol. 2, p. 583.

SEC. 271. *Stamps, how prepared and sold.* — Adhesive stamps for the purpose of paying the state tax provided for by this article shall be prepared by the State Comptroller, in such form and of such denominations and in such quantities as he may from time to time prescribe, and shall be sold by him to the person or persons desiring to purchase the same; he shall make provision for the sale of such stamps in such places and at such times as in his judgment he may deem necessary.

Source. — Former Tax L. (L. 1896, ch. 908), sec. 316, as added by L. 1895, ch. 341.

Forging state stamps, a misdemeanor. Penal Law, sec. 892.

SEC. 271-a. *Sale of Stamps.*—The proprietary interest which one has in stamps purchased under the provisions of the Stock Transfer Law is of a limited and peculiar character, and the Legislature may limit the right to sell such stamps to those who are duly licensed without violating the provisions of either the State or Federal Constitution. People ex rel. Isaacs v. Moran (1911), 74 Misc. 491.

Selling stamps without consent of Comptroller; defense. — It is no defense to one charged with selling stamps, issued pursuant to this section, as amended in 1911, without the consent of the State Comptroller, that when said amendment took effect he had in possession about $1,000 worth of stamps which he had purchased under the original statute which did not require that the seller of stamps should first obtain the written consent of the State Comptroller. People ex rel. Isaacs v. Moran (1911), 74 Misc. 491.

SEC. 272. *Penalty for failure to pay tax.* — Any person or persons liable to pay the tax by this article imposed, and any one who acts in the matter as agent or broker for such person or persons, who shall make any sale, transfer or delivery of shares or certificates of stock, without paying the tax by this article imposed, and any person who shall in pursuance of any sale, transfer or agreement, deliver any stock or evidence of the sale or transfer of or agreement to sell any stock, or bill or memorandum thereof, or who shall transfer or cause the same to be transferred upon the books or records of the association, company or corporation, and any association, company or corporation whose stock is sold or transferred, which shall transfer or cause the same to be transferred upon its books, without having the stamps provided for in this article affixed thereto, shall be deemed guilty of a misdemeanor, and upon conviction thereof shall pay a fine of not less than five hundred nor more than one thousand dollars, or be imprisoned for not more than six months or by both such fine and imprisonment, in the discretion of the court.

(Amended by L. 1911, ch. 352, and L. 1912, ch. 292, in effect May 1, 1912.)

SEC. 273. *Canceling stamps; penalty for failure.* — In every case where an adhesive stamp shall be used to denote the payment of the tax provided by this article, the person using or affixing the same shall write or stamp thereupon the initials of his name and the date upon which the same shall be attached or used, and shall cut or perforate the stamp in a substantial manner, so that such stamps cannot be again used; and if any person makes use of an adhesive stamp to denote the payment of the tax imposed by this article, without so effectually canceling the same, such person shall be deemed guilty of a misdemeanor, and upon conviction thereof shall pay a fine of not less than two hundred nor more than five hundred dollars or be imprisoned for not less than six months, or both, in the discretion of the court.

(Amended by L. 1911, ch. 352, in effect June 15th, 1911.)

SEC. 274. *Contracts for dies; expenses, how paid.* — The State Comptroller is hereby directed to make, enter into and execute for and in behalf of the state such contract or contracts for dies, plates and printing necessary for the manufacture of the stamps provided for by this article, and provide such stationery and clerk hire together with such books and blanks as in his discretion may be necessary for putting into operation the provisions of this article; he shall be the custodian of all stamps, dies, plates or other material or thing furnished by him and used in the manufacture of such state tax stamps, and all expenses incurred by him and under his direction in carrying out the provisions of this article shall be paid to him by the State Treasurer from any moneys appropriated for such purpose.

Source. — Former Tax L. (L. 1896, ch. 908), sec. 319, as added by L. 1905, ch. 24.

SEC. 275. *Illegal use of stamps; penalty.* — Any person who shall wilfully remove or alter or knowingly permit to be removed or altered the canceling or defacing marks of any stamp provided for by this article with intent to use such stamp, or who shall knowingly or wilfully buy, prepare for use, use, have in his possession or suffer to be used any washed, restored or counterfeit stamp, and any person who shall intentionally remove or cause to be removed or knowingly permit to be removed any stamp, affixed pursuant to the requirements of this article, shall be guilty of a misdemeanor and on conviction thereof shall be liable to a fine of not less than five hundred nor more than one thousand dollars, or be imprisoned for not more than one year, or by both such fine and imprisonment, at the discretion of the court. (Amended by L. 1911, ch. 12, and L. 1912, ch. 292, in effect May 1, 1912.)

SEC. 276. *Power of State Comptroller.* — Every person, firm, company, association or corporation engaged in whole or in part in the making or negotiating of sales, agreements to sell, deliveries or transfer of shares or certificates of stock, or conducting or transacting a brokerage business, shall keep or cause to be kept at some accessible place within the state of New York, a just and true book of account, in such form as may be prescribed by the comptroller, wherein shall be plainly and legibly recorded in separate columns, the date of making every sale, agreement to sell, delivery or transfer of shares or certificates of stock, the name of the stock, and the number of shares thereof, the face value of the stock, the name of the seller or transferor, the name of the purchaser or transferee and the number and face value of the adhesive stamp affixed as provided for by section two hundred and seventy of this chapter.

Every association, company or corporation shall keep or cause to be kept at some accessible place within the state of New York, a stock certificate book and a just and true book of account, transfer ledger or register, in such form as may be prescribed by the comptroller, wherein shall be plainly and legibly recorded in separate columns the date of making every transfer of stock, the name of the stock and the number of shares thereof, the serial number of each surrendered certificate, the name of the party surrendering such certificate, the serial number of the certificate issued in exchange therefor, the number of shares covered by said certificate, the name of the party to whom said certificate was issued and the number and face value of the adhesive stamps affixed, as provided by section two hundred and seventy of this chapter. It shall also retain and keep all surrendered or canceled shares or certificates of its stock and all memoranda relating to the sale or transfer of any thereof. All such books of account, transfer ledgers, registers and stock certificate books, shall be retained and kept as aforesaid for a period of at least two years subsequent to the date of the last entry made therein as herein required; and all such surrendered or canceled shares or certificates of stock and memoranda relating to the sale or transfer of stock, shall be retained and kept for a period of at least two years from the date of the delivery thereof. For the purpose of ascertaining whether the tax imposed by this article has been paid, all such books of account, transfer ledgers, registers, stock certificate books, surrendered or canceled shares or certificates of stock and memoranda relating to the sale or transfer thereof, shall at all times between the hours of ten o'clock in the forenoon and three o' clock in the afternoon, except Saturdays, Sundays and legal holidays, be open to examination by the comptroller or his duly authorized representative.

The comptroller may enforce his right to examine such books of account and bills or memoranda of sale or transfer; and such transfer ledger, register and stock certificate books and surrendered or canceled shares or certificates of stock by mandamus. If the comptroller ascertains that the tax provided for in this article has not been paid, he shall bring an action in his name as such comptroller, in any court of competent jurisdiction for the recovery of such tax and for any penalty incurred by any person under the provisions of this article.

Every person, firm, company, association or corporation who shall fail to keep such book of account or bills or memoranda of sale or transfer, or transfer ledger, register or stock certificate book or surrendered or canceled shares or certificates of stock as herein required, or who alters, cancels, obliterates or destroys any part of said records, or makes any false entry therein, or who shall refuse to permit the comptroller or any of his duly authorized representatives freely to examine any of said books, records or papers at any of the times herein provided, or who shall in any other respect violate any of the provisions of this section shall be deemed guilty of a misdemeanor and on conviction thereof shall for each and every such offense pay a fine of not less than five hundred dollars nor more than five thousand dollars, or be imprisoned not less than three months nor more than two years, or both, in the discretion of the court.

(Amended by L. 1910, ch. 453; L. 1911, ch. 352, and L. 1912, ch. 292, in effect May 1, 1912.)

Books and records. — The fact that stock books of a New York Corporation are kept at its place of business in the state of Rhode Island does not relieve the corporation from the duty imposed upon it by this section, and such corporation must keep the books and records required by said section. Rept. of Atty. Genl. Vol. 2. p. 674.

SEC. 277. *Civil penalties; how recovered.* — Any person, firm, company, association or corporation who shall violate any of the provisions of section two hundred and seventy or section two hundred and seventy-two of this chapter shall in addition to the penalties herein provided forfeit to the people of the state a civil penalty of ten dollars for each and every share of stock so sold or transferred or transferred or entered upon the books of the corporation, as the case may be, without the payment of the tax by this article imposed thereon. Any person who shall violate any of the other provisions of this article shall in addition to the penalties hereinbefore provided forfeit to the people of the state a civil penalty of five hundred dollars for each and every such violation.

The State Comptroller shall bring an action in his name as such comptroller in any court of competent jurisdiction for the recovery of any civil penalty; and all moneys collected by him shall be paid into the state treasury. In an action against a corporation or its transfer agent to recover a penalty because of its transfer of stock upon the books or records of the corporation without requiring the payment of the tax by this article imposed, the failure of the corporation or its transfer agent, on the demand of the comptroller or his duly authorized representative to produce the surrendered certificate or memoranda of sale with the required stamps attached, shall constitute prima facie proof of the nonpayment of the tax imposed by section two hundred and seventy of this chapter.

(Amended by L. 1912, ch. 292, in effect May 1, 1912.)

SEC. 278. *Effect of failure to pay tax.*—The effect of this section is not to impose upon the vendor who fails to pay the tax a forfeiture of his property, but simply denies to him the right to enforce the contract of sale, and hence the provision is not unconstitutional. Sheridan v. Tucker (1911), 145 App. Div. 145, 129 N. Y. Supp. 18.

The donee of corporate stock claiming title by gift causa mortis or inter vivos can prove such gift only in a case where the donor affixed the proper stamps to the certificates at the time of the gift and delivery thereof. Matter of Raleigh (1911), 75 Misc. 55.

Failure to pay tax must be pleaded as defense. — The statute does not provide that a person must pay this tax before he can make or bring an action to enforce a contract for the transfer of stock. Such payment is not made a condition precedent to the right to bring an action, and plaintiff is not compelled to alleged compliance, but the failure to pay the tax is matter to be pleaded as a defense. Bean v. Flint (1912), 204 N. Y. 153.

SEC. 280. *Refund of tax erroneously paid. Application.* — The face value of stock transfer stamps should not be refunded to the Standard Oil Company, although such company has surrendered certificates of stock held by it to its various subsidiary corporations and has issued new certificates to those companies. Rept. of Atty. Genl. Mch. 7, 1912.

Insurance Law

(L. 1909, chap. 33. Consol. Laws 1909, chap. 28.)

Life or Casualty Insurance Corporations upon the Co-operation or Assessment Plan.

SEC. 214. Exemption of certain societies*** from the provisions of this article.

The voluntary unincorporated associations known as the New York Stock Exchange are exempted from the provisions of this article.

Banking Law

(L. 1909, ch. 10. Consol. Laws 1909, ch. 2.)

SEC. 23. *Books, papers and affairs to be examined.*—It shall be the duty of the board of directors of every bank and trust company in the months of April and October in each year to examine or cause a committee of at least three of its members to examine fully into the books, papers, and affairs of the bank or trust company of which they are directors, into the loans and discounts thereof and particularly into the loans or discounts made directly or indirectly to officers or directors thereof, or for the benefit of such officers or directors, or for the benefit of other corporations of which such officers and directors are also officers or directors, or in which they have a beneficial interest as shareholders, auditors, or otherwise, with the special view of ascertaining the value and security thereof, and of the collateral security, if any, given in connection therewith, and into such other matters as the superintendent of banks may require. Such directors shall have power to employ such assistance in making such examination as they may deem necessary. On or before the fifteenth day of the month succeeding such examination, a report in writing thereof, sworn to by the directors making the same, shall be made to the board of directors of such bank or trust company, be placed on file in said bank or trust company, and a duplicate thereof filed in the banking department. Such report shall particularly contain a statement of the assets and liabilities of the bank or trust company, examined, as shown by the books of the bank or trust company, together with such deductions from the assets and the addition of such liabilities direct, indirect, contingent or otherwise, as such directors or committee, after such examination, may find necessary in order to determine the true condition of the bank or trust company. It shall also contain a statement showing in detail every liability to such bank or trust company, direct, indirect, contingent or otherwise, of every officer or director thereof and of every corporation of which any such officer or director is also an officer or director, or in which corporation any such officer or director is beneficially interested as a shareholder, creditor, or otherwise.

It shall also contain a statement, in detail, of loans, if any, which in their opinion are worthless or doubtful, together with their reasons for so regarding them; also a statement of loans made on collateral security which in their opinion are insufficiently secured, giving in each case the amount of the loan, the name and market value of the collateral, if it has any market value, and, if not, a statement of that fact, and its actual value as nearly as possible. Such report shall also contain a statement of overdrafts, of the names and amounts of such as they consider worthless or doubtful, and a full statement of such other matters as affect the solvency and soundness of the institution. If the directors of any bank or trust company shall fail to make, or cause to be made and filed, such report of examination in the matter, and within the time specified, such bank or trust company shall forfeit to the people of the state one hundred dollars for every day such report shall be delayed, which penalty may be recovered through an action brought by the attorney-general against such bank or trust company, in the name of the people of the state of New York. The moneys forfeited by this section, when recovered, shall be paid into the state treasury, to be used to defray the expenses of the banking department.

(Amended by Laws 1913, ch. 451. In effect May 8, 1913.)

TABLE OF CASES CITED

TABLE OF CASES CITED

(References are to pages)

A	Page
Albers v. Merchants' Exchange, 140 Mo. App., 446	3
Albers Commission Co. v. Spencer, 205 Mo., 105	2
Allen v. McConihe, 124 N. Y., 342	77
American Ins. Co. v. Fisk, 1 Paige, 90	59
Amsden v. Jacobs, 75 Hun, 311	101
Armstrong v. Bickel, 217 Pa., 173	104
Armstrong v. Danahy, 75 Hun, 405	58
Arnott v. Pittson, etc., Coal Co., 68 N. Y., 558	111
Asgood v. Bander, 75 Iowa, 550	75
Atkinson v. Rochester Printing Co., 114 N. Y., 175	195
Austin v. Hayden, Mich., 137 N. W., 317	46, 51, 52, 94, 96, 104
Ayer v. Mead, 13 Ill. App. 625	83
B	
Bach v. Tuch, 126 N. Y., 53	58
Baker v. Drake, 66 N. Y., 518	84, 87, 94
Baldwin v. Flagg, 36 N. J. Eq., 57	74
Barber v. Ellingwood, 144 App. Div., 512	53, 103, 104, 107
Barber v. Ellingwood No. 2, 137 App. Div., 704	111
Bartlett v. Bartlett & Son Co., 116 Wis., 450	7, 24
Bassett v. Irons, 8 Mo. App. 127	2
Bassett v. Perkins, 65 Misc., 103	113
Baster v. Board of Trade, 83 Ill., 146	7, 24
Bate v. McDowell, 40 N. Y. Super. Ct., 106	76, 78
Baum v. N. Y. Cotton Exch. 4 N. Y., Supp., 207	20, 23
Bean v. Flint, 204 N. Y., 153	70, 248
Benvegna v. United Surety Co., 196 N. Y., 453	230
Bernheim v. Keppler, 34 Misc., 321	6, 15, 16, 19
Bigelow v. Benedict, 70 N. Y., 204	22, 54, 75

PAGE

Birnbaum v. May, 58 App. Div., 76 79
Blaine v. Thomas, 103 App. Div., 600 90
Blodgett v. Morril, 20 Vt., 509 58
Board of Trade v. Kinsey, 130 Fed. 507; 198 U. S., 236 . 29
Board of Trade v. Nelson, 162 Ill., 431 . . . . . 2, 3, 25
Board of Trade v. Riordan, 94 Ill., App., 298 . . . 20, 25
Board of Trade v. Weare, 105 Ill. App., 289 . . . . 3, 24
Bostedo v. Board of Trade, 130 Ill. App., 560 . . . 3, 24, 27
Boyce v. Grundy, 3 Pet., 210 59
Boyle v. Henning, 121 Fed. 376 . . . . . 76, 86, 88, 104
Broad v. Hoffman, 6 Barb., 177 . . . . 56, 234
Brown, In re, 175 Fed., 769 110
Brown, In re, 185 Fed., 766 110
Brown v. Hall, 5 Lans., 177 54
Brown v. Post, 6 Robt. 111 . . . . 56, 234
Bruff v. Mali, 36 N. Y., 200 59
Buchanan v. Tilden, 18 App. Div., 123 . . . . 55, 56, 234
Buch v. Houghtaling, 110 App. Div., 52 81
Burhorn v. Lockwood, 71 App. Div., 301 affd., 177 N. Y., 539 . 81
Burnham v. Lawson, 118 App. Div., 389 . . . . . 81, 107
Byrne v. Weinfield, 113 App. Div., 451 99

C

Caldwell v. People, 67 Ill. App., 367 50
Camman v. Huntington, 89 App. Div., 99 111
Campbell v. Wright, 8 N. Y. St. Rep., 471 . . . . 53, 103
Carlisle v. Norris, 142 N. Y. Supp., 393 . . . . 75, 94, 113
Cassard v. Hinman, 1 Bosw. 207 53
Cazeaux v. Mali, 25 Barb., 578 59
Christie Grain & Stock Co. v. Board of Trade, 125 Fed., 161 . 29
Clappe v. Taylor, 125 App. Div., 605 94
Cochran v. Adams, 180 Pa. St., 289 15
Cochran v. Ellis, 107 Ill., 413 77
Cohen v. Budd, 52 Misc., 217 . . . . 3, 15
Colket v. Ellis, 10 Phila., 375 82
Commonwealth Bank v. Schuylkill Bank, 1 Pars. Eq. Cas. Pa., 180 59
Conklin v. Raymond, 127 App. Div., 663 78
Content v. Banner, 184 N. Y., 121 . . . . 89, 94
Cook v. Phillips, 56 N. Y., 310 . . . . 56, 234

PAGE
Corp. v. Brown, 2 Sand., 293 . . . . 55, 234
Cragie v. Hadley, 99 N. Y., 131 195
Crummey v. Mills, 40 Hun., 370 54
Currie In re, 185 Fed., 263 . . . . 16, 17
Curtis v. Leavitt, 15 N. Y., 9 46
Custer v. Titusville Gas Etc., Co. 63 Pa. St., 381 61

D

Davis v. Gwynne, 57 N. Y., 676 80
Day v. Holmes, 103 Mass., 306 . . . . 47, 83
Denton v. Jackson, 106 Ill., 438 85
Denton v. MacNeill L. R. 2 Eq., 352 62
Des Jardin v. Hotchkin, 141 App. Div., 845. . . . . 82, 85
Douglas v. Carpenter, 17 App. Div., 329 . . . . 46, 96, 97
Downie v. White, 12 Wis., 176 58
Dwight v. Badgley, 75 Hun. 174 54

E

Ennis, In re, 187 Fed., 720 110
Ennis v. Ross, 37 Misc., 160 113
Essen v. Linderman, 71 Pa. St., 76 86
Estes v. Perkins, 137 App. Div., 367 89
Evans v. Wrenn, 93 App. Div., 346 . . . . 79, 103
Evans v. Chamber of Commerce, 86 Minn., 448 7

F

Fairbairn v. Rausch, 104 App. Div., 259 102
Fairchild v. Flowerfelt, 79 Misc., 42 . . . . 87, 88
First National Bank of Waterloo v. Bacon, 113 App. Div., 612 98
Fisk & Robinson, In re, 185 Fed., 974 3
Fletcher v. Dold Packing Co., 169 N. Y. 571 53
Foster v. Murphy & Co., 135 Fed., 47 85
Frost v. Stokes, 55 N. Y., Super. Ct., 76 56
Fuller v. Mun. Tel. & St. Co., 117 App. Div., 352 . . . 26, 54
Furniture Co. In re, 170 Fed., 485 61

G

Galigher v. Jones, 129 U. S., 193 77
Gen. Prov. Assur. Co. In re, L. R., 9 Eq., 74 58

PAGE

Gheen v. Johnson, 90 Pa. St., 38 . . . . 76, 103
Gillet v. Whiting, 120 N. Y., 402 . . . . 94, 105
Glynn v. Conklin, 127 App. Div., 473 69
Goddard v. Merchants' Exchange, 9 Mo. App., 290 . . . 3
Gould v. Trask, 10 N. Y. Supp., 619 101
Greely v. Doran-Wright Co., 148 Mass., 116 83
Green v. Board of Trade, 174 Ill., 585 3
Gruman v. Smith, 81 N. Y., 25 . . . . 86, 94
Guffanti v. National Surety Co., 196 N. Y., 452 230

H

Haebler v. N. Y. Prod. Exch., 149 N. Y., 414 8
Haight v. Dickerman, 18 N. Y. Supp., 559 . . . . . 2, 19
Haight v. Haight & Freese Co., 46 Misc., 501; 102 App. Div., 475 . . . . 26, 50
Hall v. Baker, 66 App. Div., 131 . . . . 195, 199
Hallett's Estate, In re, L. R. 138 Ch. D., 696 109
Hardy v. Jaudon, 1 Rob., 261 45
Harris v. Pryor, 18 N. Y. Supp., 128 . . . . . 88, 93, 100
Harris v. Turnbridge, 83 N. Y., 92 76
Hawley v. Kountze, 6 App. Div., 217 . . . . . . 56, 57, 234
Hayes In re. 75 N. Y. Supp., 312 . . . . 12, 15
Heath v. Griswold, 5 Fed., 573 46
Heath v. President of Gold Exchange, 7 Abb. Pr. N. S., 251 6
Heim v. N. Y. Stock Exch., 64 Misc., 529; Affd. 138 App. Div., 96 23, 26, 28, 52
Hellman, Matter of, 174 N. Y., 254 11
Helm v. Ennis, 109 App. Div., 42 76
Hentz v. Minor, 18 N. Y. Supp., 880 54
Hess v. Rau, 95 N. Y., 359 . . . . 74, 103
Hess Malting Co. v. Warren, 15 Ill. App., 507 2
Hickok v. Cowperthwait, 137 App. Div., 94 98
Hoffman v. Livingston, 46 N. Y. Super. Ct., 552 76
Holmes v. Seaman, 184 N. Y., 486 39
Hopkins v. O'Kane, 167 Pa. St., 478 74
Horton v. Morgan, 19 N. Y., 170 . . . . 82, 83
Hunt v. Marquand, 109 App. Div., 729 99
Hurd v. Taylor, 181 N. Y., 231 . . . . 54, 77, 107
Hurlbutt, Hatch & Co. In re, 135 Fed., 504 . . . . 12, 13

PAGE

Hurst v. N. Y. Produce Exch., 100 N. Y., 605 25
Hurt v. Miller, 120 App. Div., 833 . . . . . . 77, 107
Hutchinson v. Lawrence, 67 How. Pr., 38 . . . . . 23, 25
Hyde v. Woods, 94 U. S., 523 12

I

Illingworth v. De Mott, 59 N. J. Eq., 8 76

J

Jackson v. Foote, 12 Fed., 37 75
Jones v. Gallagher, 3 Utah, 54 80
Jones v. Seaman, 133 App. Div., 127 106

K

Keller v. Halsey, 202 N. Y., 588 92
Kent v. DeCoppet, 149 App. Div., 589 32
Ketcham v. Provost, 156 App. Div., 477 . . . . . . 14, 97
Kilmer v. Hutton, 131 App. Div., 625 . . . . . . 77, 105
King v. Zell, 105 Ind., 435 74
Kingsbury v. Kirwan, 43 N. Y. Super. Ct., 451 . . . 53, 57
Kisch v. Venezuela Cent. R. Co., 34 L. J. Ch., 545 . . 62
Knowlton v. Fitch, 52 N. Y., 288 74
Konta v. St. Louis Stock Exchange, 189 Mo., 26 11
Kridel v. Bloomingdale, 149 App. Div., 605 101
Kruse v. Kennett, 181 Ill., 109 54

L

La Gar v. Carey, 12 N. Y. St. Rep., 171 54
La Grange, etc., Plank Road Co. v. Mays, 29 Mo., 64 . . 58
Lambert v. Addison, 46 L. T. Rep., 20 22
Langer v. Price, 114 App. Div., 78 88
Lawrence v. Maxwell, 53 N. Y., 19 . . . . 46, 84
Lazare v. Allen, 20 App. Div., 616 . . . . . 53, 88, 103
Leech v. Harris, 2 Brewst. (Pa.), 571 . . . . . 19, 23, 24
Lehman v. Feld, 37 Fed., 852 83
Leiter v. Thomas, 110 App. Div., 879 . . . . 88, 91
LeMarchant v. Moore, 79 Hun, 352 108
Leo v. McCormack, 142 App. Div., 741 112
Levy v. Loeb, 85 N. Y., 365 . . . . 76, 84

PAGE
Levy v. Potter, 104 App. Div., 457 113
Lewis v. Wilson, 121 N. Y., 288 . . . . 22, 25
Life Assn. of England, Re, 34 Beav., 639 58
Ling v. Malcolm, 77 Conn., 517 83
Litchfield Bank v. Church, 29 Conn., 137 58
Little v. McClain, 152 App. Div., 197 . . . . . . 81, 112
Livermore v. Bushnell, 5 Hun, 285 111
Logan v. Tel. etc. Co., 157 Fed., 570 54
Lowenberg v. Greenbaum, 99 Cal., 162 12
Lurman v. Jarvie, 8 App. Div., 37 24
Lynch v. Simmonds, 67 N. Y. Supp., 420 77

M

McCabe v. Emmons, 51 N. Y. Super. Ct., 219 . 12, 13, 219
McCabe v. Lawrence, 51 N. Y. Super, 219 12
McDearmott Commission Co. v. Board of Trade, 146 Fed. 961 29
McGinnes v. Smythe, 101 N. Y., 646 93
McIlvaine v. Egerton, 2 Rob., 422 53
McIntyre v. Whitney, 130 App. Div., 557 111
McIntyre, In re, 181 Fed., 955 110
MacDonald v. Ackley, 93 Pa. St., 277 39
MacDowell v. Ackley, 93 Pa. St., 277 39
Mangles v. Grand Collier Dock Co., 10 Sim., 519; 16 Eng. Ch., 519 58
Manning v. Heidelbach, 153 App. Div., 790 . . . . 90, 106
Markham v. Jaudon, 41 N. Y., 235 . . . . . . 83, 86, 94
Marye v. Strouse, 5 Fed., 483 . . . . 47, 78, 84
Marylebone Banking Co., Matter of, 3 De G. & S., 21 58
Mayer v. Monzo, 151 App. Div., 866 . . . . . . 46, 85, 97
Michael v. Hart (1901), 2 K. B., 867; L. T. Rep. (N. S.), 548 . . 100
Miller & Co. v. Lyons, Va. 74 S. E., 194 89
Mills v. Gould, 42 N. Y. Super. Ct., 119 2
Mills, Matter of, 125 App. Div., 730, ... 100, 106, 107; 110
Minnesota Lumber Co. v. Whitebreast Co. 160 Ill., 85 54
Moffatt v. Board of Trade, Mo., 11 S. W., 894 . . . 7, 23, 37
Moore v. Rodewald, 142 App. Div., 741 . . . . . 105, 112
Morgan v. Jaudon, 40 How. Pr., 366 93
Morris v. Grant, 34 Hun., 377 . . . . 3, 6, 9
Moyse v. N. Y. Cotton Exchange, 143 App. Div., 265 . . 25
Mullen v. Quinlan & Co., 195 N. Y., 109 107

PAGE
Muller v. Bensley, 20 Ill. App., 530 75
Mulligan, In re, 116 Fed., 715 106
Musco v. United Surety Co., 196 N. Y., 459 230

N

Nashua Savings Bank v. Abbot, 181 Mass., 531 13
Nat. League of Com. Merchants v. Hornung, 148 App. Div., 355 2, 7, 19, 20
Neilson v. James, 9 Q. B. D., 546 83
Nelson v. Board of Trade, 121 Ill., 412 . . . . . . 21, 23
Newkirch v. Keppler, 56 App. Div., 225 . . . . . 20, 21
Newman v. Lee, 87 App. Div., 116 . . . . 77, 84

O

O'Dell v. Boyden, 150 Fed., 731 . . . . 12, 13, 16

P

Pacaud v. Waite, 218 Ill., 138 . . . . 2, 7
Page, In re, 107 Fed. 89 13
Page v. Edmunds, 187 U. S., 596 12
Parish v. N. Y. Produce Exch. 169 N. Y., 34 39
Paton v. Newman, 51 La. Ann., 1428 2
Peabody v. Speyers, 56 N. Y., 230 2
Pearce v. Foote, 113 Ill., 228 54
Peck v. Doran, etc., Co. 46 Hun, 454 54
Peckham v. Ketchum, 5 Bosw., 506 111
Peckham v. Ketchum, 90 Pa. St., 38 76
Peller v. Leiter, 189 N. Y., 361 50
People v. Board of Trade, 45 Ill., 112 . . . . 2, 3
People v. Board of Trade, 80 Ill., 134 . . . . 20, 23
People v. Board of Trade, 224 Ill., 370 39
People v. Duffy-McInnerney Co., 122 App. Div. 336 . . . 69
People v. East Buffalo Live Stock Assn., 88 App. Div., 619 . 24
People v. Feitner, 167 N. Y., 1 12
People v. Goslin, 67 App. Div., 16, affd. 171, N. Y., 627 . 62, 207
People v. Meadows, 199 N. Y., 1 109
People v. N. Y. Produce Exch., 149 N. Y., 401 . . . . 20, 24
People v. Reardon, 197 N. Y., 236 69
People v. St. Nicholas Bank, 77 Hun, 159; 196

PAGE
People v. Severance, 67 Hun, 182, ... 196
People v. Todd, 51 Hun, 446 55
People v. Wade, 59 N. Y. Supp., 846 55
People ex rel. Farrington v. Mensching, 187 N. Y., 8 . . . 68
People ex rel. Hatch v. Reardon, 110 App. Div., 821, 184 N. Y. 431, 204 U. S.,152 69
People ex rel. Isaacs v. Moran, 74 Misc., 491 . . . . 240, 241
Picard v. Beers, 195 Mass., 419 77
Pickering v. Demerritt, 100 Mass., 416 . . . . . 47, 84
Pickering v. Templeton, 2 Mo. App., 424 58
Pierson v. Frenkel, 103 N. Y. Supp., 49 94
Pitcher v. Board of Trade, 121 Ill., 412 . . . . . 21, 24
Pixley v. Boynton, 79 Ill., 553 75
Platt v. Jones, 96 N. Y. 24 12
Porter v. Wormser, 94 N. Y., 431 . . . . . 47, 79, 84
Post v. Thomas, 153 App. Div., 865 80
Potter v. Malcolm, 104 N. Y. Supp., 760 83
Prout v. Chisholm, 89 Hun, 108 . . . . 60, 78
Pugh v. Moore, 44 La. Ann., 209 113

Q

Quelle Paine, 39 Misc., 712 93
Quentell v. N. Y. Cotton Exch., 56 Misc., 150 25

R

Raleigh, Matter of, 75 Misc., 55 . . . . 69, 248
Ramsey v. Muller, 202 N. Y., 72 81
Reichard v. Hutton, 138 App. Div., 122 77
Reichland v. Hutton, 148 App. Div., 813 105
Renville, Matter of, 46 App. Div., 37 29
Rice v. Davis, 136 Pa. St. 430 84
Richter v. Poe, (Md.) 71 Atl., 420 . . . . 78, 84, 100, 103
Ridgeley v. Taylor & Co., 118 App. Div., 10 80
Ritchie v. Burke, 109 Fed., 16 46
Ritter v. Cushman, 35 How. Pr., 284 86
Robinson v. Pittsburgh, etc., R. Co., 32 Pa. St., 334. . . 61
Rock v. Carpenter, 110 N. Y. Supp., 261 81
Rogers v. Wiley, 14 N. Y., Supp., 622, affd. 131 N. Y., 527 86, 93, 101

PAGE

Rorke v. San Francisco Stock and Exch., Bd., 99 Cal. 196 . 17
Rosenbaum v. Stiebel, 122 N. Y. Supp., 131 . . . 88, 108
Rosenstock v. Torney, 32 Md., 169 83
Rothschild v. Allen, 90 App. Div., 233, affd. 180 N. Y., 561 45, 46, 95, 96
Ruggles v. Brock, 6 Hun, 164 61
Russel v. N. Y. Produce Exch. 27 Misc., 381 28
Rutland R. Co. v. Haven, 62 Vt., 39 59
Ryan v. Cudahy, 157 Ill., 108 . . . . 24, 25
Ryan v. Lamson, 44 Ill. App., 204 21

S

Schulteis v. Caughey, 146 App. Div., 102 112
Seymour, Johnson & Co., Matter of, 37 Misc., 264 . . .6, 16
Shannon v. Chenay, 156 Cal., 567 12
Sheridan v. Tucker, 145 App. Div., 145 . . . . . 69, 70, 243
Shiel v. Stoneham, 77 Misc., 125 94
Shotwell v. Mali, 38 Barb., 445 59
Skiff v. Stoddard, 63 Conn., 198 . . . . 46, 96
Small v. Housman, 208 N. Y., 115 . . . . . . 87, 91, 92, 93
Smith v. Craig, 151 App. Div., 648. 88
Smith v. Savin, 141 N. Y., 515 46
Smith v. Tracy, 30 N. Y., 79 111
Soby v. People, 134 Ill., 66 50
Sonneborn v. Lavarello, 2 Hun, 201 7
Sparhawk v. Yerkes, 142 U. S., 1 12
Spear v. Hart, 3 Rob., 420 83
Sprague v. Currie, 133 App. Div., 18 . . . . 76, 81, 94, 106
Springs v. James, 137 App. Div., 110 53,82
Stanton v. Small, 3 Sandf., 230 53
Stapleton v. O'Dell, 21 Misc., 94 196
Staples v. Gould, 9 N. Y., 520 . . . . 54, 213
State v. Milwaukee Chamber of Commerce, 47 Wis., 670 . 24
Stenton v. Jerome, 54 N. Y., 480 . . . . 86, 93
Sterling v. Jaudon, 48 Barb., 459 . . . . . . 53, 103, 104
Stewart v. Drake, 46 N. Y., 449 88
Stewart v. Harris, 101 App. Div., 181 81
Stone v. Lothrop, 109 Mass., 63 82
Story v. Salomon, 71 N. Y., 420 . . . . 54, 75

PAGE

Strickland v. Magoun, 119 App. Div., 113 . . . . 45, 96, 97, 99
Swift v. San Francisco St. Exch. Board, 67 Cal., 567 . . . 39

T

Talcott v. Standard Oil Co., 149 App. Div., 694 113
Taylor v. Ketcham, 35 How. Pr. 289; 5 Rob., 507 . 77, 85, 87, 106
Thompson v. Adams, 93 Pa. St., 55 . . . . . . 2, 13, 15
Thornburgh v. Newcastle, etc. R. Co., 14 Ind., 499 62
Thorne v. Prentiss, 83 Ill., 99 2
Tompkins v. Morton Trust Co., 91 App. Div., 274 94
Tracy In re, 191 Fed., 810 . . . . 45, 99
Treadwell v. Clark, 114 App. Div., 403, affd. 190 N. Y., 51 98, 99
Tuell v. Paine, 39 Misc., 712 76
Tyler v. Barrows, 6 Rob., 104 53

U

Union Nat. Bank v. Hunt, 76 Mo., 439 62
U. S. Radiator Corp. v. State of N. Y., 208 N. Y., 144 . . 69

V

Vanderpoel v. Kearns, 2 E. D. Smith, 170 . . . . . 56, 234
Van Dusen-Harrington Co. v. Jungeblut, 75 Minn., 298 . . 83

W

Washburn v. Franklin, 28 Barb., 27 213
Waugh v. Seaboard Bank, 54 N. Y. Super. Ct., 283 . . . 3
Weare Commission Co. v. People, 209 Ill., 528 50
Weidenfeld v. Keppler, 84 App. Div., 235 23
Weir v. Dwyer, 114 N. Y. Supp., 528 . . . . 77, 90
Weld v. Cable Co., 199 N. Y. 88 54
Weston v. Ives, 97 N. Y., 222 2
West v. McLaughlin, 162 Fed., 124 110
West v. Wright, 86 Hun, 436 54
Wheeler v. Newbould, 16 N. Y., 392 87
White v. Brownell, 2 Daly, 329 . . . . . 2, 3, 13, 21, 22
White v. Smith, 54 N. Y., 522 . . . . 53, 74, 103
White Mountains R. Co. v. Eastman, 34 N. H., 124 58
Whitlock v. Seaboard Nat. Bank, 29 Misc., 84 47
Wilde, In re, 133 Fed., 562 . . . . 56, 234

PAGE

Willard v. White, 56 Hun, 581 108
Willets v. Poor, 141 App. Div., 743 61
Winston v. F. A. Longshore & Co., 116 La., 21 86
Wolff v. Lockwood, 70 App. Div., 569 107
Wood v. Fisk, 141 N. Y. Supp., 342 . . . . 98, 106
Woodward v. Stearns, 10 Abb. Pr. N. S., 395 . . . . 56, 235
Wright v. Toomey, 137 App. Div., 401 56
Wronkow v. Clews, 52 N. Y. Super. Ct., 176 80

Y

Young v. Eames, 78 App. Div., 229 . . . . 20, 26

Z

Zeller v. Leiter, 114 App. Div., 148 53
Zimmerman v. Heil, 156 N .Y., 703 77

INDEX

INDEX

(References are to pages)

PAGE

Account, agreement to carry for a definite period . . . 100
" joint 113
" stated defined 112
Accounts, essential facts of 27, 182
" of the Exchange 122, 130
" , fictitious names 27, 182
" , keeping proper 78
Accusations, method of procedure 21, 140, 142
Acting for buyer and seller. 84
" " foreign corporations 205
Acts detrimental to welfare of Exchange . . 186, 190, 191
" of partner, responsibility for 171
Additional margin, waiver of customers' default 93
Addresses of members 36, 170
Adequate margin 38, 190
Admissions, Committee on 6, 127
" " " its jurisdiction . . . . 6n.
Admission to membership 10, 133
Adopted child, gratuity to 38, 145
Advances on collateral security 56, 223
" , pledging stock for 45
" , right to, on authorized sale 111
Adverse interest, creating, custom disapproved 83
Advertisements 37, 175
" false, as to securities 60, 208
" to depress market value 62
Agents, solicitation of business by 36, 172
Agreement as to margin 91
" to carry customer's account for a definite period . . 100
Altering contracts, custom disapproved 83

INDEX

PAGE

Alternative demand for margin insufficient 86
Anti-bucket shop law 49, 199
Appeals 10, 28, 132
Application of proceeds of membership 14, 135
Applications for membership 10, 133
" " " , misstatement on 20, 140
Appointees 116, 126
Arbitrage, domestic 35, 175
" foreign 35, 176
Arbitration 6, 127
" Committee 6, 127
" " , Appeals from. 6, 128
" clause, effect of . . . . 6n.
Arrangements, Committee of 5, 126
Assessments on death of members 38
" " " , failure to pay 11, 134, 144
Assistant Chairman 5, 122
"At three days," bids and offers 25, 154
Authority to sell, discretionary 80
Authorization to sell, distinguished from order 78
" " " , makes notice unnecessary 94
Award of arbitrators, effect of . . . . 7n.

"Bank," unauthorized use of the term 198
Bankers, misconduct by 196
Banking Law, examination of books and papers 249
" " , licenses, bonds and deposits 225
" " , Constitutionality of Statute 229
Banking licenses, books to be kept and records made . . . 230
" " , penalty for conducting business without license, etc. 231
" " , perjury 232
" " , penalty for failure to make reports 233
Banks, misconduct by 196
Betting 173
Bids and offers 24, 153
" " " , rules covering 176
Bids or offers, variation 155
Bills of foreign banks, unlawful discount of 198

INDEX

PAGE

Bonds, (See "Securities," "Stocks")
Books of corporations, closing of 165
" " " , " " during deliveries . . . 158
" " Exchange 122, 130
" " members 20, 21, 141
Borrowing and lending (See "Loans")
Branch houses. 170
Branch offices 36, 170, 172
Brokerage on loans 55, 234
" " " , recovery of excess 55, 234
Broker's correspondent, his agent 103
" duty as to retaining stock purchased 94
" insolvency stock goes to customer 108
" lien 111
" own name, custom as to purchase in 82
" , right to pledge margined stock en bloc 95
Brokers, transactions by, after insolvency 51, 210
Bucket shop 27, 49, 179
" " , defined 50, 202
" " , law as to 49, 199
" " , corporations, penalty for second offence . . . 202
" " , transactions with or for, forbidden . . . 27, 179
"Bull" defined 74
"Bunching" orders prohibited 34, 183
Business Conduct, Committee on 7, 129
Business hours 23, 152
" , solicitation of 33, 36, 168, 172, 181
Buyer and Seller, acting for 84
Buyers' duties on comparison 29, 155
" options, bids and offers. 25, 154
" rights 29, 157
Buying customers' stocks 84
" on margin, valid 84
By-laws, when reasonable, sustained by courts . . . . . 3n.
" upheld when not against public policy . . . . . 3n.
" courts will construe . . . . 3n.

"Call" defined 75
Calls 153

PAGE

Capital stock, notice of increase of 33, 167
Care required 75
"Cash" bids and offers 25, 154
Certificate of stock, etc., change in form 33, 168
" " " , not a negotiable instrument 113
" " " , transfers of (See "Transfers")
Chairman 5, 122
" , Assistant 5, 122
" , gratuity fund trustees 148
Charges against members 21, 22, 142, 143
City bonds, listing 9, 131
" " , commission rate on 169, 183
Claims between partners 16, 136
" filing 15, 136
"Claims of members," meaning of . . . . 15n.
Clearances for members 180, 183
" " non-members 180
Clearing charges 180
Clearing House 30, 31, 160
" " , Committee on 8, 129
" " , orders binding 157
" " , exchange of tickets 29, 30, 156, 159
Clerk of broker as customer's agent 112
Clerks, doing business for 181
" , employment of, for business obtained forbidden . 34, 181
" , speculative transactions for 27, 181
Closing contracts "Under the Rule" 30, 31, 32, 161
(See also "Under the Rule")
" out transactions on default, custom as to. 83
Collateral security, advances on. 56, 233
" " , sale of, customs as to 82, 83
Collection of dividends, charge for 33, 167
Commission rule, money advances upon unusual terms . 35, 185
" " , penalty for violation of 35, 170
" " , relieving customer from part of stamp tax . 35
" " , special or unusual rates of interest . 35, 185
Commissions, Committee on 8, 129
" , right of suspended member 35, 170
" must be charged 34, 168

INDEX

PAGE

Commissions, must be net 34, 168
" , "bunching" orders prohibited 34, 168
" , rates of 34, 169
" , reciprocal business 35, 182
" , taking over transactions 183
" , on government securities 184
" , on mining shares 182
Committees, standing 5-10, 126
" , ad interim 121
" , fees to 118
" , vacancies in 132
Communications to Exchange 37, 174
Comparison, responsibility for losses by 37, 184
Comparisons 29, 30, 155, 184
Compulsion, to sell when broker is under no 80
Conducting transactions, statutory enactments 83
Conduct of business, rules for 23, 152
" disorderly 23, 152
Consenting to felony 47
Consideration, validity of certain agreements made without . 53, 213
Consolidated Stock Exchange, transaction of business with members prohibited 27
Constitution, alterations of 37, 174
" , Committee on 8, 130
" , signing of 11, 133
" , violation of 20, 141
Continuous quotations 175
Contracts, altering, custom disapproved 83
" , liability on 30, 155
" , maturity of, on transfer of membership . . 14, 134
" , on holidays 154
" , settlement of 30, 158
" , subject to rule of, Exchange 153
" , deposits on 32, 164
" , closing 31, 161
" , disagreements 30, 156, 164
" , written 25, 154
Conversion 45, 46, 99, 105
" , by selling without notice 87

PAGE
Conversion, sale without demand and notice 93
Coöperation with insolvent broker 51, 104
Cornering the market, illegal 111
Corporations, acting for foreign 205
" , frauds in organization of 57, 204
Correspondent, broker's his agent 103
Counsel of Exchange 5, 120
" , Gratuity Fund 150
" , professional, excluded 22, 144
Courts, interference of 21n., 22n., 23n.,
Creditor, members, rights of 17, 136
Customer's agent, notice to 92
" death 102
" stock, buying 84
Customs and usages of Exchange govern 82
" " " " " , approved 83
" " " " " , disapproved 47, 83

Damages for default, claims for. . 30, 31, 32, 158, 159, 161, 162
" , measure of, sale of stock 107
Dealing outside of Exchange prohibited 23, 152
" , suspension of 33, 168, 187
" in Exchange with non-members 20, 140
" in dividends 33, 167
" in privileges 26, 155
" in differences or quotations 26, 179
" for clerks 27, 181
" , members' transactions with himself 26, 178
" outside of business hours 23, 152
" , reckless and unbusinesslike 19, 139
Dealings, inquiry into 8, 130
Death, customer's 102
"Debts," meaning of . . . . 19n.
Deceased members 16, 17, 38, 136, 148
Decorum 37, 173
Default as to margin, waiver of 93
" in delivery (See "Deliveries")
" of customer, custom as to closing out 83
" , transactions on 83

PAGE
Defrauded customer of insolvent broker, rights of 108
Deliveries 30, 157
" , necessity for stamped sales ticket 31, 186
" by certificate or transfer 30, 157
" during "closing" of books 30, 158
" , hours for, and payment 30, 158
" , default, damage 30, 31, 158, 159
Delivery of memoranda of transactions 47, 212
Demand and notice, sale without, a conversion 93
" for margin, necessity for 86
" must be specific 86
" , alternative insufficient 86
" for money deposited 113
Deposits in insolvent bank, receiving 195
" on contracts 32, 164
" , due bills for dividends 32, 166
Differences, arbitration of 6, 128
" as to terms of contract 37, 164
" , dealing in 26, 79
" on comparison 30, 56
Disagreement on terms of contract 36, 164
Discount, unlawful, of bills of foreign banks 198
Definite order, broker must obey 77
Definition of terms 50, 74
Discretion, order to sell at 80
Discrimination by Exchange or members 52, 203
Disorderly conduct 37, 173
Disposal of membership of deceased members . . . 16, 136
" " " " expelled members . . 17, 18, 136
Dividends 33, 165
" , charge for collecting 33, 165
" , dealing in, prohibited 33, 167
Due bills 32, 166
Dues and Fines 11, 133

Elections, annual 123
" , special 126
Eligibility for membership 10, 133
" to offices 125

PAGE

Employees (See "Clerks")
Equitable principles of trade 1, 23, 117
Evidence, production of 22, 141
Exchange, objects of 1, 117
" , government and officers of 3, 117
" , hours of business 23, 152
" , minutes of 173
" , special closings 152
" , special meetings. 4, 120
" , or members, discrimination by 52, 203
Exchanges, other in New York 140, 152
Ex-dividend 33, 165
"Exhausted" margin defined 85
Exhaustion of margin 80
" " " notice of 86
" " " " " object of 87
" " " " " reasonableness of 87
Exhibiting quotations 201
Expulsion, right to provide for . . . . 19n, 23n.
" , " of courts to interfere, ... 21n, 22n, 23n.
" , " " member to notice and hearing . . 24n, 25n.
" must be contested promptly . . . . 11n.
" , effect 17, 19, 22n, 23n. 136, 139
" , readmission after 6, 127
"Ex-rights" 33, 166
Extension of time to insolvent 18, 138
" " " , misstatement 20, 140

Failure to affix stamps 31, 186
" " exchange clearing-house tickets 30, 159
" " make deposits 32, 165
" " execute orders 82
Failures, number of 43
False rumors as to stock, bonds or public funds 207
" statement or advertisement as to securities 60, 208
Fees to committees 118
Felony, manipulation of prices of securities 48
" , anti-bucket shop law 49
" , trading against customers' orders 47

PAGE

Felony, unauthorized pledging of customers' securities . . 45
Fictitious person, signing name of, to subscription . . 57, 204
" transactions 48, 49
" " , custom disapproved 83
" " forbidden 26, 155
" names accounts in 27, 182
" reporting or publishing 59, 207
Filing claims 15, 136
Finance Committee 8, 130
Finances of Exchange 8, 130
" " gratuity fund 149
Fines 11, 133
"Fly-power" defined 75
Foreign arbitrage 176
" corporations acting for 205
" partnerships 35, 36, 170, 172
Fraud or fraudulent acts 21, 140
Frauds in organization of corporations 57, 204
Fraudulent issue of stocks and bonds 58, 204
Futures, contracts in, not illegal 53
" , dealings in 55
" , options in, when valid 54

Gambling transactions 53, 54
Good faith and care required 75
Governing Committee 3, 4, 118
" " , vacancies in 119
" " , quorum 119
" " , adjourned meetings 120
" " , special meetings 6, 120
" " , resolutions of, violation of . . 21, 141
Government of Exchange 3, 117
" securities, listing of 9, 131
Gratuity Fund 37, 38, 144
" " , its trustees 39, 148
" " , purposes 145
" " , liability of Exchange and members . . . 147
" " , assessments. 144
" " , reduction of 147

PAGE

Gratuity Fund, beneficiaries 145
" " , benefits not part of estate of member . . 147
" " , investments 148, 149
" " , " , organization of 148
" " , officers 149
" " , vacancies 148
" " , amendment of rules 39
Guaranteeing stock 111

Half-holidays, contracts falling due on 154
" " , loans of money or securities on day preceding 155
" " , deposits called on 165
Holidays, closing Exchange 152
(See also "Half-holidays")
Hours of business 23, 152
Hypothecation, when larceny 106
(See also "Pledging")

Improper use of customer's securities 37, 190, 191
Indebtedness, disputed prior 77
Indecorous conduct or language 37, 173
Initiation fee 10, 133
Insolvencies, committee on 8, 130
Insolvency 17, 137
" , transactions by brokers after 51, 210
" , of broker, stock goes to customer 108
Insolvent members, announcement by 17, 137
" bank receiving deposits in 195
" broker, coöperating with 51, 104
" broker, rights of defrauded customer of 108
" member, closing contracts of 31, 161
" " , extension of time 18, 137
" " , " " " misstatement on application 21, 140
" " , reinstatement 18, 137, 138
" " , list of creditors 18, 19, 138, 139
" " , commission rates to 34, 170
" " , reckless and unbusinesslike dealings . 19, 139
" , when broker is 51
Insurance law, exemption of Exchange from 243

INDEX

PAGE

Interest 37, 165, 167, 185
" , creating adverse, custom disapproved 83
" , payment of, without effecting loan 185
" , permitted on advances on collateral security. . . 56, 233
" , Rates of 35
Investigations 119
Irregularity in securities 37, 164
Issue of stocks and bonds, fraudulent 58, 204

Joint account 113, 169, 176
" deposits 32, 164, 165
Just and equitable principles of trade . . 1, 7n. 23, 117, 141

Keeping proper accounts 78

Larceny 45
" , where securities hypothecated 106
Law Committee 9, 130
Laws and Decisions, summary of 43
Laws covering stockbrokers, scope of 43
Lender of securities (see "Loans")
Lien, broker's 111
Loans of money or securities not effected 167, 185
" subject to rule of Exchange 153
" of money or securities, closing under rule . 31, 32, 158, 163
" of money or securities due on holidays 154
" " " " " , notice of return 159
" , brokerage on 55, 234
" , recovery of excess 55, 235
" , restitution a bar to further penalties 235

Manager of branch office 36, 172
Manager's acts, broker bound by 76
Manipulation of prices of securities 48, 208
Manner of Sale 79
Margin, adequate 38, 190
" , broker's course on exhaustion of 80
" , buying on, valid 84
" , defined 74, 85

PAGE
Margin, necessity for demand for 86
" , demand for must be specific 86
" , " " alternative, insufficient 86
" , notice of exhaustion of 86
" , " " , object of 87
" , " " , sufficiency of 87
" , reasonable time to make good 88
" , special agreement as to 91
" , waiver of customer's default as to 93
Margined stock, sub-pledging en bloc 46
" " , must be purchased 84
" " , broker's right to pledge 95
" " , " " " " en bloc 95
" " , sale of sufficiently 85
Market, cornering, the, illegal 111
" , quotations, transactions on basis of 49
" , sale at the 101
Maturity of contracts on transfer of membership . . 12, 134
Measure of damages 107
Member of Exchange, (See "Membership")
" " " , dealings of, inquiry into 9, 130
" " " , " on other exchanges . . 23, 152
" " " , " with non-members . . 23, 140
" " " , " with one's self , . . . 178
" " " , debts of 14, 135
Members, discrimination by 52, 203
" number of 10
Membership, admission to 10, 133
" , application for 10, 133
" , eligibility for 10, 133
" , transfer of 11, 134
" , how increased 10, 133
" , readmission 6, 127
" , reinstatement 18, 138
" , application of proceeds of 14, 135
" , of deceased member, disposal of 16, 136
Memoranda of transactions, delivery of 47, 212
Mining shares, commission on 182
Minor offence, procedure 22, 143

INDEX

PAGE

Minutes 37, 173
Misconduct by banks and bankers 196
Misdemeanor, failure to deliver memoranda of transactions 48, 212
Money deposited, demand for 113
" loans, (See "Loans")
Mutual deposits 32, 164

Names of persons dealt with to be forwarded to customers . 49
Nominal margin, agreement as to 92
" positions for employees 181
Nominating Committee. 123
Non-members, arbitration by 6, 127
" " , commission rates to 34, 169
Notice, loans, return of 30, 159
" , closing of contracts under rule 31, 162
" , mutual deposits 32, 164
" , time contract 25, 154
" , of transactions to customer 76
" of exhaustion of margin 86
" " " " " , object of 87
" " " " " , reasonableness of 87
" of time and place of sale, sufficiency of 89
" , not necessary when direct authorization to sell . . 94
" to customer's agent 92
" , waiver of reservation in contract to close without . 89
Number of members 10n. 133
" " " , increase of 10, 133

Officers of Exchange, powers and duties 4
" " " , eligibility 125
" " " , removal 9, 126
" " " , compensation 118
Offices of members (See "Branch Offices")
"Option" defined 74
Options in futures, when valid 54
Options sometimes prohibited by statute 54
Order, broker must obey definite 77
" , distinguished from authorization to sell 78
" , proof of receipt of 79

PAGE
Order, to sell at, discretion 80
Orders, customers, trading against 47, 209
Orders, failure to execute 82
" , waiver or revocation of 82
Organization of corporations, frauds in 57, 204

Partners, commission rate to 169
" , general and special 36, 171
" , foreign 36, 171
" , responsibility for acts of 36, 172
" , persons ineligible as 36, 171
" , claims between 16, 136
Partnerships (See also "Partners") 36, 171
" , registration of and changes in 36, 171
" , undesirable 36, 171
" , dissolution of 36, 171
Payment 30, 157
" before delivery 30, 77
Penalties, violation of commission law 34, 170
" , " " provision of Constitution . . . 22, 141
" , " " rule of Governing Committee . . 22, 141
" , violation of partnership rule 36, 172
" , " " branch office rule 36, 172
" for non-payment of dues and fines . . 11, 133, 134
Period, agreement to carry account for a definite 100
"Personal Liability" securities 29, 157
Place of sale, sufficiency of notice of 89
" " transaction, customer to be notified of 49
Pledgee from broker, right of 99
Pledge of margined stock, right of 95
" " stocks, en bloc 95
Pledging stock 97
" " , waiver of pledgee's lien 98
" " , for advances 45
" " , left for safe keeping 52
Pledging of customer's securities, unauthorized 44, 211
Pooled stock 79
Premiums 165, 167
President 4, 120

PAGE

Presumption of value 78
Price of securities, manipulation of 48, 208
Principal and agent, acting as 47
" , duty on comparisons 29, 156
" , substitution of 29, 157
" , undisclosed 113
Prior indebtedness, disputed 77
Privileges, dealing in, forbidden 26, 155
" for non-member, commission on 190
Proceeds of membership, application of 14, 135
Proof of receipt of order 79
Prospectus, subscribing name of another in 57, 204
Publishing or reporting fictitious transactions . . . 59, 207
Purchase in broker's own name, as to 82
Purpose of Stock Exchange. 1
"Put" defined 75

Quorum of Committees 132
" " Exchange 125
" " Governing Committee 119
" " Gratuity Fund trustees 149
Quotation service 127
Quotations, dealing in 29n, 179
" , continuous or frequent 175
" , exhibiting 201

Ratification of unauthorized pledge 46
" " transaction 81
Readmission to membership 6, 127
Reasonable time to make margin good 88
Rebatement of assessments to members 147
" " commissions 34, 168
Receipt of order, proof of 79
Receiver of securities, rights and duties of 158
" " " , must not deduct damage 159
Receiving deposits in insolvent bank 195
Reckless and unbusinesslike dealing 37, 190, 191
Reclamation 164
Reëstablishment of contract (See "Under the Rule")

INDEX

PAGE

Registration of address 36, 170
" , branch office 36, 170
" , partnership and changes 36, 171
" , securities 33, 167
" , wire connections 28, 189
Registry office of corporation 33, 167
"Regular way" bids and offers 25, 154
Reinstatement 18, 137
Removal of appointees, clerks, etc. 126
" " officers of Exchange 126
" " Trustees of Gratuity Fund 151
" " securities from list 9, 131
Reporting or publishing fictitious transactions . . . 59, 207
" transactions 29, 155
Resolutions of Governing Committee, violation of . . 22, 141
Responsibility for accounts 182
Return of loans (See "Loans")
Revenue tax 186
Rights of defrauded customer of insolvent broker 108
" " receiver or seller of securities 32, 166
" pertaining to securities 32, 166
Rules of Exchange as between broker and customer 82
" " " " " members 2
" , power of Exchange to make 3
" , member cannot deny reasonableness of 3
Rumors, false, as to stocks, etc. 207

Salary of employees in branch offices 36, 172
" " " for procuring business 34, 168
" " " of Clearing House 129
" " " of officers and appointees 118
Sale at the market 101
" , manner of 79
" of collateral security, customs as to 82, 83
" , sufficiently margined stock 85
" , unauthorized 111
" with no change of ownership 191
" , without demand and notice, a conversion 93
Sales, short 103

INDEX

PAGE

Sales, tickets, revenue stamp on 31, 186
Same security, orders to buy and sell 26, 176
Seat on Exchange, is property . . . . . 11n, 12n, 13n.
" " " , disposal of, on insolvency . . . . . 12n.
" " " , consent to transfer necessary . . . . 12n.
" " " , cannot be sold as collateral . . . . . 14n.
" " " , trustee in bankruptcy gets title to . . . 12n.
Secret profits 76
" " , ratification of taking of 81
Secretary of Exchange 5, 122
" " Gratuity Fund 149
Securities Committee on 9, 131
" " " its jurisdiction . . . . 9n.
" , manipulation of prices of 208
" , suspension of dealing in 33, 168
" , removal from list 33, 168, 187
" , change in form of certificate 33, 155
" , commissions on transactions in 169
" , contracts, rules for settlement 9, 131
" , deliveries (See "Deliveries," "Under the Rule")
" , increase of capitalization 33, 167
" , listing of 9, 131
" , loans of (See "Loans") . . .
" , payment for. 30, 157
" , rights pertaining to 33, 166
" , transfer and registry 33, 165
" , unauthorized pledging or other disposition of customer's securities 44, 211
Seller and buyer, acting for 84
" , rights of 32, 165
" , duties on comparison 29, 156
"Seller's" options, bids and offers 25, 154
Settlement of contracts 30, 158
Shares of stock, transfers of (See "Transfers")
"Short sale" defined 74
Short sales 103
Short selling valid 53
Signature to Constitution, effect of 133
Smaller quantity than ordered, purchase of 78

PAGE
Solicitation of business 36, 172
Special agreement as to margin 91
" committees. 132
" partners 36, 171
Specialists 26, 178
Stamp Tax (See "Stock Transfer Stamp Tax") 186
Stamps, failure to affix. 31, 186
Standing Committees 5-10, 126
Statement, false, as to securities 60, 208
" of transactions 201
State securities, listing of 9, 131
" " , commission rates on 169
Statutory enactments, disregarding custom disapproved . . 83
Stock certificate not a negotiable instrument 113
" goes to customer on broker's insolvency 108
" , guaranteeing 111
" , margined, must be purchased 84
" , pledging 97
" , " , waiver of pledgee's lien. 98
" , pooled 79
" , tender of 93
" , transfers of certificates and shares of (see "Transfers")
" , list, Committee on 9, 131
" , listing of securities, dealt in 9, 131
" , list removal from 9, 131
Stock Transfer Tax Law 236
" " " " , amount of tax 65, 236
" " " " , application 65, 237
" " " " , effect of amendment of 1911 . 68, 238
" " " " , taxable transfers 65, 239
" " " " , compromise of claims 240
" " " " , stamps, how prepared and sold . 66, 240
" " " " , selling stamps without consent of comptroller 240
" " " " , penalty for failure to pay tax . 66, 241
" " " " , canceling stamps, penalty for failure 66, 242
" " " " , contracts for dies; expenses, how paid 242
" " " " , illegal use of stamps, penalty . . 66, 243
" " " " , power of state comptroller . . 67, 243

PAGE

Stock Transfer Tax Law, books and records . . . 67, 69, 246
" " " ", civil penalties, how recovered . . 246
" " " ", effect of failure to pay tax . . 68, 247
" " " ", refund of tax erroneously paid . . 248
" " " ", summary 65
(See "Commision rule")
Stocks (See "Securities")
" , buying customer's 84
" , false rumors as to, etc. 207
" and bonds, fraudulent issue of 58, 204
"Stop order" defined 78
Sub-pledging margined stock en bloc 46
Subscribing name of another in prospectus, etc . . . 57, 204
Subscription receipts, listing of 9, 131
" rights, commission rates 169
Subscription, signing name of fictitious person to . . 57, 204
Subscriptions for collateral purposes only 58
Substitute principal 29, 157
Sufficiently margined stock, sale of 85
Summary of Laws and Decisions 43
" proceedings 22, 143
Suspension of members, . . . 17, 18, 19, 20, 21 22, 137, 139
" " ", how period determined 19
" " ", for what imposed 20, 21
" " ", committees finding final 22
" " ", announcement of 22
" " ", effect of 22
" of dealings in securities 34, 168

Table of cases cited 253
Taking over position, commission rate 183
Tax law, transfer, summary 65
Telegraph and telephone connections with non-members 28, 187, 189
" " " " " Consolidated; connection with Exchange operator, pay of 189
Telephone (see "Telegraph")
Tender of stock 93
Testimony, requirement to give 22, 141
Time and place of sale, sufficiency of notice of 89

PAGE

Time and place of, transaction to be furnished to customer . 49
" " " " contracts (see "Written Contracts")
" " " " extension of (see "Insolvent")
Trading against customer's orders 47, 209
Transaction, ratification of unauthorized 81
Transactions (see "Dealings")
" by brokers after insolvency 51, 210
" , closing out on defendant, custom as to . . 83
" , delivery of memoranda of 47, 212
" , fictitious 48
" , notice of, to customer 76
" , statement of 201
Transfer agency of corporation 33, 167
" books, closing of 33, 165
" of membership 11, 134
" " " , maturity of contracts on 12, 134
Transfers of certificate and share of stock 62, 213
" " " , how title transferred 62, 214
Transfers of powers of those lacking full legal capacity and of fiduciaries not enlarged 62, 124
" , corporations not forbidden to treat registered holder as owner 63, 215
" , title derived from certificate extinguishes title derived from a separate document 63, 215
" , who may deliver a certificate 63, 216
" , effectuality of indorsement 63, 216
" , rescission of transfer 63, 217
" , " " " does not invalidate subsequent transfer by transferee in possession 63, 217
" , delivery of unindorsed certificate imposes obligation to
" , indorse 63, 218
ineffectual attempt to transfer amounts to a promise to transfer 63, 218
" , warranties on sale of certificate 63, 219
" , no warranty implied from accepting payment of a debt 64, 219
" , no attachment or levy upon shares unless certificate surrendered or transfer enjoined 64, 220
" , creditors' remedies to reach certificate 64, 220
" , no lien or restriction unless indicated on certificate 64, 220

PAGE

Transfers, alteration of certificate does not divest title to shares 64, 221
" , lost or destroyed certificate 64, 221
" , rule for cases not provided for by the act . . . 221
" , interpretation 222
" , definition of indorsement 222
" , definition of person appearing to be the owner of certificate 223
" , other definitions 223
" , article does not apply to existing certificates . . 65, 224
" , inconsistent legislation repealed 224
Treasurer of Exchange 5, 121
" " Gratuity Fund 149
Trials, minor offenses, summary proceedings 22, 143
" , major offenses 22, 142
" , adjournment of 119
" , counsel excluded 22, 144
Trust companies, doing business for clerks of 27, 181
" " , Gratuity Fund 150
" " , mutual deposits 32, 164
Trustees of bond issues 33, 168
" " Gratuity Fund (see "Gratuity Fund")

Unauthorized pledge of customers' securities 44, 211
" " ratification of 46
" sale, right to advances, etc. 111
" transaction, ratification of 81
" use of the term "bank" 198
Unbusinesslike dealings 19, 139
"Under the rule", contracts of insolvents 31, 161
" " " , duties of chairman 31, 161, 163
" " " , notice of intention 32, 161
" " " , notice of closing 162
" " " , parties in interest 162
" " " , settlement price if not closed out . . 32, 162
" " " , damages resulting from securities pledged for loan 32, 163
Undisclosed principal 113
Unlawful discount of bills of foreign banks intention by one party only 54, 198

INDEX

PAGE

Usages of Exchange govern. 82
Usury 56

Vacancies in Governing Committee 119
" " offices 125
" " chairmanship 122
" " Committees 132
" " Gratuity Fund 148
Validity of certain agreements made without consideration 53, 213
Vice-President 4, 121
" " , Vacancy in office 126
Violation of branch office or partnership law 36, 172
" commission law 35, 170
" provision of Constitution 22, 141
" resolution of Governing Committee. 22, 141
" rules covering bids and offers 155
Visitors 37, 173, 174
Voting power, pertaining to securities 33, 166

Wager 53-55
Waiver of customer's default 93
" " pledgee's lien 98
" " reservation to close without notice 89
Welfare of Exchange, act detrimental to. 22, 142
Wire connections, approval of by committee of arrangements 28, 189
(see also "Telegraph and Telephone")
Witness, requirement to testify 22, 141
" , right to produce, etc. 22, 141
Written contracts, when they must be made 25, 154
" " , notice under 25, 154
" " , liability fixed 29, 157

THE COUNTRY LIFE PRESS
GARDEN CITY, N. Y.

Made in the USA
Monee, IL
20 October 2026

66035308R00174